INTRODUCTION TO CRIMINAL
JUSTICE RESEARCH METHODS

ABOUT THE AUTHORS

Gennaro F. Vito is a Professor, Vice Chair and Graduate Program Coordinator in the Department of Justice Administration at the University of Louisville. He also serves as a faculty member in the Administrative Officer's Course at the Southern Police Institute. He holds a Ph.D. in Public Administration from The Ohio State University. Active in professional organizations, he is a past President and Fellow of the Academy of Criminal Justice Sciences. He is also the recipient of the Educator of the Year Award from the Southern Criminal Justice Association (1991) and the Dean's Outstanding Performance Award for Research and Scholarly Activities from the former College of Urban and Public Affairs at U of L (1990), the Dean's Award for Outstanding Research from the College of Arts and Sciences and the President's Distinguished Faculty Award for Excellence in Research (2002). He is the author of over 65 professional, refereed journal articles (in such journals as *Criminology, The Journal of Criminal Law and Criminology, Justice Quarterly, Police Quarterly,* and *The Prison Journal* and over 40 technical research reports. He has published on such topics as: capital sentencing, police consolidation, police traffic stops (racial profiling), policing strategies for drug problems in public housing, attitudes toward capital punishment, and the effectiveness of criminal justice programs, such as drug elimination programs, drug courts, and drug testing of probationers and parolees. He is to co-author of nine textbooks in criminal justice and criminology including *Organizational Behavior and Management in Law Enforcement* (Prentice Hall) and *Criminology: Theory, Research, and Practice* (Jones & Bartlett).

Julie C. Kunselman is Associate Professor and Chair of the Department of Political Science and Criminal Justice at Northern Kentucky University. She earned a B.S. in Mathematics from Gannon University and an M.P.A. and Ph.D. in Urban and Public Affairs from the University of Louisville in 2000. Dr. Kunselman has co-authored more than 20 peer-reviewed publications, most recently in the areas of criminal justice education, policy analysis and administration.

Richard Tewksbury is Professor of Justice Administration at the University of Louisville and editor of the journal Justice Quarterly. He holds a PhD from The Ohio State University. Dr. Tewksbury is a recipient of ACA's Peter P. Lejins Correctional Research Award. He serves as Chair of the American Correctional Association Research Council. He has previously worked for both the Ohio Department of Rehabilitation and Corrections and Kentucky Department of Corrections, and consulted with numerous state and local agencies across the nation. He is author/editor of 13 books and more than 200 articles, chapters and reports.

Second Edition

INTRODUCTION TO CRIMINAL JUSTICE RESEARCH METHODS

An Applied Approach

By

GENNARO F. VITO, Ph.D.

Professor
Department of Justice Administration
University of Louisville

JULIE C. KUNSELMAN, Ph.D.

Associate Professor
Department of Political Science and Criminal Justice
Northern Kentucky University

RICHARD TEWKSBURY, Ph.D.

Professor
Department of Justice Administration
University of Louisville

CHARLES C THOMAS • PUBLISHER, LTD.
Springfield • Illinois • U.S.A.

Published and Distributed Throughout the World by

CHARLES C THOMAS • PUBLISHER, LTD.
2600 South First Street
Springfield, Illinois 62704

© 2008 by CHARLES C THOMAS • PUBLISHER, LTD.

ISBN 978-0-398-07813-3 (hard)
ISBN 978-0-398-07814-0 (paper)

Library of Congress Catalog Card Number: 2008008610

Printed in the United States of America
LAH-R-3

Library of Congress Cataloging-in-Publication Data

Vito, Gennaro F.
 Introduction to criminal justice research methods : an applied approach. --
2nd Ed. / by Gennaro F. Vito, Julie C. Kunselman, Richard Tewksbury.
     p. cm.
 Includes bibliographical references and index.
 ISBN 978-0-398-07813-3 (hard) -- ISBN 978-0-398-07814-0 (pbk.)
 1. Criminal justice, Administration of--Research--Methodology. I. Kunselman, Julie C. II. Tewksbury, Richard A. III. Title.

 HV7419.5.V58 2008
 364.072--dc22

                                                              2008008610

PREFACE

Introduction to Criminal Justice Research Methods: An Applied Approach is a text designed to assist criminal justice students and practitioners to conduct research on problems and issues facing the criminal justice system. It is based upon our collective experience as researchers and instructors in criminal justice research and policy analysis. It is our hope that our definitions and examples will help students and practitioners to both comprehend research articles and reports and to conduct their own research.

Each of the authors brought specific areas of expertise to this effort. We are familiar with the research process and have worked together on several published studies. The text is designed for persons with little or no research background and provides real world examples and clear definitions of terms and concepts. The text focuses upon policy and program analysis in the hope that accurate information will improve and reform criminal justice operations.

G.F.V.
J.C.K.
R.T.

CONTENTS

INTRODUCTION TO CRIMINAL JUSTICE RESEARCH METHODS

Chapter 1

THE PURPOSE OF CRIMINAL JUSTICE RESEARCH

CHAPTER OVERVIEW

This text is designed as an introduction to research methods in criminal justice. Research is really about the generation of information that is both accurate and objective for the purpose of guiding decision making. Without research, we have no knowledge about crime: What it is, where it happens, how it happens, and why it happens. Information either guides the development or determines the validity of theory (Criminology) and the effectiveness of crime policies and programs (Criminal Justice). Information provides guidance on how to combat crime and the selection of the best possible approach. Research is also the way to evaluate the effectiveness of the approach considered. Without information, we have no guidance.

THE PURPOSE OF RESEARCH

The detailed information that is generated by research is a management tool that has become a significant part of criminal justice operations. For example, problem solving has become a key component of police operations at all levels of the organization – from the community and the street cop to the chief executive. Research informs the problem solving function. Police managers must be able to assess agency performance (both individually and collectively), analyze and solve community problems and judge the competency of programs designed to address them.[1] It can guide decision making in the following manner:

> Research can provide useful and exciting insights into community problems and how police agencies operate. It can reveal potentially useful programs and strategies for dealing with problems. It can show which programs are successful and which are not. It can suggest new strategies to deal with old issues. It can provide information needed to improve existing programs. And it can inform the public and elected officials. In short, research is a tool for police managers who want to make rational, informed decisions.[2]

Police research is designed to provide information to answer specific questions and to inform police management decisions.[3] Specifically, research can guide management decisions to allocate resources in the department and to the community. How should the department deal with calls for service, routine patrol, crime investigation and prevention, and engage in problem solving? Efficient allocation of resources requires information.[4]

The Goals of Research

Research can be classified by purpose, according to the aims of the project. Thus the research may involve: exploration, description, explanation and evaluation. The goal of **exploratory research** is to examine the forces at work in some new area of crime where little about the subject is known. This type of research can generate information that could lead to more detailed analysis of the subject in the future. For example, identity theft is a new form of crime. It involves someone wrongfully obtaining and using another's personal data (your name, Social Security number, credit card number, bank account number, telephone calling card number, or other identifying information) to commit fraud or deception for economic gain.[5] Exploratory research on identity theft reveals that its costs are substantial. Estimates from 2003 indicate that thieves who used personal information to establish new credit and bank accounts cost victims and financial institutions over $33 billion.[6] The victims of these crimes are not only faced with financial losses. They must also contend with the loss of identity and restoration of their good financial name in terms of their credit rating. Exploratory research on identity theft has led to further analysis. For example, research findings from one large municipal police department in Florida found that the number of reported incidents of identity theft increased at a higher rate than other more typical theft crimes. It was also determined that the average identity theft offender was African American, female, unemployed, working alone, and unknown to the victims. White males were most likely to be the victims of this crime.[7]

Descriptive research is designed to answer three basic questions:[8]

1. How big is the problem?
2. Whom does the problem effect?
3. What causes the problem?

Descriptive research is aimed at detailing situations and events that are somewhat new and unique. It attempts to uncover facts and describe reality. For example, consider the research findings on the drug, methamphetamine – a powerful central nervous system stimulant that produces a short, intense "rush" when used due to release of high levels of dopamine from the brain. It can be smoked (in its granulated, crystal form known as "ice"), snorted, orally ingested or injected.[9] Chronic abuse of methamphetamine abuse can lead to psychotic behavior – intense paranoia, visual and auditory hallucinations (including the delusion that "crank bugs" are crawling under the user's skin), and out of control violent rages. Physically, the drug can result in inflammation of the heart lining, rapid heart rate, irregular heartbeat, increased blood pressure, damage to the small blood vessels of the brain and even acute lead poisoning.[10] Plus, the manufacture of methamphetamine has a severe effect upon the environment. Brewing one pound of methamphetamine also releases poisonous gas and produces 5 to 7 pounds of toxic waste that is typically carelessly dumped into the lab's environment without regard to its impact.

Use of this drug is rapidly increasing. In 2003, almost 8 percent of high school students, about 9 percent of young adults (aged 19–28) and almost 6 percent of college students surveyed nationwide reported using methamphetamine at least once during their lifetime. Similarly, national data (39 states in 25 sites) from the 2003 Arrestee Drug Abuse Monitoring Program (ADAM) recorded a median rate (50th percentile – half of the arrestees) of 4.7 percent of adult males and 8.8 percent of adult females testing positive for methamphetamine upon entry to jail. Between 1992 and 2002, yearly rates admission to drug treatment for methamphetamine abuse increased from 1 to 5.5 percent.[11] During the same time frame, U.S. hospitals reported 69 percent increase in methamphetamine induced emergency room visits (from 10,447 to 17,696).[12]

During 2001, the DEA made over 7,000 methamphetamine related arrests (about 22 percent of the total number of drug arrests the agency made). In 2003, Federal courts sentenced almost 4,500 offenders on methamphetamine-related charges. Of these offenders, the majority were white (59.3%) and male (85.9%). Over eleven percent of these offenders had a weapon involved in their drug offense.[13]

Control over trafficking in methamphetamines has changed in recent years. Traditionally, outlaw motorcycle gangs and independent operators have run meth labs and sold the drug. Beginning in 1994, Mexican drug trafficking organizations began to dominate this drug market. Their established drug trafficking routes and smuggling methods coupled with the establishment of "super labs" (capable of producing in excess of 10 pounds of meth in one 24-hour production cycle) has made this takeover possible.[14]

Explanatory research involves the determination of how or why an event has occurred. Typically, it involves the search for the causes of crime by examining the relationship between variables. This type of research can be applied through the problem solving perspective. For example, street level prostitution creates an environment where other crimes can flourish – the sale of illegal drugs, the generation of profits for organized crime groups, and bringing strangers in contact with offenders who are primed to commit robbery. Determination of the sources of a problem lead to the creation of a response to it. Police crackdowns on street level prostitution can thus involve:[15]

1. Enforcing laws prohibiting soliciting, patronizing, and loitering for the purposes of prostitution.
2. Enhancing fines/penalties for prostitution-related offenses committed within a specified high-activity zone.
3. Banning prostitutes or clients from geographic areas.
4. Encouraging community members to publicly protest against prostitutes and/or clients.
5. Identifying and targeting the worst offenders.

In this fashion, explanatory research can examine a problem and generate approaches to deal with it. Valid information can provided guidance to criminal justice operations.

Evaluation research is concerned with the application of research knowledge. It is a specialized form of research that aims to determine the effectiveness of a policy or program. This subject is covered in detail in Chapter Ten. For example, the Lifer's Program at a state prison in Rahway, New Jersey (the famous "Scared Straight" documentary) was one of several programs designed around organized visits to prisons by at-risk juveniles. The aim was to deter them from further involvement in delinquency. Petrosino and his colleagues conducted a detailed review of studies (experimental designs conducted over 25 years in eight different jurisdictions and involving nearly 1,000 participants) to determine the effectiveness of these programs. They found that, rather than aiding their juvenile subjects, the programs were likely to be more harmful than doing nothing.[16] Evaluation research is designed to publicize the track record of criminal justice interventions so that good programs proliferate and poor ones do not.

Research methodology involves the use of the proper plans and tools to produce accurate information. We will provide an overview of the basic tools available to conduct and comprehend research reports. Students must be able to conduct research and comprehend the worth of research reports. The criminal justice professional must be able to comprehend and implement policy based upon valid information. Students must have the ability to read and comprehend research reports and to make some reasoned judgment about the conclusions that are drawn.

In order to judge the value of research, the reader must be able to understand the best method to conduct it. How the study was done, how the research sample was selected, and the type of research design used are research methodology issues that can affect the information generated by the research. In fact, many of these concepts are familiar to you right now. There is a very practical and "common sense" aura to these terms. But the terminology of research is unknown and strange to you.

BASIC CHARACTERISTICS OF THE SCIENTIFIC METHOD

Research methods consist of a number of techniques that have been established over time in many disciplines. Again, they are designed to generate information. Like criminal investigation methods, they are techniques for finding out what has taken place. Essentially, the research design is the plan (or blueprint) for carrying out the inquiry. Typically, it is very thorough, logically outlining the procedures to be followed to conduct the research including: methods of data collection (or observation), measurement of key variables and the method of analysis that will be used.

Inductive and Deductive Reasoning

Typically, criminal justice research begins with the rather simple process of identifying a problem – the identification of a concern to the community – and testing the statements surrounding it. Problem statements are usually data driven and provide symptoms of the problem at hand. Using **induction**, observations based upon information collected are made to provide evidence that a problem exists and to explain its nature. Thus, the process of induction begins with observations about the problem made on the basis of data analysis and then arrives at **generalizations**. Generalizations are based upon the belief that the observations made are representative of similar problems that exist elsewhere. These inferences also presume that the events observed in one location are applicable to those in others. Thus, problems faced by different agencies in different locales may be addressed through the use of approaches that have proven to be effective elsewhere.

The **deductive method** takes a different approach. It applies theory to a problem to explain its existence and provide a method to deal with it. Here, research is designed to test the validity of predictions deduced from theory.

What both methods have in common is a faith in reason and the belief that the world operates according to certain laws that can be ascertained through careful study and the collection of empirical evidence. These "laws" will be carefully developed over time as researchers examining the same phenomenon using similar methods (**replication**) to verify the findings of previous studies.

Problem Statements

The emphasis here is on the logical analysis of problems and devising the appropriate method to obtain evidence. For example, in policing, a problem could be considered as the basic unit of police work –

a group or pattern of crimes, cases, calls or incidents.[17] Burglaries in a precinct could be considered a problem. How could this "problem" be reduced to a researchable level? Burglary is a **concept** – a categorization within a concern (crime). During the research process, it is necessary to transform concepts into variables by precisely stating what is meant by the concept under study. A **Variable** is an attribute that has more than one possible value. Researchers must determine how variables will be measured. Naturally, some variables are more difficult to measure than others. The **operational definition** of a variable simply refers to the manner in which the variable was measured. In terms of our burglary example, burglary is the concept. The variable is the frequency of burglaries and the operational definition (measurement) is the number of burglaries reported to the police.

From these data, the precinct captain can deduce the extent (frequency of occurrence) and nature of residential burglary as a problem. Is there a consistent pattern in terms of when, where and how burglaries occurred in the area? On the basis of these patterns a method of police response can be established. For example, the captain may decide to increase patrols in the area at the times and days of the week when burglaries were committed. The captain might also enlist the services of residents in the area by establishing a Neighborhood Watch Program – where community members patrol their streets and keep a watchful eye on residences.

Issues to consider when determining the nature of a crime problem are presented in Table 1.1.

Table 1.1

DETERMINING THE NATURE OF A CRIME PROBLEM

ISSUES	MEASUREMENT METHODS
What is the extent of the crime problem?	Crime rates by type of crime
What is the direction and magnitude of the crime problem over time?	Crime rates by type of crime and year. Rate of change in the crime rate over time.
Where and when is the incidence of crime highest?	Frequency and rates of crime by type of crime and location (both time and place). Use of Crime Mapping.
Who is most seriously victimized by the crime?	Victimization data (age, race, sex, education, income, place of residence).

Units of Analysis

Another important issue in the definition of a research problem is deciding on what is the **unit of analysis** of concern to the study. Units of analysis are defined as: "the specific objects or elements whose characteristics we wish to describe or explain and about which we will collect data."[18] The most common units of analysis used in criminal justice studies are individuals, groups, organizations and social artifacts.[19] For example, if we decide to study the level of job satisfaction among police officers, the individual unit of analysis would be the police officer. The group level would be all of the police officers in a particular precinct. The organizational level would be the entire police department under study. Social artifacts that could be used would be newsletters and other relevant public documents from the local police union organization or bargaining representative. The research should make proper conclusions based upon the unit of analysis under study. Individuals cannot represent the entire organization so careful generalizations must be made.

Hypothesis Testing

Hypothesis testing is another basic aspect of the scientific method. A hypothesis is typically defined as a statement about the nature of things (in this case crime and criminal behavior) that is derived from a theory. For example, consider the following statement:

> If convicted murderers are executed, the number of homicides after the execution will decrease.

Where does such a hypothesis come from? In criminological theory, deterrence theory tells us that crime is the result of action freely taken by a rational individual after a careful assessment of the potential benefits of committing the crime in comparison to its potential costs. Theoretically, the executions of murderers would enter into the calculations made by other offenders. To a rational offender, the cost (dying) outweighs the benefits of the crime. Following an execution, the criminal justice researcher could develop a research design which would test not only the impact of the execution, but the validity of deterrence theory.

Independent and Dependent Variables

Hypothesis testing is built upon the concept of independent and dependent variables. Again, a **variable** is a concept that can take on different quantitative or qualitative values. For example, the crime rate (measured by the number of crimes reported to the police in a year) can take on different values. Therefore, the crime rate is a variable.

For example, let's examine the relationship between the jail incarceration rate and the crime rate. Here, both the jail incarceration rate and the crime rate are variables. We are interested in testing the following hypothesis:

> Does locking up criminals affect the crime rate? The size of the jail population may affect the crime rate by deterring and/or incapacitating criminals. An increase in the size of the jail population would cause the crime rate to go down.

Here, note that we have stated a temporal relationship between the jail population and crime rates. In order to test for a deterrent or incapacitative effect, the change in the jail population must occur before we examine the potential impact upon the crime rate – the change in the jail population precedes the change the in crime rate. Therefore, the change in the crime rate is dependent upon the change in the jail population. The change in the crime rate is a consequence of the change in the jail population. In this case, the jail population is not dependent upon the crime rate.

In research terminology, this hypothesis means that crime rate is the **dependent variable**. The jail population is the independent variable – it precedes the crime rate in time and may produce an effect in the crime rate. Using this hypothesis, we will test the relationship between these two variables and attempt to determine if locking up criminals affects the crime rate. To objectively verify a research hypothesis, it is necessary to operationally define both the independent and dependent variables. For example, one study of this relationship examined the change in the jail population in one year and the change in the crime rate (for different types of crime) in the following year for the cities served by the largest jails (the top 100) in the United States.[20] Providing these measurements and specifying the conditions for the research, makes our hypothesis about jail population and crime rates testable. Since both the variables and their measurement have been specified, this relationship can be objectively verified through research.

This example is also a **causal hypothesis** – a cause and effect relationship is assumed between the independent and dependent variables. If increasing the jail population has a deterrent or incapacitative effect upon crime, the crime rate in the area should go down following an increase in the jail incarceration rate. Causation within such a relationship cannot be positively proven but can be approximated. Many factors other than the jail incarceration rate can affect the crime rate. However, to even partially address the issue of causation, the relationship between the independent and dependent variables must occur in a certain way. Here, the change in the jail incarceration rate must precede the measurement of change in the crime rate. This is the requirement of **causal time order**. For the independent variable (X) to produce an effect in the dependent variable (Y), it must precede it in time. If this time order is not maintained, then causation cannot even be addressed.

In addition, this hypothesis stipulates the direction of the relationship between the independent and dependent variables. Recall that the policy premise behind our hypothesis is that an increase in the size of the jail population would cause the crime rate to go down. This is a **directional research hypothesis**. It is stated in terms of the predicted relationships between the variables. On the other hand, a **non-directional research hypothesis** is one that does not specify the direction of expected relationships or differences between variables.

In this fashion, hypothesis testing provides direction for the research by specifying relationships between variables and then testing their accuracy through the research process itself.

ISSUES AND TRADITIONS IN CRIMINAL JUSTICE RESEARCH

Researchers in criminal justice are concerned with the study of criminal behavior and the policies and programs that are developed to deal with crime. Criminology provides the theoretical basis for criminal justice research. In this section, we shall review the basic premises of criminological theory and their contribution to and effect upon research methodology.

The Classical School

The basic theoretical premise of the Classical School of Criminology is deterrence. Deterrence presumes that people are rational and they will follow the course of action that gives them the greatest amount of pleasure and the least amount of pain. There are two forms of deterrence:

1. **General deterrence** in which the criminal is punished as an example to others who may contemplate committing a crime and
2. **Specific deterrence** – where the offender is punished in order to deter any future crimes undertaken by this individual. One form of specific deterrence is incapacitation. Here, the offender is targeted for punishment that will prevent him or her from committing crimes in the future. One example of an incapacitative punishment is the Career Criminal Laws like California's "Three Strikes" Law where offenders receiving a third felony conviction are eligible for a sentence of life without parole.

To classical theorists like **Cesare Beccaria** and **Jeremy Bentham**, criminal behavior is based upon rationalism and free will. People choose to commit crime because they perceive that benefits that they can derive are greater than the pain that punishment will inflict. In order to deter crime, we must establish and then enforce laws that generate punishments that would outweigh the benefits of crime.

In addition, the Classical School had a "due process" aspect that emphasized fairness and equity in the law. When Beccaria wrote that laws should be known, he was not simply speaking to the rational offender but was also protesting a penal system that often reflected the political whims of the ruler. The legal code should be just, not arbitrary, in order to maximize the deterrent effect of punishment. After all, how can punishment have a deterrent effect, if offenders do not know what crimes are worth in terms of punishment?

The Classical School has had a dramatic impact upon criminal justice research. All of our previous examples, the citizen's crime watch (block watch), the execution of convicted murderers, and the potential effect of jail incarceration on the crime rate are examples of deterrence research. Deterrence stresses that the presence of a just punishment, equitably and efficiently applied, will prevent crime.

However, there are a number of problems associated with deterrence theory research. First of all, how do we know how many potential offenders there are in the general population? How can we estimate how many persons know the penalty for a particular crime? For example, how do we know how many persons are actually deterred by an execution? Do deterred persons call the police station to report that they were thinking about killing someone (like their mean, old professor) but the possibility of execution changed their mind? Also, it is difficult for researchers to manipulate deterrent punishments in order to measure their effectiveness. We cannot remove or eliminate a certain law for a period of time and then put it back into place. Nevertheless, deterrence theory has been thoroughly researched and will continue to serve as a focal point as we search for effective and just methods of crime control.

The Positivist School

The Positivist School of criminology is related to the research tradition of the natural sciences. In fact, a "positivist" is a scientist who is concerned with the generation of scientific knowledge. The Positivist School attempted to develop and construct general laws to explain and predict criminal behavior.[21] Founded by **Cesare Lombroso**, the Positivist School sought to determine the causes of crime through careful, controlled and scientific study. The hope was that research could lead to the effective treatment of the offender. The focus of study was the individual criminal to determine the attributes related to criminal behavior. Lombroso was an Italian physician who studied prisoners. The Positivist School rests upon a correctional perspective or Medical Model that served as the basis for the hope of rehabilitation of prisoners. Once the causes of crime were identified, something could be done to reduce or eliminate it.

Lombroso's analysis was based upon the biological studies of Charles Darwin and emphasized the determination of physical attributes associated with crime. Lombroso viewed crime as a problem of "defective individuals": "Crime can be controlled through a criminal justice system that apprehends, adjudicates and rehabilitates the individual offender. The emphasis upon treatment overshadows any perceived need for any structural changes in society.[22] Yet, the Positivist tradition is not limited to the biological approach to crime. Typical studies using this approach are concerned with such topics as: the comparison of delinquents to non-delinquents, the evaluation of treatment methods, and the prediction of crime and delinquency, and probation and parole success.

The Positivist School was responsible for the introduction of the scientific method to the study of crime. Lombroso, along with his French counterparts, Queletet and Guerry, utilized direct measurement of crime and statistical analysis of individuals to study criminology. His studies were "'objective' in method, often statistical" and "'positive' in the sense of deterministic." The Positivist School also introduced the idea of multiple factor causation – the thought that crime was the result of several factors, some natural to man and his world, some biological and others environmental.

However, the Positivist School also presents a number of methodological problems. Although Lombroso made the careful attempt to measure the biological attributes of criminals (prisoners) and then compare them to non-criminals (soldiers – as a control group), the basic flaw in this comparison has been with criminology ever since. The "**Lombrosian fallacy**" is the acceptance of the state or legal definition of crime as a starting point. Do prisoners constitute a true and accurate sample of the actual population of criminals? Or do they simply represent a selective sample of those individuals who have been apprehended and convicted? The use of adjudicated delinquents or convicted prisoners as the research sample reflects this basic problem. Yet, on the other hand, where does one go to find a sample of lawbreakers? The problem is that the use of prisoners as a research sample ignores the fact that the criminal justice system itself is a very selective process and that any patterns observed as a result of the research may be the result of that process, not a true difference which exists in the criminal population. In other words, the incarcerated population could reflect the result of bias in the criminal justice process and in American society in general.

In fact, this type of research may promote a distorted view of crime patterns. For example, white-collar criminals seldom end up in prison and the poor and minority populations are traditionally over represented in the prison population. Research in the Positivist tradition can lead to a "kinds of people" interpretation of criminality; that crime is largely a product of individuals who are somehow different from the "normal" citizenry. This type of research fails to question the equity of the criminal justice process and to critically examine the sources of bias in the system. Thus, the Positivist School emphasizes the prediction and control of crime and overlooks the social process of law enforcement.

The Social Process School

In contrast, the Social Process School concentrates upon the manner in which laws are made and enforced. It is a combination of a number of criminological theories that critically examine the criminal justice process. They share the common theme of questioning the status quo in criminology (i.e., the "Chicago School" of criminology, Labeling theory, Conflict theory, Anomie theory, Marxist criminology). This tradition views crime from the perspective of the criminal or the actor (different functionaries in the criminal justice system).

It uses Max Weber's concept of **verstehen**: empathetic understanding of the individual. The legal definition of crime is viewed as a process that can be used against certain elements of society. Unlike the view of the Positivist School, the legal definition of crime is not accepted as a legitimate starting point for research. It recognizes that the criminal law can be exercised in a biased fashion that protects the interests of the dominant classes in society. It focuses upon such topics as: the creation of legal norms, the manner in which crime functions to maintain social solidarity, the interrelationship between crime and the criminal justice system, and the development of criminal careers. Unlike the Classical and Positivist Schools, this tradition utilizes both quantitative and qualitative methodologies to study crime.

The most telling criticism of this school is that it provides a "romanticized view of powerless deviants" and ignores the fact that crime is not completely determined by the social process. Certain behaviors (i.e., murder) would never be accepted by society, even though it is possible that not all murderers are treated in the same manner in the criminal justice system. The critical edge provided by this school of criminology, while substantial, must be tempered by objectivity.

In addition, Gilsinian summarized the "common threads" of these schools of criminology in the following manner:

1. Tendency Toward Combinations: People tend to combine things. An undesirable result (crime) is viewed as caused by a pathological condition.

2. Determinism: Given a certain pre-existing condition, crime will almost inevitably result.
3. Rationalism: The belief in the essentially orderly, understandable nature of human society. The discovery of the "laws" of criminality could lead to control of the crime problem.[24]

We add another attribute to this list. Criminology is not simply aimed at theory construction. Every school seeks to improve the social condition and do something about crime. The Classical School emphasized deterrence for the purpose of crime prevention and crime control (i.e., capital punishment, mandatory sentencing, and incapacitation of career criminals). The Positivist School provided a basis for the Medical Model (rehabilitation) of corrections. The Social Process School promoted the reform of laws (decriminalization: i.e., "status" offenses for juveniles) or even the restructuring of the social order (Marxist) and the critical examination of the discretionary powers of the criminal justice system, from the use of force by police right up to the imposition of capital punishment. Theory feeds research. Criminal justice research utilizes criminology to analyze the causes of crime, the manner in which the system operates, and the evaluation of programs that the system offers.

This brief summary of criminological theory provides an introduction to the linkage between theory and research. These theoretical traditions have affected both the subject matter and methodology of research in criminal justice.

CRIMINOLOGY AS AN APPLIED SOCIAL SCIENCE

An applied social science is one that seeks knowledge that can be put to use in the solution of social problems. The applied nature of criminology is illustrated by the research questions that are addressed. In particular, criminologists frequently conduct policy and program evaluations to determine whether or not a particular crime control method is effective.

Example: The Kansas City Preventive Patrol Experiment

Under the Professional Model of policing, police departments respond to incidents. As a result, patrol operations consume the majority of departmental resources. The effectiveness and deterrent value of patrolling was an unquestioned, traditional value of police administrators. O.W. Wilson sponsored this dogma of policing. Wilson believed that patrol created the impression of police omnipresence. It would convince most offenders that the opportunity for crime did not exist.[25] Patrol would also make citizens feel safer because the police could respond quickly to calls for service. In this manner, preventive patrol and quick response time became the major concerns of modern police departments. Administrators devoted their resources to more personnel, cars, and technological advances to speed communications and cut response time. As budgets became strained, police administrators questioned these assumptions and wanted to know if they justified the expense.[26]

These assumptions formed the basis for the Kansas City Preventive Patrol Experiment. It was designed to measure the impact of preventive patrol on the incidence and the public's fear of crime. Between October 1, 1972 and September 30, 1973, three controlled levels of routine preventive patrol were used in the experimental areas of Kansas City (15 beats). The first "reactive" area received no preventive patrol. Officers entered the area only in response to citizen calls for assistance. When they were not responding to calls, officers patrolled the boundaries of this area or patrolled the adjacent beats in the proactive area. In the second "proactive" area, police visibility was increased two to three times its usual level. In the third "control" area, the normal level of patrol was maintained. In effect, the police presence in the first and third areas was confined to responding to calls. Their visibility on the street was limited.

The results of the experiment produced no significant differences in the amount of crime, police response time, citizen satisfaction with police services or the rate at which they reported crimes to the police. Citizens were no more afraid of crime in the unpatrolled beats than they were in the Reactive Area. In particular, the experimental conditions had no significant effect on the most preventable crimes: burglaries, auto thefts, larcenies, robberies, or vandalism.[27]

Although there was considerable criticism of the experiment, a major tenet of policing, the effectiveness of preventitive patrol, received no support from the Kansas City findings.[28] In fact, subsequent research on police patrol tactics has supported the Kansas City findings. The type of patrol (even plainclothes or team policing) seems to have little effect on crime.[29] In her review of program findings, Newton reported that, with few exceptions, police anticrime efforts like preventitive patrol have failed to reduce crime. Other police programs like the daypatrol component of the Nashville saturation patrol; the Nashville home burglary saturation patrol, the Kansas City apprehensionoriented patrol, the Minnesota Crime Watch, operation identification programs have not had the desired crime reducing effect.[30] She warned that most crime prevention efforts are susceptible to **displacement**: due to specialized patrol or other enforcement efforts, crime may be reduced in one area because it has been displaced to other areas, targets, or times. This is known as the **"spillover effect."** Dis-placement theory states that, if the police presence is increased in one area, crime may actually be displaced rather than reduced. It will simply move over into neighboring areas were the "heats off." There was no indication of a spillover effect in the Kansas City Preventive Patrol Experiment.

A second Kansas City study questioned another major traditional patrol value – quick response to citizen's calls for service. It concluded that because citizens generally take so long to report crimes, even the quickest responses to most calls yield few arrests.[31] Overall, the results of the experiment raised serious doubts about the effectiveness and efficiency of preventive patrol. The need for patrol cars cruising the streets at random to prevent crime and quickly responding to citizen calls for service was now open to question.

The Kansas City Preventive Patrol Experiment has been criticized for its failure to isolate the effects of its treatment (proactive patrolling). The neighborhoods in the control group may have been exposed to the treatment. Police serving the control group areas were supposed to provide traditional reactive patrolling – responding to incoming calls for service and patrolling only the perimeter of the beat or an adjacent proactive, experimental neighborhood beat. The problem is that the 15 neighborhoods in the study were adjacent to one another and shared common boarders. Therefore, the control neighborhoods may have been exposed to the proactive patrolling (treatment) from the experimental neighborhoods.[32] The importance of this issue will be discussed in our analysis of research design.

The Executive Committee of the International Association of Chiefs of Police wrote that the results of the experiment could only be cautiously applied to other communities due to different enforcement problems and needs, varying populations, and different police agencies. They noted some flaws in how the research was conducted, particularly: maintaining the experimental conditions of the study (e.g., intended versus actual police activity in the reactive areas), lack of teamwork and conflict between department personnel and the research team; lack of personal data on the participating officers; the small sample size and the absence of some important variables. They note that some of the outcomes should be viewed as "inconclusive" rather than "nonsignificant." They suggest that the findings did not provide sufficient justification for concluding that patrol is not an important function in contemporary law enforcement and they do not justify decisions to reduce the number of police officers.[33]

Larson developed statistical models to estimate the frequency of police patrols and response time in the experimental areas. He found that patrols in Kansas City were not large enough to reach the intensity level of other cities. Patrol levels in the reactive areas were almost as large as the levels they experienced during high workload periods prior to the experiment. On the positive side, Larson noted that the experiment demonstrated that police administrators could shift officers from one area to another without adverse effects. The police could stop preventive patrol activities in a neighborhood for a year and not be missed by the residents. They could focus their manpower to combat certain crimes in certain areas, focus on special problems, and use their resources in innovative ways.

In sum, the Kansas City Experiment demonstrated that police departments could actively engage in research that will result in valid and valuable information that can provide guidance for operations. Strategies in policing and police management can be tested and their effectiveness considered rather than assumed. Research can guide policy and operations.

Example: Racial Disparities in Capital Sentencing

Historically, race has played a role in capital sentencing in this country. In *Furman* v. *Georgia*, several U.S. Supreme Court justices raised serious questions about arbitrariness and discrimination in the application of the death penalty.[35] For example, Justice William O. Douglas stated that the death penalty was "pregnant with discrimination" because it was selectively applied to minorities.

At that time, a massive body of research indicated that racial bias clouded the capital sentencing process. In particular, it clearly demonstrated that blacks were far more likely to be sentenced to death than were whites.[36] Other studies found that capital sentencing was determined by the interaction between the race of the offender and the race of the victim. Blacks who killed (or raped) whites were mostly likely to receive a death sentence.[37] This evidence served as the backdrop for the *Furman* decision. It did not outlaw but it questioned the results of the unbridled discretion typically at work in capital sentencing. In 1976, the court issued the *Gregg* v. *Georgia* decision. The justices ruled that Georgia's guided discretion statue provided adequate protection against bias in capital sentencing.

However, research on capital sentencing following *Gregg* indicated that race is still a dominant factor in the decision to execute. For example, studies based in Florida revealed that blacks that killed whites had the greatest probability of receiving a death sentence.[38] Similar results were discovered in Arkansas, Georgia, Illinois, Kentucky, Mississippi, New Jersey, North Carolina, Ohio, Oklahoma, South Carolina, Texas, and Virginia. This pattern of discrimination held fast even when the severity of the homicide was taken into account.[40]

This research was reviewed by the U.S. General Accounting Office to determine if the race of either the victim or the defendant influences the likelihood that offenders were sentenced to die. The GAO examined 53 studies of capital sentencing and excluded those that did not contain empirical data or were duplicative. The GAO then reviewed 28 studies that they judged methodologically sound and concluded that:

- In 82 percent of the studies, race of the victim was found to influence the likelihood of being charged with capital murder or receiving the death penalty for who murdered whites.
- The influence of the race of the victim was found at all levels of the criminal justice process. This evidence was stronger at the earlier stages of this process (e.g., the prosecutorial decision to seek the death penalty or to proceed to trial rather than plea bargain) than in the later stages.
- Legally relevant variables (e.g., aggravating circumstances, prior record, culpability level, heinousness of the crime, and the number of victims) were influential but did not fully explain the reasons for racial disparity in capital sentencing.

• More than three-fourths of the studies that identified race of the
defendant effect found that black defendants were more likely to
be sentenced to die.

Since this review, studies of capital sentencing have continued to confirm these conclusions. In Kentucky, research found that blacks who
killed whites were more likely to be the target and recipient of a capital sentence.[42] Kentucky later passed a bill, the Racial Justice Act,
which allowed defendants in capital cases to use statistical evidence of
racial discrimination to show that race influenced the decision to seek
the death penalty. If the judge finds that race was a factor, the death
penalty would be barred.

A Maryland study examined nearly 6,000 homicide prosecutions
where the death penalty might have been applied between 1978 and
1999. In 1,311 death penalty eligible cases, 180 cases went to trial,
resulting in 76 death sentences. Again, when the race of both the victim and offender were examined together, the disparities began to surface. The study showed blacks that killed whites were two times more
likely to get a death sentence as whites that killed whites. Blacks who
killed whites were four times as likely to get a death sentence as blacks
that killed blacks. This study led Maryland Attorney General J. Joseph
Curran to ask the governor to abolish the death penalty.[43] Together,
these studies illustrate the ability of research to inform public policy.
The findings on capital sentencing were consistent across locations
and times. Both the scope and accuracy of these studies led to solid
recommendations, supported by research evidence.

As these examples suggest, criminological studies must be interpreted with caution. These examples demonstrate how difficult it is to
accurately draw policy implications from research findings. Sound
policy can only follow accurate research. Research should be replicated in other locations to be certain that results generated in one area
apply to others. For these reasons, criminologists are often reluctant to
reach definite conclusions based upon their studies.

Criminologists can and do adopt public policy analysis as a research
framework. It focuses on the study of policy formation and application. It attempts to inform public opinion and decision makers about
the consequences of public policy. Limitations of the study must be
taken into account but the findings should lead to recommendations
concerning the management of the crime problem. The full implica-

tions of research findings and their potential impact upon persons must be carefully stated. These are duties that criminologists cannot ignore.

CONCLUSION

This overview of basic research principles and theoretical concepts provides an introduction to the body of this text. Research has an important place in the criminal justice system. The information provided by research reports can provide a basis for reform and improvement. This information must be provided in an accurate manner with reliable results. The policy implications of research findings must be carefully drawn and the limitations of the study must be kept in mind.

KEY TERMS

Exploratory Research
Descriptive Research
Explanatory Research
Evaluation Research
Induction
Generalizations
Deductive method
Replication
Concept
Variable
Operational definition
Dependent variable
Independent variable
Causal hypothesis
Causal time order
Directional research hypothesis
Non-directional research hypothesis
General deterrence
Specific deterrence
Incapacitation
Cesare Beccaria

Jeremy Bentham
Cesare Lombroso
Multiple factor causation
Lombrosian fallacy
Verstehen
Displacement
Spillover effect

REVIEW QUESTIONS

1. What is the value and purpose of criminal justice research? Give examples to support your answer.
2. What is an operational definition and what is its purpose?
3. What is the difference between the inductive and deductive methods?
4. Give an example of a research hypothesis and identify the independent and dependent variables.
5. In your answer to the previous question, was your hypothesis directional or non-directional? Why?
6. Identify the major assumptions of the:
   a. Classical School
   b. Positivist School
   c. Social Process School
7. Is it possible for studies to be "value-free"?
8. Summarize the major findings of the research studies and discuss their policy implications.
9. What is the problem with displacement or the "spillover effect"?
10. Do you agree with the Maryland Attorney General that the research indicates that the death penalty should be abolished? Why?

REFERENCES

1. Eck, J.E. and La Vigne, N.G. (1994). *Using research: A primer for law enforcement managers.* Washington, D.C.: Police Executive Research Forum, p. 2.
2. Ibid.
3. Ibid., p. 4.
4. Spelman, W. (1988). *Beyond bean counting: New approaches for managing crime data,* Washington, D.C.: Police Executive Research Forum, p. 13.

5. U.S. Department of Justice, "Identity Theft and Fraud," (7/25/05) http://www.usdoj.com/criminal/fraud/idtheft.html; Federal Trade Commission, "ID Theft Home," http://www.consumer.gov/idtheft/.

6. Synovate, *Federal Trade Commission – Identity theft survey report* (Washington, D.C.: Federal Trade Commission, 2003): 6.

7. Allison, S.F., Schuck, A.M., and Lersch, K.M. (2005). Exploring the crime of identity theft: Prevalence, clearance rates, and victim/offender characteristics. *Journal of Criminal Justice*, 33:19–29.

8. Eck and La Vigne, *Using Research*, p. 12.

9. ONDCP Drug Policy Clearinghouse Fact Sheet, *Methamphetamine* (Washington, D.C.: Executive Office of the President, Office on National Drug Control Policy, 2003): 1; Office of National Drug Control Policy, *Drug Facts – Methamphetamine* (7/6/2005), http://www.whitehousedrugpolicy.gov/drugfact/methamphetamine/index.html.

10. Ibid.

11. Office of National Drug Control Policy, *Drug Facts*.

12. Ibid.

13. Ibid.

14. Ibid.

15. Scott, M.S. (2002). *Street prostitution – Problem-oriented guides for police series, no. 2*, Washington, D.C., U.S. Department of Justice, Office of Community Policing Services, pp. 16–21.

16. Petrosino, A., Turpin-Petrosino, C., and Buehler, J. (2003). *Scared Straight* and other juvenile awareness programs for preventing juvenile delinquency: A systematic review of the randomized experimental evidence. *Annals of the Academy of Political and Social Science*, 589:41–62.

17. Cincinnati Police. (2007). *Problem-solving guide*, Cincinnati, OH: Chief Thomas H. Streicher, p. 6.

18. Monette, D.R., Sullivan, T.J., and DeJong, C.R. (2005). *Applied social research: A tool for the human services*, Belmont, CA: Brooks/Cole – Thomson Learning, p. 86.

19. Senese, J.D. (1997). *Applied research methods in criminal justice*, Chicago: Nelson-Hall, p. 30.

20. Sykes, G.W., Vito, G.F., and McElrath, K. (1987). Jail populations and crime rates: An exploratory analysis. *Journal of Police Science and Administration*, 15:72–77.

21. See Vito, G.F., Maahs, J.R., and Holmes, R.M. (2007). *Criminology: Theory, research and policy*, Boston: Jones and Bartlett.

22. Poveda, T.G., and Schaffer, E. (1975). "Positivism and interactionism: Two traditions of research in criminology," in Viano, E. ed., *Criminal justice research*, Lexington, MA: Lexington Books.

23. Ibid.

24. Gilsinian, J.F. (1982). *Doing justice*, Englewood Cliffs, NJ: Prentice-Hall.

25. Kelling, G.L., Pate, T., Dieckman, D. and Brown, C.E. (1974). *The Kansas City preventive patrol experiment*, Washington, D.C.: Police Foundation, p. 1.

26. Petersilia, J. (1987). *The influence of criminal justice research*, Santa Monica, CA: RAND Corporation, p. vii.

27. Kelling, Pate, Dieckman, and Brown, *Kansas City Experiment*.

28. Larson, R.C. (1975). What happened to patrol operations in Kansas City? A review of the Kansas City preventive patrol experiment, *Journal of Criminal Justice*, 3:267–297.

29. Szynkowski, L.J. (1981). Preventive patrol: Traditional versus specialized, *Journal of Police Science and Administration*, 9:167–183.

30. Newton, A.M. (1978). Prevention of crime and delinquency, *Criminal Justice Abstracts*, 10:245–266.

31. Krajick, K. (1978). Does patrol prevent crime? *Police Magazine*, 1:4–16.

32. Farrington, D.P. (1983). "Randomized experiments in crime and justice," in Tonry, M. and Morris, N. eds., *Crime and justice*, Chicago: University of Chicago Press, 257–308.

33. International Association of Chiefs of Police Executive Committee. (1975). IACP position paper on the Kansas City preventive patrol experiment, *Police Chief*, 42:16–20.

34. Larson, "What happened to patrol operations in Kansas City?"; Petersilia, *Influence*, p. 9–10. Similarly, the authors of the Kansas City experiment noted that their results indicated that police administrators could be more flexible in officer allocation. Pate, T., Kelling, G.L. and Brown, C. (1976). A response to: What happened to patrol operations in Kansas City, *Journal of Criminal Justice*, 3:299–320.

35. Bowers, W.J. (1983). The pervasiveness of arbitrariness and discrimination under post-Furman capital statutes, *Journal of Criminal Law and Criminology*. 74:1067–1100; Bowers, W.J. (1993). Research note: Capital punishment and contemporary values: People's misgivings and the court's misperceptions, *Law and Society Review*, 27:156–176.

36. Brearley, H. (1930). The negro and homicides, *Social Forces*, 9:247–253; Magnum, C.S. (1941). *The legal status of the negro*, Chapel Hill, NC: University of North Carolina Press; Garfinkle, H. (1949). Research note on inter and intraracial homicides, *Social Forces*, 27:369–381; Johnson, E.H. (1957). Selective forces in capital punishment, *Social Forces*, 36:165–169.

37. Zimring, F., Eigen, J. and O'Malley, S. (1976). Punishing homicides in Philadelphia: Perspectives on the death penalty, *University of Chicago Law Review*, 43:227–252; Wolfgang, M.E. and Riedel, M. (1973). Race, judicial discretion, and the death penalty, *The Annals of the American Academy of Political and Social Science*, 407:119–133.

38. Arkin, S.D. (1980). Discrimination and arbitrariness in capital punishment: An analysis of post-Furman murder cases in Dade County, Florida, 1973–1976, *Stanford Law Review*, 33:75–101; Radelet, M.L. (1981). Racial characteristics and the imposition of the death penalty, *American Sociological Review*, 46:918–927; Radelet, M.L. and Pierce, G.L. (1990). Race and prosecutorial discretion in homicide cases, *Law and Society Review*, 19:587–621; Zeisel, H. (1976). Race bias in the administration of the death penalty, *Harvard Law Review*, 43:227–252.

39. Baldus, D.C., Pulaski, C. and Woodworth, G. (1983). Comparative review of death sentences: An empirical study of the Georgia experience, *Journal of*

Criminal Law and Criminology, 74:661–753; Bienin, L.B., Weiner, N.A., Denno, D.W., Allison, P.D., and Mills, D.L. (1988). The reimposition of capital punishment in New Jersey: The role of prosecutorial discretion, *Rutgers Law Review*, 41:27–372; Eckland-Olson, S. (1988). Structured discretion, racial bias, and the death penalty: The first decade after Furman in Texas, *Social Science Quarterly*, 69:853–873; Gross, S.R., and Mauro, R. (1988). *Death and Discrimination*, Boston: Northeastern University Press; Keil, T.J., and Vito, G.F. (1990). Race and the death penalty in Kentucky murder trials: An analysis of post-Gregg outcomes, *Justice Quarterly*, 7:189–207; Paternoster, R. (1983). Race of the victim and location of the crime: The decision to seek the death penalty in South Carolina, *Journal of Criminal Law and Criminology*, 74:754–785; Smith, M.D. (1987). Patterns of discrimination in assessments of the death penalty: The case of Louisiana, *Journal of Criminal Justice*, 15:279–286.

40. Barnett, A. (1985). Some distribution patterns for the Georgia death sentence, *U.C. Davis Law Review*, 18:1375–1384; Keil, T.J., and Vito, G.F. (1989). Race, homicide severity and the application of the death penalty: A consideration of the Barnett scale, *Criminology*, 27:511–531.

41. U.S. General Accounting Office. (1990). *Death penalty sentencing: Research indicates a pattern of racial disparities*, Washington, DC: U.S. General Accounting Office.

42. Keil, T.J. and Vito, G.F. (1995). Race and the death penalty in Kentucky murder trials, 1976–1991, *American Journal of Criminal Justice*, 20:17–36.

43. Paternoster, R. and Brame, R. (2002). *An empirical analysis of Maryland's death sentencing system with respect to the influence of race and legal jurisdiction*, College Park, MD: University of Maryland.

Chapter 2

LIBRARY RESEARCH AND LITERATURE REVIEWS

CHAPTER OVERVIEW

In this chapter you will learn about the purpose, process and uses of research that focuses on identifying what information is already known about a particular topic or question. One of the important things to remember about criminal justice research is that all research is about adding to the existing body of knowledge that exists about a particular topic or question. Researchers rely on what previous studies have shown to guide their own studies. In this way we can think of any new piece of research as adding to the knowledge that is already known. Research studies that are done today do not replace the knowledge that was learned by studies done last year; instead, today's studies add to our knowledge base and help to understand things in more detail, from different perspectives or simply make our confidence in knowledge stronger (because more studies have found similar results).

The information from previous studies can be found in several ways, and from a variety of sources. When researchers talk about doing background research – or "reviewing the literature" – they are talking about the basic processes of what is also called library research. Working in libraries and with library resources are experiences and skills that most people first have in elementary school. These same skills are used, although in some refined and more focused ways, by researchers throughout their careers to start all of their research projects.

WHAT IS LIBRARY RESEARCH?

Library research is the process of searching for, finding and using existing information (including both previous research studies and theoretical discussions) to help in planning and understanding current research. The goals of doing library research are to identify what is already known about a topic or research question, and to provide researchers with guidance about what gaps exist in our current knowledge, what data collection methods have previously been shown to be effective and efficient for particular topics or questions, and what problems researchers should be aware of as they embark on their own research process.

Doing library research on the topic or question that a researcher is interested in provides background information that guides the researcher in setting up her own study. By knowing what is already known, how previous researchers have defined their variables, from whom data on questions has previously been collected, and what processes have and have not worked well, a researcher can avoid making the mistakes that others have made and she can design and conduct a study that will add to the knowledge base about her topic of interest.

DOING LIBRARY RESEARCH

The actual practice of doing library research involves searching for information in a variety of places, knowing where to look for information and being able to narrow the focus of information that is collected, read and used for guidance. The first thing that researchers doing background research on a topic need to know is where to look for information on previous research.

Sources of Research Literature

There are a number of types of resources that can provide researchers with information to guide their work and to get a thorough understanding of what is already known about a topic or research question. Each of the types of sources, however, tends to provide a different type of information, and varying degrees of depth and detail.

Books can be useful resources, especially when looking for theoretical understandings of an issue and in-depth, thorough discussions of a topic. Books can also provide discussions (usually very detailed) about large scale research projects. When a researcher says that she uses books in her review of the literature she means what is also referred to as "research monographs." These types of books are discussions devoted to the comprehensive presentation of one study, not a collection of multiple studies that are all reviewed or discussed only briefly.

One source of information that is tempting for many beginning researchers to use is textbooks. The textbooks that students use in classes (such as this one you are reading right now) are obviously useful and efficient ways to learn many pieces of information about a topic. However, textbooks are not considered true scholarly sources for a couple of reasons. First, the information presented in textbooks tends to be broad, and not deep. This means that lots of information ("facts") is presented, but not much detail about the way this information was discovered is presented. Therefore, it is difficult for a researcher to assess the quality of the research process that is behind the discovery of this information. (Or, said differently, knowing whether or not the research that produced a particular fact/finding was high quality research is very difficult without more information than is typically reported in a textbook.) A second problem with using textbooks as a source of information is that the information presented in a textbook is all filtered and based on the interpretations of the textbook author(s); it is not the actual work of the researchers who did the studies being discussed. This leaves the information open to possible errors, omissions and mis-interpretations. With all of this being said, it is important to realize that textbooks can be useful, however, as a place to identify major studies that the researcher can then obtain and read and review for themselves.

The most common type of information that most criminal justice researchers use when reviewing what is already known about a topic or question is the **scholarly journal article**. Articles that are published in scholarly journals are (almost always) reports of individual research projects. Each journal article will typically be focused on a very specific research question, and the findings of the individual study on that research question. For most criminal justice researchers, and most social scientists generally, the primary way that research results are reported is through articles in scholarly journals.

A scholarly journal article will include several important sections. First there is an introduction and a review of the existing research literature that pertains to the question being studied in the project. This in itself can be very useful to researchers, as this makes available a summary and review of what was known at a given point in time about the topic in question. In many ways, this is like finding a mini-textbook about the topic or question that is the focus of the article. Following the review of literature is the detailed discussion of the research methods that were used to study the question. This is a very important part of the journal article, as this is where the reader gets the information that allows him to assess whether the research was done in a high quality way, and is likely to produce valid, reliable and generalizable results/findings. After the detailed discussion of the research methods the article will include the presentation of the findings or results of the project. And, finally, the conclusion (or "discussion") section of the article will explain the relevance of the results and inform the reader about how these results fit into the bigger picture of knowledge about the topic.

Another critically important thing to understand about research that is reported in scholarly journal articles is that the articles that are published in these outlets have all undergone a rigorous process of quality assurance. The **peer review process** in scholarly publishing is when a researcher submits her finished research report (a "manuscript") to a journal for the editor to consider it for publication. When an editor receives a manuscript she then submits it (usually "blinded," or with all information identifying the author[s]) to a panel of other scholars who are knowledgeable about the specific topic. It is the job of this panel of scholars to carefully review the research being reported, looking for problems in how the research was conducted, how the results/findings are reported and how the theoretical explanation/argument of the results are presented. This process is designed to ensure that only well-done research, which is valid, reliable and explained in theoretically and practically sound ways, ends up being published. The peer review process is the way that scientists work to ensure that only high quality research is publicized and widely available. Box 2-1 lists some of the top journals in Criminal Justice and Criminology.

Scholarly journal articles are not only important sources of knowledge, but they are also usually very specific in what they address. As

---

Box 2-1
TOP JOURNALS IN CRIMINAL JUSTICE AND CRIMINOLOGY

Crime and Delinquency
Criminal Justice and Behavior
Criminal Justice Review
Criminal Justice Policy Review
Criminology
Criminology and Public Policy
Federal Probation Quarterly
Journal of Contemporary Criminal Justice
Journal of Criminal Justice Education
Journal of Criminal Justice
Journal of Criminal Law and Criminology
Journal of Research in Crime and Delinquency
Journal of Quantitative Criminology
Justice Quarterly
Law and Society Review
Police Quarterly
The Prison Journal

---

a study of a particular, specific research question they information that is reported in a journal article may either be perfect for assisting a current researcher understand what is known about his topic, or it can be frustrating that the study is related to what he is interested in, but based on a different population, or from a too-different-to-be-relevant location or uses variables defined in different ways and therefore only somewhat informative. Scholarly journal articles are the first place that most research appears for public access and consumption however, and in criminal justice it is the most common source of information about what is known about a particular topic.

A third source of information, but one that can be a bit more difficult to access than books or scholarly journal articles, are **research reports** from criminal justice agencies. Many agencies, especially larger ones, will occasionally do their own research on a topic, question, problem or policy issue that is relevant to their operations. Typically this research is used for internal agency decision-making and guidance for operations of the organization, and hence is not usually written up as a journal article or book. Especially when a researcher is interested in a question about operations or policies of criminal justice agencies the existing research from agencies can be a great resource. This type of resource is most easily identified and accessed by reviewing the websites of individual agencies and organizations. So, if a researcher is interested in job satisfaction of prison staff, she might find it useful to check the websites of the 50 state departments of corrections, to see if any of the agencies have done internal studies of employee job satisfaction. This is almost always information that would not be found elsewhere.

A fourth source of information, but one that is likely to have limited value, is the reporting of information in **trade publications** (newsletters, magazines, etc. written for persons in particular professions). These publications will report on research results that pertain to particular questions and topics germane to that profession, but the information reported tends to be in simple language and to lack the details about what the research process included and specifics of the results. However, if a researcher was interested in studying the effectiveness of various methods of recruitment for police departments, she might find it useful to skim through past issues of *Police Chief* magazine or newsletters from the International Association of Chiefs of Police to see if there are any stories about whether or not particular recruitment methods are more or less effective. If she does find relevant stories, she should use this information as a starting point for trying to then locate more detailed information about the studies being reported. Hence, she could check the specific agency's website or contact either the article author or agency where the reported project was done to ask for more information. Trade publications can be useful starting points to locate information, but very rarely are the actual articles in them sufficiently detailed to be useful as sources themselves. Additionally, trade publications are not subject to the peer-review process that journal articles undergo. Therefore, the information reported in trade publication articles may need to be viewed with a degree of skepticism.

In addition to books, scholarly journal articles, agency research reports and trade publications there are a number of other sources of information that may or may not be relevant and useful to researchers looking to review the state of knowledge about a particular topic or research question. Included among these other types of sources are papers presented by researchers at academic and professional conferences. The papers presented at conferences have (in almost all instances) not yet been published in any outlet, and are usually the most recent research findings that exist. Often the papers presented at conferences are works in progress, preliminary findings or projects that the researcher has completed but is still working with to identify the full range of implications and conclusions. Other sources include student research in the form of doctoral dissertations and master's theses. In most social science disciplines and at most universities dissertations and theses are required to be original research. Often these sources (especially theses) do not get rewritten and published in any form, meaning that the only place this work can be found is in the dissertation or thesis. Additionally, some researchers find it useful to use book reviews in their process of identifying and reviewing existing research. Book reviews are most useful for providing the researcher with information about whether or not a research monograph is truly on point for her interests, reviews provide a brief summary of the book's content, and reviews provide at least one other scholar's evaluation of the quality of the research (or theoretical discussion) reported in the book.

What is important to keep in mind about the range of types of sources of information is that it is essential to search for information in a variety of types of places, and the types of sources are likely to provide different types of information. Some of these sources of information can be fairly easy to identify and access, others can be more challenging. The next section discusses ways to find the information you need to develop a well-rounded and thorough understanding of a particular topic or question, and where you should look for information.

How to Find Previous Research

The ways that researchers can and do find previous research will vary based on what types of sources are being sought (or, said differently, each approach to searching for previous research is likely to yield different types of sources of information). As early as elementary school most of us were taught how to find basic information in the library. While the tools used for that information have changed significantly over the years (does anyone remember the card catalogue?), the strategies and approaches for searching remain basically the same. The places that we look for identifying what is available are the same today as they were 10, 20, even perhaps 50 years ago, but the form that those sources take have changed.

Today the vast majority of library research is conducted electronically. However, as recently as the mid-1990s many (if not most) researchers were still working with actual paper and books to locate information. The move to electronic versions of the basic search tools has made the process of library research much quicker, more efficient and likely to yield larger bodies of information than was the norm previously. Suffice it to say that the two oldest authors of this book remember well being students and having to actually walk to the library (or, in some cases multiple libraries on campus), sit in front of a long line of thick books that listed the newly published research by key words, thumb through book after book after book of listings of abstracts, write down the citation for the articles and reports that seemed important, and then walk through the library collecting the bound copies of journals which then had to be taken to a photocopy machine so coins could be deposited and copies could be made of the various pieces. Today's students probably find the description of this process to be quaint, and completely foreign. Today a researcher can sit at a computer, anywhere in the world, at any time of day or night, and quickly search for, find, and print copies of stacks of articles. And, all of this is done for no cost.

So, what are the tools that can be used to find and access background research? The first important tool to be familiar with is the electronic version of **abstract databases**. These are collections of brief summaries of the goals, methods and findings of published (and in some databases agency reports and conference presentations) research reports that can be searched using key words, by author and depending on the specific database sometimes other variables as well. The brief summaries are what are known as the article's/report's **abstract**. These databases are usually discipline specific, or include sources from several closely related disciplines. Criminal justice researchers usually start their search for background information in Criminal Justice Abstracts, and often also look in databases focused on sociology, psychology, political science and law.

There are some unique abstract databases with which criminal justice researchers also should be familiar. One of these is the abstract database maintained by the National Criminal Justice Reference Service (NCJRS). This is a division of U.S. Department of Justice. Included in this web-based database are published research reports and a significant portion of agency produced research reports and some trade publications.

Another important database with which to be familiar is called Digital Dissertations. This is the new version of what some students may remember as Dissertations Abstracts. This database is devoted to providing access to the vast majority of doctoral dissertations and many masters' theses completed by students at American universities. Each source included in the database includes a detailed abstract (usually significantly longer than the abstracts included elsewhere for journal articles) and information about who completed the research, for what degree and at what educational institution.

A third important database that does not provide access to abstracts or summaries of research articles, reports, etc., but which can quickly move a researcher along in the process of identifying everything on a particular topic is the source known as Social Science Citation Index. The focus of this database is to provide a listing of all of the references included in a research article. The database can be searched and used in several ways. This includes looking up the sources that a particular article cites. Or, the database can be searched to find all articles, reports, etc. that include a particular citation in their reference list. This can be a very productive strategy for finding what is available on a particular topic, especially if there is a classic or extremely influential piece of research on a particular topic. For instance, if a researcher is interested in doing a project to look at the impacts of various types of police patrol strategies, he would already known (from reading Chapter One in this book) that Kelling, Pate, Dieckman and Brown's 1974 report for the Police Foundation is a classic study in this area. Using Social Science Citation Index the researcher could search to see all of the articles, reports, etc. published since that time that includes citations to this report. The pieces identified by this process could then be checked to see if they in fact are studies of effectiveness of various police patrol practices. (For anyone familiar with the process of legal research, in which lawyers track case precedents and citation strings, the process of working with Social Science Citation Abstracts is very similar.)

Another productive, but more simplistic version of this approach is for a researcher to carefully review the reference list in any and all articles, books, reports, etc. that they do identify for their background research. Simply reading through the reference lists of the first few pieces of literature you find can direct you to many more relevant pieces in a very short period of time. The thing to remember here, however, is that if the first few articles, reports, etc. that you encounter are not very recent, reviewing the reference lists of these pieces will not provide you with more recent pieces; after all, only things available at the time the piece whose reference list you are reading were available have a chance of being included in that reference list.

Another important place to look for information, especially statistics about the operations of criminal justice agencies are the websites of both government research agencies and criminal justice agencies. At the federal level, the Bureau of Justice Statistics is a wealth of information about criminal justice organizations' operations, staffing, cases handled, and many other issues. The Federal Bureau of Investigation maintains the Uniform Crime Reports which is the major source of information about crimes reported to law enforcement agencies. The National Crime Victimization Survey is the major source of information about the number of crimes (and characteristics of victims, perpetrators and incidents) reported by victims, but not necessarily to law enforcement. The federal Office for Victims of Crime also provides a range of statistical information about crime victims and criminal events.

Other types of government agencies also can be rich sources of information. As discussed earlier, actual criminal justice agencies (especially larger ones) will often have a research unit or department that does and posts research reports. Other types of government agencies also maintain collections and databases of research reports. For researchers interested in corrections issues the National Institute of Corrections maintains a database with summaries (and many full text documents) of published and unpublished research and many reports of research and programs produced by corrections agencies.

It is also worthwhile to check the websites of professional organizations in topical and practice areas in which one is interested in conducting research. For instance, both the International Association of Chiefs of Police and the American Probation and Parole Association have entire sections of their websites devoted to research they have done themselves and that they have identified from others. Many other criminal justice professional organizations also maintain collections of both internally and externally produced research pertaining to their professional membership and audience.

Finally, and perhaps most familiar for many students, there is the general internet search via a commercial search engine. As most everyone today knows, doing a general internet search for almost any topic will produce dozens, hundreds or many thousands of "hits" on documents and websites that at least to a minimal degree mention or address a particular topic (e.g., keyword). Researchers often use general internet searches only as a way to check for hard-to-find documents that may not come up in other more rigorous types of searches. Extreme caution needs to be used in finding and using sources from the internet. Whereas earlier it was explained that the peer review process ensures that scholarly journal articles meet a criterion of scientific value, there is no such check and balance on the information and materials that can be found on the internet. In very simple terms, anyone can post anything on a webpage. Just because someone went to the trouble of typing something and then uploading it to a webpage does not mean that the information is accurate or has any value in scientific research.

Of course, the first step in the design of a study is the selection of a topic.

SELECTING A TOPIC

The first suggestion that you should follow is to choose a topic that you are interested in. The starting point might be a criminological theory that you wish to test or your practical experience (either working or observing) in the criminal justice system. You must be careful, however, to guard against bias. The very fact that you are interested in a topic indicates that you feel about it in some way. The research that you conduct should be as free of bias as possible. Your thoughts about a topic, let's choose capital punishment as an example, must not guide the research in such a way that it influences the final results. You must be prepared to have your initial beliefs rejected or supported by the research findings. Since research requires a strong commitment of time, money, and energy.[1] For these reasons, you must be willing to make these substantial investments in your topic.

A second suggestion is that the topic should be significant. It should contribute to knowledge and inform public policy regarding crime and justice. Research provides information that can be used to solve crime problems and insure that justice is provided across the system. Problem solving is a key element of applied research.[2]

Finally, the research should be viable and feasible. Are you able to conduct the study and obtain the data that are required? Will it take too much time and/or too much money?

Now that you have selected the topic, it is necessary to refine it further – to narrow its scope and focus and provide a purpose for your study. For example, if you go to the *Criminal Justice Abstracts* (an automated list of citations of journal articles, books, and reports in criminal justice and criminology) and conduct a search on our selected topic "capital punishment," you will generate a list of 1,512 abstracts of books and articles on this subject and 375 web sites.[3] Capital punishment is a very broad topic. Our list of the first ten "hits" has everything from "capital punishment views in China and the United States" to "juvenile capital offenders in Texas."[4] This topic must be narrowed down to make it more manageable and to provide focus for our study. We decide that we are actually more interested in the death penalty for juveniles. This is a much more specific topic. When it is submitted to the *Criminal Justice Abstracts*, the number of "hits" (14 articles and books and 0 web sites) demonstrates how much more in focus our topic of interest has become.[5]

LITERATURE REVIEWS

Once a researcher has identified and collected the relevant existing research pertaining to his topic or research question the task becomes reviewing the information for guidance in the current project and writing a **literature review**. The review of the literature is the discussion of the theoretical and content issues that are known about the research question at the center of the current effort. This discussion has multiple purposes, and serves several goals

Goals for literature reviews include:

- Providing a summary of the known information related to the research question
- Identifying gaps in the existing knowledge where additional information is needed
- Assessing the generalizability of the body of existing knowledge to other populations and settings
- Evaluating the adequacy of the theoretical explanations that have been offered for understanding the topic in question
- Identifying methodological approaches that do and do work effectively and efficiently when studying the topic of interest

The most obvious contribution that a review of the literature provides is to provide the researcher (and later readers of the review) with a thorough understanding of what is known about the topic in question. This includes understanding what variables have been previously shown to be (or not to be) related to the dependent variable (and each other), the prevalence and/or incidence of a phenomena in the community, what aspects of programs/initiatives/organizations work well (or not well) under various conditions, and generally what can be said definitively about how a phenomena exists in society.

The summary of what is known is directly related to the second goal for literature reviews, pointing out what is not known. When a researcher can identify these gaps in the existing literature, this means that the knowledge base about a topic lacks some piece(s) of information that therefore limits our ability to have a complete understanding of the topic being studied. These are topics and questions that then should or need to be the focus of additional research. This is important to know. Knowing what is unknown may be even more informative than knowing what is known.

A literature review will often serve the purpose of assessing the previously completed research regarding the persons and places from which data was collected, and hence to which the findings of a study can be generalized. By considering from whom and where data for studies whose findings are available come it is possible to identify gaps in knowledge about to which the findings can be applied more broadly. Consider for example a researcher interested in whether deaf individuals can effectively work as law enforcement officers. If, after reviewing all of the literature she can identify about persons with disabilities serving in law enforcement and the types of jobs for which deaf persons do and do not effectively work, a researcher realizes all of the research available has been done in cities with a population of one million or more, there is a clear gap in generalizability of these findings. This would suggest that additional research should be done in smaller cities, suburban areas and rural communities. If the body of research that has been identified presents strong arguments that deaf individuals make very good police officers in major cities, can we trust that this would hold true in rural west Texas, central Montana or the Appalachian regions of Kentucky and Tennessee? Based on the research available, we would not be able to say. Therefore, a review of the literature should point out this limitation of the existing research.

This also serves as a way of showing the importance and need for a research project.

As explained in Chapter One, criminal justice research is guided by theory. As the foundation of understanding and explaining the criminal justice system, the actions of those who work in, are served by and are processed by the criminal justice system, theory is critical to explaining the relevance of research findings. As one goal of a review of the literature is an examination of if and how well the findings of previous research projects are explained by (or fit) theoretical propositions and perspectives. This approach involves assessing whether the findings reported in previous research studies fit with what a particular theory says are the necessary/important types of variables and relationships. If the findings of previous research do show that the way a theory suggests something operates is in fact the way that things seem to be occurring, then the review of the literature would be supportive of such a theory.

Finally, reviews of literature regarding a particular topic or question should look at what types of data collection and analysis processes have been used in previous research, and where researchers have reported difficulties and problems. Additionally, this approach to a review of the literature will look at how key concepts and variables are defined and operationalized (or, how measurements of variable X are made), to see if when researchers use different definitions they end up with different results.

Regardless of the purposes that a review of the literature fulfill the ultimate goal of the final written document that is the literature review is to lead a reader from a starting point of "oh, this might be an interesting topic" to the point of understanding why a researcher does the study he does, and how it will contribute to a developing body of knowledge about the particular topic. This means that a review of the literature needs to develop ideas and move a reader along a path of greater understanding. How this movement and development of understanding is constructed is the focus of the final section of this chapter.

Writing the Literature Review

The process of actually writing a review of the literature includes reading and taking notes on all of the relevant pieces of research that are identified, organizing the information uncovered into conceptual groups, outlining a logical progression of ideas from general to showing the need for the research to which the review of literature is leading, and then writing a conceptually-focused discussion of the research that is available.

When writing a review of the literature it is important focus on the ideas and concepts that are revealed in the available research, not to focus on the specific findings and minute details of studies. It is also important to write the review of literature at a level of discussing ideas, not simply summarizing one study/article after another. When minute details are the focus and/or summaries of studies are present one after another, there is no connection or central idea that a reader takes away.

In writing a review of the literature the researcher should begin the process by identifying what he wants the reader to learn from the document. Highlighting a central message, or three or four main points that should be understood can help a researcher write a review of the literature that is focused and leads the reader from a point of general interest in a topic to understanding what is known and what remains to be known about the topic or research question that is the core of a research project/product.

CONCLUSION

Background research, including identifying previous research on the topic of interest to a current researcher and reviews of that literature, provide important contributions to the design, conduct and reporting of any research project. There are a variety of places that research is reported, and all of which may provide insights and contributions to a researcher planning a research project. The purpose of finding, reading and reviewing research about a topic that has been previously done is to allow a researcher to thoroughly understand the knowledge based about a topic, and to plan a research project while taking advantage of the lessons learned in previous research.

Library research, and literature reviews that are written with the information gathered via library research, both inform the design of a research project and functions to show consumers of a research product that there is a need for the information and findings of a research project. Without reviews of the literature there would be no easy way to know what is known about a topic and if, how and where any particular research project and it's findings contribute to the body of knowledge about a topic.

KEY TERMS

Library research
Scholarly journal article
Peer review process
Research reports
Trade publications
Abstract databases
Abstract
Literature review

REVIEW QUESTIONS

1. What is the purpose of the literature review?
2. Why are journal articles a valuable source of information?
3. Why are research reports from agencies relevant to the research process?

REFERENCES

1. Delbert C. Miller, ed. (1991). *Handbook of research design and social measurement.* Newbury Park, CA: Sage, p. 17.
2. Leonard Bickman and Debra J. Rog, eds. (1998). *Handbook of applied social research methods.* Newbury Park, CA: Sage, p. x.
3. *Criminal Justice Abstracts* contains abstracts of current books, journal articles, government reports and dissertations from the world over. We conducted this search on July 11, 2007 using the on-line service provided by the University of Louisville. The abstracts themselves are published and presented by CSA Illumina.
4. Jiang, S., Lambert, E.G., and Wang, J. (2007). Capital punishment views in China and the United States: A preliminary study among college students. *International Journal of Offender Therapy and Comparative Criminology,* 51:84–97; Mikhail, D. (2006). Refining and resolving the blur of Gault for juvenile capital

offenders in Texas: A world without the juvenile death penalty. *Victims & Offenders*, 11: 99–121.

5. For example, first two articles cited in the *Criminal Justice Abstracts* were: Vito, G.F., and Keil, T.J. (2004). Dangerousness and the death penalty: An examination of juvenile homicides in Kentucky. *The Prison Journal*, 84:436–451; Moon, M.M., Wright, J.P., Cullen, F.T. et al. (2000). Putting kids to death: Specifying public support for juvenile capital punishment. *Justice Quarterly*, 17:663–684.

Chapter 3

ETHICAL ISSUES IN CRIMINAL JUSTICE RESEARCH

CHAPTER OVERVIEW

The nature of criminal justice research lends itself to ethical situations before, during, and after a research project. **Ethics** refers to the study of moral principles between what is right and what is wrong or standards of good conduct. All research raises certain ethical issues and concerns. Ethics in research is a means of achieving and upholding moral values while engaging in research, avoiding research strategies that may endanger these values, and balancing conflicting values that confront the researcher.[1] The central element of the conflict posed by the research process is how to balance moral values and principles with the need for scientific knowledge and "methodological rigor."[2] Ethics is associated with whether there is harm to research participants and whether or not suggested harm outweighs the potential benefits of the study. Ethics is concerned with the behavior of the researcher as he/she is engaged in the field. Consider a study of obedience by **Stanley Milgrim**.[3] This study observed whether research participants who were deceived into believing that they were actually shocking and hurting another individual in an adjoining room were inherently obedient to authority. The role of the researcher in Milgrim's study was that of the authority figure; when questioned by the subjects, he provided responses such as "please continue" and "I'm responsible for what happens" in an attempt to measure the level of obedience of the subjects.[4] The behavior of the researcher in Milgrim's study is still questioned today. However, one might argue that the findings of this study (i.e., that the majority of the subjects completed the entire range of shocks), in addition to the realization that this presented the only way of measuring obedience (i.e., through deception of subjects), warrant the behavior of the researcher in this classic study.

Although it is not entirely possible for a researcher to be able to determine the potential harm or impact of a stimulus, it is his/her responsibility to "think through" the research process in an attempt to address any ethical concerns that may arise. Serious thought must be given to the treatment of human subjects as well as the researcher's responsibility for the outcomes or consequences of his or her work. Researchers have an obligation to conduct their research in such a way that minimal risks will be posed to participants. Some decisions must be made about the benefits to the research that follows from the exposure of the participants to situations that could produce harm or put them at potential risk of harm.

In preparation of a study, researchers must think about decisions related to the participants, the field involved, and his/her role in the research. For example, research conducted on juvenile delinquents requires certain parental provisions in addition to outlining more generally, no harm will come to these juvenile participants. Similarly, "protected populations" such as prisoners (as well as children) may only volunteer to be included in the research. **Voluntary participation** and **no harm to participants** are two ethics-related issues that must be addressed prior to research being conducted which involves human subjects.

A researcher must also weigh decisions associated with the research environment prior to beginning the research. That is, will research be conducted in an open setting where individuals are unaware they are being observed? If so, is this ethical? The role of the researcher must also be decided; determining the role of the researcher will be discussed thoroughly in Chapter Nine, however, from an ethical standpoint, what if the researcher is a covert observer, meaning the participants are unaware they are being observed? Ethical issues surround these questions and the decisions made may have implications on the outcomes of a study.

Finally, the researcher must make ethical decisions in analyzing their data and their findings. What if the researcher is hired by state government to evaluate a program and his findings are not "politically correct"? Have you ever heard someone say that it is possible to lie with statistics or make numbers say what you want them to say? These suggestions make it necessary for researchers to choose the appropriate statistical analyses for their data and research questions. Additionally, it is important for the researcher to not **whitewash** unfavorable findings, meaning that she should not minimize any significant or major findings when reporting her research.

ETHICS IN RESEARCH

Largely in response to the biomedical experiments conducted during World War II, governments and the scientific community have adopted policies for addressing the ethical concerns related to research with human subjects.[5]

> The best known of these codes are the **Nuremberg Code of 1947**, the **Helsinki Declaration of 1964** (revised in 1975), and the 1971 Guidelines (codified into Federal Regulations in 1974) issued by the U.S. Department of Health, Education, and Welfare Codes for the conduct of social and behavioral research have also been adopted, the best known being that of the American Psychological Association, published in 1973.[6]

The National Research Act[7] in 1974 created the National Commission for the Protection of Human Subjects of Biomedical and Behavioral Research whose major charge was to determine which ethical principles should ground scientific research involving human subjects.

The Belmont Report

The Belmont Report[8] is a summary of the Commission's work and outlines basic ethical principles for evaluating proposed research involving human subjects. The report highlights the need for **respect for persons**, **beneficence**, and **justice** as suggested in the following:[9]

> Some persons are in need of extensive protection, even to the point of excluding them from activities which may harm them; other persons require little protection beyond making sure they undertake activities freely and with awareness of possible adverse consequence. The extent of protection afforded should depend upon the risk of harm and the likelihood of benefit. . . . In most cases of research involving human subjects, respect for persons demands that subjects enter into the research voluntarily and with adequate information. . . .
> Two general rules have been formulated as complementary expressions of

beneficent actions in this sense: (1) do not harm and (2) maximize possible benefits and minimize possible harms. . . .

Who ought to receive the benefits of research and bear its burdens? This is a question of justice, in the sense of "fairness in distribution" or "what is deserved." An injustice occurs when some benefit to which a person is entitled is denied without good reason or when some burden is imposed unduly.

There are many ways researchers may incorporate the general ethical principles set forth in the Belmont Report when conducting research. Specifically, in proposals for research involving human subjects, the researcher will address: (1) Anonymity; (2) Confidentiality; (3) Potential Harm to Subjects; (4) Deceiving Subjects; (5) Voluntary Participation; (6) Informed Consent; and (7) Legal liability. As discussed above, problems in these areas are confronted at every phase of the research process.

ADDRESSING GENERAL ETHICAL PRINCIPLES IN RESEARCH

Anonymity

Oftentimes social scientists conduct studies with human subjects that assure individuals **anonymity** if they choose to participate in the study. Anonymity does not allow for the data obtained to be matched to an individual participant. That is, no one, including the researcher, is able to determine who in the sample or population participated in the study and if an individual did participate, then what his/her responses were. Why is "the guarantee" of anonymity important in research? It allows for increased reliability and validity in research conducted with hard to reach populations, as well as in research where individuals may be less likely to participate if they think they can be "identified." Consider, for example, if you were asked to participate in a study about GHB use among college students and one of the eligibility criteria to participate was that you use illicit drugs. Are you likely to participate if you know someone can match you with your responses? Thus, ethics also affect the validity of research.

While use of anonymity is beneficial in attracting individuals to participate in a study and increasing the validity and reliability of self-report data, there are some drawbacks. Consider, for example, a study where individuals are asked to answer questions about their knowledge of prisoner rights. They are asked not to include their names on their answer sheet. After completing the questions, the following week the individuals watch a documentary on the subject of prisoner rights. They are then given an opportunity to answer the same bank of questions, again, without including their name. In this example, the participants are anonymous. Given anonymity in this research, then: (1) how do we know that the same group of individuals completed the pre and post questionnaires; (2) how do we know that any statistical differences found in the pre and post measures are for the same group of individuals; (3) how do we measure any individual gains that may have occurred between the pre and post questionnaire; and (4) how do we match an individual's pre and post questionnaire. Furthermore, when anonymity is used in survey research it is *not* possible to know who in the sample or population participated (i.e., returned response card or questionnaire), which requires the researcher to send second mailings to, or complete follow-up actions with, all eligible individuals. Thus, while anonymity is an important ethical issue to not overlook, it sometimes may not be appropriate for a research design that is being used.

Confidentiality

In situations when anonymity may not be appropriate, researchers may instead maintain **confidentiality** of their participants and the reported data. Confidentiality allows for the data obtained by the researcher to be matched to an individual participant, but guarantees that the relationship will not be identified in any written or verbal communication. Data may be analyzed individually or in aggregate, but when the data are reported no identifying characteristics allow for individual level data/responses to be matched with a participant. Consider questionnaires you have received which provide you with a "code letter" or "code number" on the return envelope or the questionnaire itself; this is an example of one way researchers attempt to ensure confidentiality.

In criminal justice research the sensitivity of information is paramount. For example, self-report surveys of criminal activity, victimization surveys, studies of police corruption, or studies of criminal career patterns all address information about individuals that could result in harm or embarrassment to a participant if his/her identity was disclosed or discovered. Some studies may intrude on private settings or privileged relationships. Consider research in the areas of domestic violence, plea bargaining, gang behavior, or inmate life; each area requires a researcher to determine the best method of collecting data while at the same time recognizing the need to maintain anonymity or confidentiality.

Research may also be directed toward behaviors or beliefs, or values or attitudes of individuals or groups. For example, questionnaires may include items that ask individuals to respond to questions about victimization, deviant behavior, race and crime, or criminal activity:

> Did the respondent use any object that placed you in imminent fear of danger?[10]
> Have you ever used drugs to have sex with someone?[11]
> Most violent crimes are committed by black males (Strongly Agree, . . ., Strongly Disagree)[12]
> Were you "high" on drugs when committing any of these offenses?[13]

It is the responsibility of the researcher to protect the rights of the respondents, which includes confidentiality of their responses.

Potential Harm to Subjects

The research topic, findings, and in some instances, the sponsor must be taken into account in determining the **potential harm to subjects** in a proposed study. While the harm or potential harm to subjects which may follow from research is not intentional, the researcher must be aware of the potential consequences and make decisions as a means of resolving the conflict associated with potential harm and scholarly rewards. When the area of interest is deviant or criminal behavior, then the potential harm to subjects is increased.

Furthermore, harmful effects to subjects may be realized immediately or after some amount of time following an experiment involving exposure to mental or psychological stress, undue hardship, or physical abuse. Similarly, harm may follow from a participant's non-exposure to a given environment, stimulus, or treatment. This may exist in a study evaluating opportunities for prisoners, where some prisoners are locked in individual cells for 23 hours a day and others are provided recreational and educational opportunities outside of their cell for eight hours each day. In both cases, exposure to harm or non-exposure to opportunities, there exists a potential for both short- and long-term consequences for the subjects.

Researchers have different beliefs about the justification of harm to subjects. Some have argued that harm is acceptable if it is necessary to obtain research results and further knowledge development. However, this can lead to serious abuse of the rights of individuals and distrust of researchers and the research process. Another position is that harm that is infrequent, rare, or minimal may be justified as long as the participants are aware of the risks. This too, however, may be problematic as it requires researchers to estimate the probability and the extent of harm to participants. Consider, for example, the **Stanford Prison Experiment** in which Zimbardo and his colleagues attempted to study the strength of social-situational variables on behaviors.[14]

In the Stanford Prison Experiment, a simulated prison environment was created in the basement of a university building. Student participants were randomly assigned roles as either prison guards or prisoners. The project was scheduled to run for two weeks, but was terminated after six days when the students, who had all been pre-screened to ensure for "normal" subjects, began to exhibit stereotypical role behavior. For example, the guards were verbally and physically abusive to the inmates and seemed to enjoy their power and misuse of power. The prisoners were subjected to the abuse and became subservient and powerless. The experiment was too stressful for some prisoners and they had to be released even prior to the sixth day.[15] It is doubtful that Zimbardo might have predicted the extreme behaviors and the consequent harm that resulted from the prison experiment. Nonetheless, if harm occurs, the researcher is responsible for that harm.

Deceiving Subjects

Participants may give their permission to be studied, but may be purposely misinformed about the nature of the research. This is the use of **deception** in research and may take many forms. Most deception in criminal justice and criminology research is utilized in field studies. These are studies in which the researcher enters the world of his or her participants and studies their behavior in a natural setting. If the world being entered is an attempt to study deviant behavior, then the researcher may use deception to as a means of observing without the individuals knowing they are being studied. This may mean that the researcher poses as a member of a deviant group or as someone other than a researcher. It may also mean that the participants are given false information about the research; that is, they know they are participating in a research project, but they do not know what the research is truly about.

For example, suppose you had a friend in law enforcement and you wanted to do a ride-a-long as part of a class assignment you had to do on deviant behavior for research methods class. You ask your friend if you could shadow her in order to observe instances of deviant behavior among the citizens involved in calls for service or perceived criminal activity. She agrees; however, your observation will not only include the deviant behavior among the citizens that night, but will also include the police officer! Is this deception? Do you think it is possible for you, the researcher in this case, to disclose to your friend prior to the research that this is your intention *and* if you do so, then you will get the same, unadulterated, observational data?

As mentioned at the beginning of this chapter, a very famous study by Stanley Milgrim attempted to study the impact of authority on individual decision making.[16] In this study, participants were asked to deliver an increasing level of electric shock to an individual in another room when he incorrectly answered a question. Of course, the individual in the other room answering the questions was really not hooked up to the voltage machine, but the participant did not know this and the response to being shocked by the individual in the next room was delivered very real.[17] Although the Milgrim study may never be replicated, one's ability to think that such behavior on the part of participants may exist or realize that it did exist, could not have been validated without the use of deception.

In some studies, participants may not know that they are being studied or involved in research at all. Most studies which use this form of deception are field studies. As discussed in Chapter Nine, field studies involve the observation of individuals or groups in their natural setting. Oftentimes, the researcher will assume a false identity solely for the purpose of studying a group or individual. Consider NBC's *Dateline*, where the news show features "To Catch a Predator" series. This is an example where the researcher, in this case the investigative reporter, presents himself as a child or juvenile in an online chat environment. While representing himself as a child or juvenile, the reporter suggests that he is willing to engage in sexual behavior with the individual he is chatting with online. When the individual shows up at the proposed meeting place to meet the child he thinks he has been corresponding with online, the true identity of the reporter is disclosed.

In recent years, closed circuit television (CCTV) cameras have been proposed by cities in an attempt to curb crime in public areas. Many locals are also using CCTV to catch motorists who run traffic lights. Goold discusses CCTV as the "unobservable observer" and questions whether they intrude on an individual's expectation of privacy in public spaces.[18] For a social science researcher studying deviant behavior, the question might be how reliable an individual self-reports deviant behavior, and whether the self-report may or may not be validated through CCTV (i.e., covert observation). Is it possible that individuals will act or behave differently if they think they are not being observed? And, if this is the case, then is deception by the researcher a viable alternative to gathering data?

The use of deception as a necessary component of research has been justified in a number of ways. Generally, deception is supported when a researcher attempts to obtain realistic, accurate responses from individual respondents, and deception is defined as the only means to obtain the information. Furthermore, deception might be used when researchers attempt to obtain information from certain types of individuals and/or on specific types of behavior (e.g., illicit drug use). In such cases, deception allows the researcher to observe individuals or behaviors in a natural environment.

Sometimes deception is used for pragmatic reasons. Researchers may not have the time, money, or ability to study a behavior except through the use of deception. For example, field studies of gang behavior or the homeless may not be possible unless a researcher uses deception. Members of these groups may not be likely to trust outsiders and may not respond in a natural way among an outsider, even when the outsider has gained entrée. Consequently, the researcher may masquerade as a member of the group to gather information; many of Tewksbury's studies on deviant behavior are examples of this.[19-23] One study, **The Tearoom Trade**, is a classic example of a researcher masquerading as a participant in order to gather information.[24] Humphreys was interested in understanding the sexual encounters that took place between male strangers in public restrooms. In his research he served as the lookout or "watch queen," during the partic-

ipants' sexual encounters. While in the "tearoom" Humphreys recorded the license plates of the participants, later obtained their home
addresses, and then went to their homes under disguise and false pre-
tense in order to gain personal information about the participants.[25]
Sometimes the researcher may perform deviant acts in order to
establish trust or to observe the behavior of deviants. Goode has conducted three studies in which he experiences sexual relationships with
informants.[26] When discussing whether it was necessary to have sex
with informants in his research to find what he did, he suggests:[27]

> Of course not, although at the times when I did so, it seemed perfectly natur-
> al; in fact, to have done otherwise would have felt awkward and out of step with
> everything that was going on. By doing so, I felt a natural and organic part of
> the tribes I was studying, much as Cesara, Gearing, and Wade did. Does shar-
> ing intimate moments with informants lend an authenticity to the researcher's
> vision that might otherwise have been less authoritative? Discounting the pos-
> sible social disruption that such experiences may cause, yes, I believe so.

How far should a researcher go to obtain data? Do researchers become
accessories to criminal acts if they fail to repeat or stop the activities
that they observe? What guarantees can researchers provide participants if their records are requested by the courts or another legal or
legislative entity?

EVALUATING ETHICAL PRINCIPLES IN RESEARCH

Institutional Review Board

The **institutional review board (IRB)** in institutes of higher education and in all research organizations was established to review research methodology and scrutinize the research for potential risks to
participants. The IRB reviews all research involving human subjects
which is conducted at an institution. The IRB usually includes faculty
representatives from each college in the university, an administrator,
and a community member. Research that is proposed for specific populations (e.g., for prisoner research), an individual representing the
population (e.g., an inmate advocate) may also be included on the
IRB. The IRB is charged with ensuring all research conducted by faculty and students affiliated with the institution falls within ethical
guidelines. To this end, the IRB process is one that reduces legal liability associated with the research.

Informed Consent

One part of the contract that is established in the research involves **informed consent** of participants. Informed consent means that the participants in the research voluntarily agree to participate. Informed consent provides individuals with the decision to participate in the study by informing the participants of the potential risks involved in participation, the focus of the study, and the ability to withdraw their consent to participate at any point during the course of the research. Thus, it allows participants who believe they might be harmed to not participate, and ideally increases trust and respect for science by showing potential participants that the researchers and the institution have reviewed and taken action(s) to minimize any potential harm.

Informed consent of all participants must be obtained prior to the involvement of any individuals in the research. This means prior to the beginning of any face to face interview, before the experiment begins, or before a questionnaire is completed as part of an online survey, participants have to be given the opportunity to make an "informed" decision about their participation. Informed consent forms are the most common way researchers provide this opportunity. See an example informed consent form in Figure 3.1. The informed consent form is provided to the potential participant and he/she signs it if he/she agrees to participate.

As mentioned above, informed consent is the voluntary participation of individuals in a research project. In making the decision to participate, individuals are informed of the risks involved in the research prior to their involvement and are given the right to withdraw their consent at any time during the research. This knowledge of risk and adequate information to make an informed decision to participate means that the subjects must have at a minimum, the following information (Find these items on the informed consent form provided in Figure 3.1):

1. Purpose of the research.
2. The role of the participants in the research: What will participants be expected to do?
3. Why were these particular participants selected?
4. Information about the procedures: Time, date, place of the research, who will be involved, what will occur (e.g., is it an interview, questionnaire, or observation?).

5. Any potential risk or discomfort that might impact the participant during or after the research.
6. Any potential benefits or lack of benefits to the participants.
7. Notice to the participants that they may ask any questions to clarify information about the project or their involvement in the project.
8. A guarantee to participants that they may withdraw their participation in the project at any time.
9. A promise of either anonymity or confidentiality so that each participant's identity will be protected.
10. An explanation of how the data will be utilized.
11. Contact information for the researcher and the sponsor of the research, if applicable.

Figure 3.1. Example Informed Consent Form[28]

Informed Consent Form

Title of Research: Club Drug Use by University Students: A Trend Analysis

I.   Federal and university regulations require us to obtain signed consent for participation on research involving human participants. After reading the statements in section II through IV below, please indicate your consent by signing and dating this form.

II.   **Statement of Procedure**: Thank you for your interest in htis research project being conducted by Drs. Julie Kunselman and Kathrine Johnson of the University of West Florida. This stage of the research project involves conducting personal interviews with UWF students. These interviews will take place twice each adademic year in a private setting conducive to completing an interview. The major aspects of the study are described in the statements below, including the risks and benefits of participating. your information will be kept in strict confidence with only the researchers having access to the results of the survey.

I understand that:

(1) I will be answering questions concerning illegal drug use and other deviant behaviors that I, or someone I know, have been or are currently engaged. The length of each interview will be approximately 30 minutes.

(2) There are no identifying names on the interview schedule. Each participant will be assigned a control number that will be on the interview. All information obtained in the interview will remain confidential. Often the primary researchers will have access to the name and control number inventory.

(3) Any statements that indicate I plan to harm myself or any other individual will not be kept confidential.

Continued on next page

Figure 3.1 (continued)

(4) I understand that follow-up counseling and/or information is available to me by contacting the Counseling Center at (850)474-2420 or visit the Center in Building 19, West Entrance, Monday through Friday, 8:00 a.m. - 5:00 p.m. If you need to talk with someone immediately and the Center is closed, you may contact the UWF switchboard at 474-2000 and inform the operator that you need to speak with someone from the Counseling Center. All information about your contact with the Counseling Center is confidential and not part of University records. Information will not be released to any person or agency, including university personnel, without your written permission. The only exceptions to this are in the event of life threatening or child abuse situations.

(5) I may discontinue my participation in this study at any time without penalties or repercussions. I will simply indicate that I no longer want to be interviewed.

III. **Potential Risks of the Study**: The nature of deviant behavior study includes some risk to individual participants (e.g., admitting to illegal behavior). Further, limitations in methodology and research design clearly do have some affect on the disparity of reported incidence of deviant behavior. However, it is not anticipated that the procedures used in this study will result in any immediate or long-range risks to the participants. The proposed research design attempts to overcome methodology and design barriers by using a student-driven methodological approach. For example, the design focuses on the ability of student researchers to gain entrance into the environment, in addition to building a sense of trust and rapport with participants. These are critical elements that are needed (but often not present) in deviant behavior field research, and elements that will work to minimize the risks associated with disclosing such behavior. Again, although there exists a risk of using student researchers, the Co-Pis will train and work in cooperation with the student researchers. These students will be required to have had, or be currently enrolled in a research methods course and will also complete field research training.

IV. **Potential Benefits of the Study**: The data obtained from this study may provide some insight into the patterns and trends of club drug use by university students. Given this type of data, prevention and treatment options can best be considered.

V. **Statement of Consent**: I certify that I have read and fully understand the statement of procedure given above and agree to participate as a subject in the research described therin. Premission is given voluntarily and without coercion or under influence. I understand that I may discontinue participation any time. I will be provided a signed copy of this consent form.

If you have any questions or concerns please call Dr. Julie Kunselman at 850-857-6197 or Dr. Kathrine Johnson at 850-863-6588.

_____   _____

Participant's Signature   Date

_____

Participant's Name

As you can see, informed consent forms also include information about services to address harm (if harm presents itself) as well as referral information for services. Obtaining informed consent from special populations of individuals must be given additional consideration and oftentimes the informed consent process includes steps beyond an informed consent form. Special populations are groups of individuals who, because of their status, may not be able to give voluntary or knowledgeable consent. Groups include, but are not limited to, children, students, inmates, or mentally ill individuals. Sometimes the need to obtain informed consent can be waived. For example, informed consent may be waived in studies where the role of the researcher includes deception or covert observation.

The question of when is consent necessary is one which criminal justice and criminology researchers address in a number of different ways. In general, criminal justice researchers who observe public behavior or use public documents are not required to obtain informed consent. However, especially in the case of public documents, researchers are required to protect the identity of any individuals identified by or named in these documents. If the researcher is interested in sensitive or personal information or information that might be potentially harmful to an individual, informed consent is required. Similarly, if the research involves exposing the participant to risks, then the informed consent of the participant must be obtained.

RESEARCHER RESPONSIBILITY AND LEGAL ISSUES

Confidentiality between individuals in certain relationships has been deemed essential and is respected. The attorney-client, doctor-patient, and psychologist-client relationships are protected relationships. However, while the researcher-participant relationship also requires confidentiality, it does not have the same legal protections. Researchers are vulnerable to attempts that force them to violate the confidences inherent in the research process.

Demands for researcher data may come in the form of subpoena from the courts, or from legislative or administrative bodies. Other requests may come from state agencies, project sponsors, or law enforcement. While all of these entities may have an interest in obtaining access to the information, the researcher has an interest in protecting the confidentiality or anonymity of the participants. Protection of confidentiality and anonymity is not only used to protect the interests of the participants, but it also promotes scientific research and the acquisition of knowledge. For example, researchers studying victims of domestic violence may request information about the criminal offense, as well as demographic and court related data in an attempt to determine court processes and outcomes in domestic violence cases. This is especially important in evaluating whether there are differences in court dispositions by type of incident or whether a weapon was involved; but, further consider the implications if there are differences by location of victim residence (e.g., victim lives more than 10 miles from the courthouse) or by income (e.g., victim's only income is tied to perpetrator). Again, this highlights the importance of confidentiality and anonymity for the acquisition of knowledge.

The legal rationale for protection of confidentiality or the use of anonymity is based on the constitutional rights of freedom of expression, privacy, and the constitutional rights of the criminal defendant. These are protections for the participants. The right to privacy may also provide protection for the researcher. The **Fourth Amendment** protection against search and seizure and the **Fifth Amendment** protection against self-incrimination protect the researcher's ability to sustain confidentiality. The protections provided by these two amendments also protect the researcher's records and the researcher's right to refuse to testify or respond.

Researchers are not usually bound by criminal defendant protections as to do so would be extremely detrimental to the research process. However, when information about criminal activities is disclosed to a researcher, then a researcher is vulnerable to a subpoena requiring testimony or records. [Note this "clause" or "disclaimer" in the informed consent form above.] Thus, it is advisable that a researcher terminate an interview when the interviewee discloses information about undetected criminal activity or criminal activity that has not yet been discontinued.[29]

CONCLUSION

This chapter discussed the ethical considerations which researchers must take into account when designing and implementing a research project. What can be done to prevent unethical research that results in abuse of participants and the research process? What prevents researchers from violating ethical standards for their own interests or the interests of the research tradition? Many professional associations have developed codes of ethics (see the Academy of Criminal Justice Sciences[30]). Institutions of higher education use an administrative review process, the Institutional Review Board, which screens research projects involving human subjects. The IRB was instituted by the Department of Health, Education, and Welfare (now split into the Department of Education and the Department of Health and Human Services).

Some research practices can be identified as posing ethical dilemmas and require careful review and consideration, including harm to the subject, lack of informed consent, no guarantee of confidentiality or anonymity, misrepresentation of the findings, tampering with data, lack of voluntary participation, withholding treatment, and restrictions on the dissemination of findings.[31]

The social science research process is not conducted in a void. The impact of the project on society, the participants, and the researcher must be taken into account. Many times it may be impossible to foresee all possible outcomes or potential harm to participants. Nonetheless, it is incumbent upon the researcher to address, as completely as possible, the risks and benefits to society and his or her subject when designing and implementing a research project.

KEY TERMS

Ethics
Stanley Milgrim
Voluntary Participation
No Harm to Participants
Whitewash
Nuremburg Code of 1947
Helsinki Declaration of 1964
The Belmont Report
Respect for Persons
Beneficence
Justice

Anonymity
Confidentiality
Potential Harm to Subjects
Stanford Prison Experiment
Deception
The Tearoom Trade
Institutional Review Board (IRB)
Informed Consent
Fourth Amendment
Fifth Amendment

REVIEW QUESTIONS

1. Discuss the differences between confidentiality and anonymity?
2. Identify and analyze at least two (2) research hypotheses that might be appropriate for a researcher to use deception. Then, discuss what you considered in making your decision.
3. Why is deception sometimes used in research?
4. Discuss the purposes of (1) the Institutional Review Board and (2) informed consent.
5. What strategies may a researcher use to protect the confidentiality of participants?
6. What are the strengths and weaknesses of the strategies presented to minimize unethical research? Discuss which strategy you think is best.
7. Discuss whether or not there exist legal reasons for protecting the privacy of individual participants.
8. Is it possible for researchers to "justify" potential harm to subjects in order for research to be completed? Discuss.
9. Discuss whether or not researchers and their data are protected under the law.
10. In the *Tearoom Trade*, what rights of the observed were intruded upon by Humphreys? Discuss the reasons why his study would/would not pass review by an Institutional Review Board today.
11. In Milgrim's study on obedience to authority, what rights of the observed were intruded upon by Milgrim? Discuss the reasons why his study would/would not pass review by an Institutional Re-

view Board today.

12. In the Stanford Prison Experiment, what rights of the observed were intruded upon by Zimbardo? Discuss the reasons why his study would/would not pass review by an Institutional Review Board today.

13. In the Goode's study, what rights of the observed were intruded upon by the researcher? Discuss the reasons why his study would/would not pass review by an Institutional Review Board today.

14. One of the ethical issues in research relates to minimizing or no harm to participants. This means:
    a) Not depriving a participant a benefit entitled to him or her without good reason.
    b) Maintaining confidentiality or anonymity of the participants.
    c) Allowing participants to voluntarily participate in the research.
    d) Having respect for the well-being of each participant.
    e) All of these (a-d)
    f) Responses a, b, and c *only*

15. One of the methods universities use to help ensure ethical behavior in research and ethical research is the use of an Institutional Review Board (IRB). The IRB must review all research involving

    _____.

16. Please list at least four (4) of the different parts of an informed consent form.

17. Discuss two issues specifically related to the ethics of analysis and reporting research. Discuss them both by providing an example.

18. Deceiving subjects is another ethical issue in research. We talked about Laud Humphrey's research *The Tearoom Trade*. What was the deceptive part of his research?

REFERENCES

1. Diener, E. and Crandall, R. (1978). *Ethics in social and behavioral research.* Chicago, IL: University of Chicago Press.
2. Douglas, J.D. (1979). Living morality versus bureaucratic fiat, in Klockars, C. and O'Connor, F. eds., *Deviance and decency,* Beverly Hills, CA: Sage, 13–34.
3. Milgrim, S. (1974). *Obedience to authority; An experimental view.* New York: Harper & Row.
4. Ibid.

5. *The Belmont Report: Ethical principles and guidelines for the protection of human subjects of research* (Washington, D.C.: Department of Health, Education, and Welfare, 4/18/1979): OS78-0013 and OS78-0014, http://www.hhs.gov/ohrp/human subjects/guidance/belmont.htm.

6. Ibid.

7. The National Research Act (Pub. L. 93-348).

8. Department of Health, Education, and Welfare, *The Belmont Report.*

9. Ibid.

10. Scott, D. and Kunselman, J.C. (2007). Using profile analysis for assessing need in domestic violence courts, *American Journal of Criminal Justice*, 31:81–91.

11. Kunselman, J.C. and Johnson, K.A. *Club drug use among university students.* Unpublished manuscript.

12. Miller, A.J. *Police officers' perceptions of race, homosexuality, and crime.* Unpublished manuscript.

13. Kunselman, J.C., and Scott, D. *Female offender participation in a therapeutic community.* Unpublished manuscript.

14. Zimbardo, P.G. and Ebbesen, E.B. (1970). *Influencing attitudes and changing behavior; A basic introduction to relevant methodology, theory, and applications.* Reading, MA: Addison-Wesley.

15. Ibid.

16. Milgrim, *Obedience to authority.*

17. Ibid.

18. Goold, B.J. (2002). Privacy rights and public spaces: CCTV and the problem of the "unobservable observer," *Criminal Justice Ethics*, 21:21–27.

19. Tewksbury, R. (1996). Cruising for sex in public places: The structure and language of men's hidden, erotic worlds, *Deviant Behavior*, 17:1–19.

20. Tewksbury, R. (1995). Adventures in the Erotic oasis: Sex and danger in men's same-sex, public, sexual encounters, *Journal of Men's Studies*, 4:9–24.

21. Tewksbury, R. (2002). Bathhouse intercourse: Structural and behavioral aspects of an erotic oasis, *Deviant Behavior*, 23:75–112.

22. Erickson, D.J., and Tewksbury, R. (2000). The gentlemen in the club: A typology of strip club patrons, *Deviant Behavior*, 21:271–293.

23. DeMichele, M.T., and Tewksbury, R. (2004). Sociological explorations in site-specific social control: The role of the strip club bouncer, *Deviant Behavior*, 25:537–558.

24. Humphreys, L. (1975). *Tearoom trade: Impersonal sex in public places.* New York: Aldine.

25. Ibid.

26. Goode, E. (1999). Sex with informants as deviant behavior: An account and commentary, *Deviant Behavior*, 20:301–324.

27. Ibid.

28. Example form template (general text and format) created by the Office of Research and Sponsored Programs, University of West Florida, for use by institutional faculty in preparing informed consent forms. Research project specific content written by Kunselman, J.C. and Johnson, K.A. Unpublished research on Club Drug Use among University Students.

29. Kirkpatrick, A. M. (1964). Privileged communication in the correction services, *Criminal Law Quarterly*, 7:305.
30. Academy of Criminal Justice Sciences, *Code of Ethics*, http://www.acjs.org/pubs/167_664_8214.cfm.
31. Longmire, D. (1983). Ethical dilemmas in the research setting: A survey of experiences and responses in the criminological community, *Criminology*, 21:333–348.

Chapter Four

MEASURING CRIME: THE VALIDITY AND RELIABILITY OF CRIME DATA SOURCES

the government are [sic] very keen on amassing statistics. They collect them, raise them to the nth power, take the cube root and prepare wonderful diagrams. But you must never forget that every one of these figures comes in the first instance from the village watchman who puts down what he damn well pleases.

—Sir Josiah Stamp[1]

Every statistic (and this includes survey as well as police figures) is shaped by the process which operationally defines it, the procedures which capture it, and the organization which processes and interprets it.

—Wesley G. Skogan[2]

These quotations accurately reflect the real tensions that criminal justice researchers face. Their basic subject matter, crime and criminality, often defies accurate measurement. In this chapter, we will examine the problems faced in the measurement of crime through the examination of some sources of crime data. First, we must define the key concepts of measurement, validity and reliability.

CHAPTER OVERVIEW

Key Measurement Concepts

The measurement of a societal phenomenon like crime involves the conscious, controlled and rigorous classification of the observations made. Measurement generally involves the assignment of a numerical value to the observation for the simple purpose of counting and the more complex business of statistical analysis of the phenomenon in order to search for causative factors.

The ability and value of a selected form of measurement is directly related to two key concepts. The first, **validity**, is defined as the accuracy with which a measure gauges the concept under consideration.[3] One of the pitfalls concerning validity is that if the designated measurement procedure fails to measure the actual object of interest (i.e., crime), the resulting figure will be inaccurate and meaningless.[4] The researcher must be careful that the procedure for measuring crime accurately reflects the amount of crime committed rather than the impact of other factors? For example, does a decline in the number of reported burglaries indicate that a Citizen's Crime Watch Program has succeeded or have citizens suddenly stopped reporting burglaries to the police because they feel that nothing will be done? We will consider these "other factors" in some detail as the different methods of measuring crime are considered.

There are several different types of validity; two of which directly relate to the measurement of crime. The first is termed **face validity** –the "common sense" nature of a measure. For example, do crimes reported to the police (UCR) seem, on the face of it, to be an accurate indication of the amount crime in society? The second type of validity, **content validity**, requires that an instrument measures the phenomenon under study. As we shall see, the Uniform Crime Reports contains a "Crime Index" which purports to serve as an indicator of the level of serious crime in America. One of the weaknesses of the Crime Index is that it counts the theft of a bicycle on the same level as a murder. Due to the absence of some way to distinguish the seriousness of crimes, the content validity of the Crime Index is seriously affected.

The second key measurement concept, **reliability**, refers to the consistency with which a measurement device yields the same numbers upon repeated applications. A measure is reliable if different people (or the same people at different times) record the event the same way. Reliability deals with the ability to reproduce findings. For example, we can attempt to gauge the extent to which various police patrol teams classify the same events (types of crime) in the same manner. This procedure would be a test of the reliability of crime measurement.

It is important to note that these concepts are interrelated. Validity requires reliability, but a reliable tool may not be a valid one. A gauge that measures consistently may still not be measuring what it is supposed to count. The accurate measurement of crime for purposes of policy analysis requires careful attention to these concepts–validity and reliability. Naturally, if the selected indicator of crime fails on one or both counts, the subsequent analysis will suffer and be misleading at best.

With these concepts in mind, let us turn to a consideration of some of the standard sources of information about crime and criminality. They follow a generally commonsense point of view about acquiring information about crime. If one wishes to obtain data about crime, one would either go to the police (Uniform Crime Reports), to victims (National Crime Survey) or to the offenders themselves (Self-Report Studies). The assessment of these sources in terms of their validity and reliability requires close attention so that the criminal justice researcher can make the best possible choice in the selection of a crime measure. As we shall see, each measure has both strengths and potential problems regarding validity and reliability.

THE UNIFORM CRIME REPORTS (UCR)

The Uniform Crime Reporting program, compiled by the Federal Bureau of Investigation, is the oldest source of crime statistics in America. Enacted by Congressional legislation in 1930, the UCR program is a voluntary, national program which is dependent upon the cooperation of law enforcement agencies. Their contribution of reported crimes (crimes known to the police) is published each year. The UCR data are provided from nearly 17,000 law enforcement agencies across the United States.[5] There is no doubt that the prestige of the FBI facilitates the collection of these data. It is doubtful that any other agency could enjoy such success and obtain such cooperation from law enforcement agencies across the country.

Index Crimes

The UCR program has a number of distinctive characteristics. First, there is a procedure which attempts to standardize crime statistics in order to transcend differences between jurisdictions in terms of their legal definitions. Otherwise, a burglary in one jurisdiction may be classified as a misdemeanor theft in another. To accomplish this goal, the committee on Uniform Crime Records established a standard classification of crime to be used for purposes of reporting offenses known to the police. The selected crimes were those that: (1) were serious in nature, (2) were most likely to come to the attention of the police with sufficient regularity to provide an adequate basis for comparison and (3) were geographically pervasive.[6] These offenses became known as Part I offenses: murder and non-negligent manslaughter, forcible rape, robbery, aggravated assault, burglary, larceny-theft, and motor vehicle theft. These offenses were traditionally referred to as "crime index" offenses and they came to be used as a national indicator of crime much like the cost of living index is for the U.S. economy.[7]

Selected UCR Findings

For our purposes, we will focus upon the Crime Index, although the UCR does contain data on other material as well. Again, it must be stressed that the number of index crimes presented reflects the volume of serious crime which was known to the police. That is, the crime was either reported to, or directly discovered by the police. A summary of the data on the crime index for 2005 is presented in Table 4.1.

The data in Table 4.1 reveal that the UCR contains two basic forms of crime information: the actual count of crimes reported to the police and the offense rate per 100,000 inhabitants. Each year, these data are compared to figures from the preceding year and the percent change is noted. The **crime rate** per 100,000 is the only attempt made by the UCR to control for the effect of an important variable – the size of the population (i.e., other variables which could affect the number of crimes reported to the police, but which are not controlled for in the UCR include: population density, age, mobility of population, economic and cultural conditions, climate, strength of law enforcement agencies, administrative and investigative emphases of law enforcement, attitudes of the citizenry toward crime, and the crime reporting practices of the citizenry) upon the incidence of reported crime. This step is taken to make it somewhat easier to make limited comparisons of crime rates across jurisdictions, regions and other cities in the country.

Table 4.1

**CRIME INDEX OFFENSES REPORTED IN THE
UNITED STATES, 2004-2005**

Crime Index Offenses	Year	Number of Offenses	Percent Change	Rate per 100,000	Percent Change
Murder and Non-negligent Manslaughter	2004	16,148		5.5	
			+3.4		+2.4
	2005	16,692		5.6	
Forcible Rape	2004	95,089		32.4	
			-1.2		-2.1
	2005	93,934		31.7	
Robbery	2004	401,470		136.7	
			+3.9		+2.9
	2005	417,122		140.7	
Aggravated Assault	2004	847,381		288.6	
			+1.8		+0.9
	2005	862,947		291.1	
VIOLENT CRIME	2004	1,360,088		463.2	
			+2.3		+1.3
	2005	1,390,695		469.2	
Burglary	2004	2,144,446		730.3	
			+0.5		-0.5
	2005	2,154,126		726.7	
Larceny-theft	2004	6,937,089		2362.3	
			+2.3		-3.2
	2005	6,776,807		2286.3	
Motor Vehicle Theft	2004	1,237,851		421.5	
			-0.2		-1.1
	2005	1,235,226		416.7	
PROPERTY CRIME	2004	10,319,386		3513.1	
			-1.5		-2.4
	2005	10,166,159		3429.8	

The data in Table 4.1 reveal the following patterns:[8]

- The estimated number of violent crimes (Murder, Rape, Robbery, Aggravated Assault) was 1,390,695 – an increase of 2.3 percent over the estimated total for 2004.
- Among violent crimes, Robbery registered the greatest increase over 2004 – 3.9 percent.
- All violent crimes, with the exception of Forcible Rape (1.2 percent decrease), increased in 2005.

• The murder rate was 5.6/100,000 inhabitants in 2005 – a 2.4 percent increase over the 2004 murder rate.
• The estimated number of property crimes (Burglary, Larceny-theft, Motor Vehicle Theft) was 10,166,159 – a decrease of 1.5 percent over the estimated total for 2004.
• Larceny-theft had the greatest decrease (2.3 percent).
• Burglary was the only property crime that increased (0.5 percent).

Limitations of the Uniform Crime Reports

It is obvious that the number of crimes reported to the police represents only a portion of the actual amount of crime actually committed. The basic problem is that it is difficult, if not impossible, to gauge the amount of unreported crime. This problem, which is common to all the attempts to measure the incidence of crime, is termed the "dark figure of crime."

An examination of the chain of events leading to the reporting and recording of a crime reveals some of the sources of error in UCR statistics. Seidman and Couzens offer the following description:[9]

1. An event occurs, which could be interpreted as a crime.
2. It, or its consequence, is observed, by the victim or perhaps by someone else (i.e., neighbor or the police themselves).
3. The victim (or observer) notifies the police.
4. The police decide whether the reported action is to be considered a crime and, if so, how it should be described.
5. Sometimes, this description is reviewed (and can be dismissed) at another point in the police hierarchy.
6. The police decide which of the FBI categories is appropriate.
7. The statistics are made public.

In short, the sources of invalidity in the UCR statistics can be attributed to three basic sources: factors influencing the reporting of the crime to the police, recording practices of the police themselves, and subsequent problems in the official presentation and interpretation of the UCR statistics.

The first source of invalidity which influences the reporting of crimes to the police is the attitude of the victim. Here are some possible circumstances in which victims are unlikely to report a crime to the police:[10]

1. The victim consents or agrees to the act (i.e., gambling, drug use, prostitution).
2. The victim believes the crime is trivial.
3. The victim does not wish to embarrass the offender who may be a relative, school friend, acquaintance, or fellow employee.
4. The victim is in an embarrassing situation (i.e., the married man on a business trip who is robbed by a prostitute).
5. The victim does not regard the law enforcement process as effective.
6. The victim is unaware that he/she is involved in crime due to the skill of the offender. For example, an offender could steal your identity without your knowledge.

In this fashion, victims could selectively report crimes to the police and could thus affect subsequent UCR crime rates.

The second source of invalidity is that the police selectively act upon (and hence record) certain events as crime. Part of the police procedure in this area is to "unfound" crimes. **Unfounding** is defined as the process in which events are excluded:[11]

> from crime records for want of any plausible evidence that a crime was in fact committed. . . . [The police] are in a position to provide some independent corroboration of a citizen's complaints and to eliminate those misfortunes that do not amount to crimes (e.g., the abusive landlord) or those fantasies that have no basis in fact (e.g., the imagined prowler).

When the crime is founded, the police have the power to make an arrest. Studies of police arrest practices have demonstrated that the decision to arrest is influenced by: the seriousness of the crime, the expressed preference of the complainant (arrest or release of the suspect), the relationship between the complainant and the suspect (more likely to report strangers), and the attitude of the complainant towards the police. Recognition of these factors has led Quinney to conclude that UCR statistics reflect the policies and behaviors of the police themselves and should be considered as "society's production figures" on crime rather than an accurate indication of how much crime exists at a particular time.[12]

Even when police agencies have received information about a crime, their recording practices have an effect upon the accuracy of the UCR statistics. Some of the problem is due to differences, or mistakes made in the classification of offenses under UCR categories.

This problem was indicated in a study by Ferracuti, Hernandez, and Wolfgang.[13] These authors surveyed 86 Puerto Rican personnel directly involved in crime reporting and asked them to identify and classify 22 crime stories and rank them in order of their seriousness. It was discovered that only the four crimes of murder, abandonment of children, prostitution, and violation of liquor laws were correctly identified by all subjects. The largest number of errors was recorded by the crime of robbery (41.7 percent wrong). The authors concluded that errors in recording are a relevant factor in any reference to crime statistics and that their evidence is additional proof of the low validity of crime reporting statistics and the need for specific training of police personnel.

Since police agencies have direct control over their crime recording policies and practices, they are also in a position to manipulate these figures in such a way that their performance will be viewed in a positive light. Seidman and Couzens studied UCR crime rate files for Washington, D.C. to determine whether a crime suppression program instituted at the behest of the chief (and the Nixon administration) or a change in crime recording practices by the department had produced a decrease in the amount of reported crime.[14] The authors focused upon three Index Crimes (Larceny-theft, Burglary and Robbery) because they, due to the ambiguity of the UCR definitions, offered the best opportunity for manipulation. For example, with larceny-theft, the key aspect in the classification process is the dollar value of the stolen property – the cutoff point is $50. Thus, through property valuation, the police can partially determine the level of UCR statistics and can "downgrade" offenses in order to suit their purposes. Statistical analysis of the D.C. UCR statistics for this time period in comparison to other cities revealed that "at least part of the decline in the crime statistics is attributable to the increased downgrading of larcenies and, to a lesser extent, burglaries." In short, the UCR reporting system could be manipulated and is open to tampering by police departments who wish to do so for political reasons.

Given these influences upon victims and the police in terms of crime reporting, the validity of UCR data is directly related to the type of crime under consideration. For example, a crime like rape is likely to be underreported because of the social pressures placed upon the victim. On the other hand, victims are likely to report burglaries because of home insurance requirements. Similarly, homicide is unlikely to go unreported by the police or the public because of the severity of the offense. For this reason, researchers must consider the type of crime under analysis when utilizing UCR data.

Finally, the presentation of UCR statistics can often lead to misinterpretation. First, the Crime Index, which is meant to portray the level of serious crime in this country, contains no information concerning white collar offenses, distorting the impact of "street level" crime, and thus giving a false impression of the seriousness of crime in America. The Index also counts attempts on the same level as completed acts with certain crimes (i.e., forcible rape, robbery, aggravated assault, burglary, and motor vehicle theft). The Index also has problems with multiple offenses – when more than one offense occurs, the one which is considered "more serious" (higher in the rank order of the Index offenses) is the only offense counted. Wolfgang cites the following example and directions given from the 1960 UCR Handbook:[16]

> Problem: A holdup man forces a husband and his wife to get out of their automobile. He shoots the husband, gun whips and rapes the wife and leaves the automobile after taking the money from the husband. The husband dies as a result of the shooting. Solution: In the problem, we can recognize robbery, aggravated assault, rape, murder, as well as auto theft and larceny. . . . From the several crimes in the problem, you recognize . . . murder and non-negligent manslaughter as the first crime on the list. Stop at that classification – it is the only one that will be used for scoring the problem.

The Index also has problems counting the number of victims of a crime. Here, again a particular counting method is used: for personal crimes (murder, forcible rape, aggravated assault, robbery), the number of listed offenses equals the number of persons injured and for property crimes (burglary, larceny-theft, and motor vehicle theft) each operation is a single offense-the number of victims is not indicated. As previously mentioned, the Crime Index totals are misleading because each offense represents one unit regardless of the seriousness of the offense – a homicide has the same value as the theft of a $51 bicycle. Thus, the total Crime Index fails to represent a clear picture of crime severity.

The manner in which UCR data are presented can also affect its interpretation. The figures in Table 4.1 (the percentage change this year and the rate per 100,000) are particularly inaccurate since no attempt is made to control for the effects of changes in the size of the

U.S. population. The UCR often wishes to broadcast is that crime has greatly increased. Here, the most blatant example in the UCR is the **Crime Clock**. Here are the Crime Clock figures for 2005:[17]

- **Every 22.7 seconds**   **One Violent Crime**
  - o Every 31.5 minutes   One Murder
  - o Every 5.6 minutes   One Forcible Rape
  - o Every 1.3 minutes   One Robbery
  - o Every 36.5 seconds   One Aggravated Assault

- **Every 4.1 seconds**   **One Property Crime**
  - o Every 14.6 seconds   One Burglary
  - o Every 4.7 seconds   One Larceny-theft
  - o Every 25.5 seconds   One Motor Vehicle Theft

Since these figures misrepresent the probability of crime victimization, the purpose of this information is to alarm the reader as to the extent of American crime. Not every American has an equal chance of becoming a victim of these crimes.

Conclusions Concerning UCR

Given these weaknesses, what is the value of the UCR to criminal justice researchers? As a data source, the UCR consists of crimes known to the police (KTP) and highlights the Index Offenses. Crime rates per 100,000 inhabitants are also reported.

The limitations of UCR data include the fact that the reporting practices of victims and the police are subject to some pressures. Police recording practices also affect the quality of the data and since police agencies are responsible for data collection, the data can be manipulated. Finally, the data is presented in the UCR (i.e., the Crime Clock) in a misleading fashion.

It is important to recognize that the UCR statistics are the product of the interaction between offenders, victims, and the police. Zolbe reminds us that many of the constraints and limitations of the UCR data exist because the UCR was designed and created to meet the needs of the police, not the research community.[18]

An awareness of the limitations of the UCR data should enable researchers to gauge them accurately and utilize them properly. The UCR does provide a nationwide data set on a yearly basis for different cities and states. On this scope, there is no substitute for this source of crime information.

THE NATIONAL INCIDENT-BASED REPORTING SYSTEM
(NIBRS)

In 1991, the UCR program began to change its system of data collection to generate more information to conduct crime analysis. This new system is known as the **National Incident-Based Reporting System**. It is designed to collect more details about crimes reported to the police, such as where and when the offense occurred, victim information (on the harm caused by the crime) and if arrests are made, data on the offenders. NIBRS contains information on both reported crime and arrests. These elements were all missing from the UCR system. NIBRS will eventually replace the UCR as the official source of crime information from police departments as reported to the FBI.

The NIBRS data collection contains data for 22 crime categories and 56 variables including: the types of offenses in the incident; reported age, sex, and race of victims, offenders, and arrestees; weapons used; and other information (e.g., location). Currently, approximately 20 percent of the Nation's law enforcement agencies voluntarily report crime data to the FBI in the NIBRS format.

One example of the type of information that is possible to generate through the NIBRS system is crime in schools and colleges. Over a five year study (2000-2004), there were a total of 17,065,074 such crime incidents reported via the NIBRS. Of these incidents, 558,219, or 3.3 percent, occurred at schools. Based on the data received for the incidents at schools, there were 589,534 offenses committed by 688,612 offenders; 181,468 persons were arrested in connection with the incidents. An analysis of known characteristics of offenders reported during the 5-year period revealed that:

- Most offenders (38.0 percent) were 13 to 15 years old. Offenders comprising the second largest age group (30.7 percent) were 16 to 18 years old, followed by those offenders aged 19 years or older (18.2 percent) and those 10 to 12 years old (11.0 percent). Offenders 9 years of age and under accounted for 2.1 percent of the offenders.
- Males accounted for 76.7 percent of offenders who committed school crimes.

When examining victim-to-offender relationships, acquaintance was the most frequently reported relationship type for crime in schools, occurring in 52.1 percent of the instances in which the relationship was known, followed by otherwise known (not related) at 24.5 percent. Where weapon type was known, the weapon type most frequently reported was personal weapons (hands, fists, and feet, etc.), which comprised 77.5 percent of weapons used in school incidents. Knives accounted for 8.6 percent of the weapon total and guns, 2.7 percent.[19]

Thus, NIBRS has the potential to illuminate the crime incident by providing more information than the UCR. In sum, NIBRS:

- Make a distinction between attempted and completed crimes
- Provide more inclusive definitions of crime (i.e., the definition of rape has been expanded to include male victims)
- Counts all offenses that occur during an incident rather than concentrating upon only the most serious crime as the UCR did. For example, if an offender held up a liquor store and shot and killed the person working there, the UCR would count the homicide but not the robbery. Now, both offenses will be tallied.

The major distinction in NIBRS is the focus upon the crime incident itself.

THE NATIONAL CRIME VICTIMIZATION SURVEY (NCVS)

Another possible source of information on the extent of crime is the victim. Interviewing victims offers a greater potential for accuracy than police crime reports because the researcher is eliminating the "middleman" (the police) and going directly to the primary source of information (the victim). Such an approach can help to overcome the problem of unreported crime and thus illuminate the "dark figure of crime."

Since 1972, the National Crime Victimization Survey has been conducted for the Bureau of Justice Statistics by the U.S. Census Bureau. The primary purposes of the NCVS are:[20]

1. To measure the incidence of crime.
2. To measure the changes in crime rates over time.
3. To characterize the socioeconomic aspects of criminal events and their victims.
4. To identify high-risk subgroups in the population and to estimate the rate of multiple victimization.

5. To provide a measure of victim risk.
6. To calibrate the UCR data produced by the FBI.
7. To index changes in the reporting behavior of victims.
8. To measure the effectiveness of new criminal justice programs.

The methodology utilized in this survey is particularly relevant to the student since it demonstrates a number of significant principles including: sampling, interviewing techniques and the structured questionnaire. These topics will be referred to in other chapters of this text.

Features of the NCVS

The NCVS is based upon a scientifically selected, probability sample (sampling is presented in Chapter Five) of housing units. The panel consists of addresses of six independently selected samples of about 10,000 households with 22,000 individuals (total 60,000 households and over 130,000 individuals). Interviewers return to the same housing units every six months for information. If the occupants have moved, the new residents are interviewed. Housing units in the panel are visited a maximum of seven times, after which they are rotated out of the panel and replaced by a new, independent probability sample.[21] In sum, the National Crime Victimization Survey is designed to elicit responses on criminal victimization which are representative of the nation as a whole.

The household portion of the survey focuses upon some of the same offenses covered by the UCR Crime Index (burglary, motor vehicle theft, rape, robbery, assault and larceny of property and larceny from the person). In each household, a knowledgeable adult is selected to answer background questions about the household. Each individual household member over age 14 is personally interviewed about victimizations he or she may have suffered during the past year.

The validity of the information provided by the respondents is limited by two particular types of memory bias. First, there is the problem of **forgetting** (**memory decay**) – the failure to recall an event at all. Victims tend to forget crime incidents as a function of the time period between when the crime occurred and when the interview takes place. Thus, the longer the time lag, the greater the potential of forgetting.

The second problem is called **telescoping**. Telescoping can be forward or backward: an event may be remembered as having occurred more recently than it actually did, or it may be remembered as having occurred outside the time frame asked in the survey.[22] Telescoping would affect the results of the survey by including events which should not be included or by excluding those which should be included.

In order to deal with these problems, the NCVS uses a **bounding technique** in which respondents are interviewed every six months. In this fashion, the first interview serves as a benchmark and the records of each successive interview aids in the avoidance of duplication in the reports and as a check against which responses can be ascertained.

In addition to the previously mentioned crimes, the NCVS also provides data about the characteristics of the victim, the crime itself, and, with certain crimes, about offenders. Demographic characteristics of the victim are presented, including: age, race, sex, educational level, and income. Information on the characteristics of the crime are: where and when it occurred, the extent of injury and economic loss suffered by the victim, the relationship between the victim and the person committing the crime, the characteristics of the offender as perceived by the victim and whether or not the crime was reported to the police. Unlike the UCR, NCVS does not provide data on particular cities and counties, but it does provide data on suburban and urban victims and crimes, and for four major geographic regions (North, South, East, and West). It also presents NCVS victimization rates per 1,000 population.

One feature of the NCVS that is designed to serve an attention getting device, similar to the UCR Crime Index, is the measure – **households touched by crime**. It takes into account all of the six previously-mentioned crimes and is an indication of the risk of victimization in this country.

Selected NCVS Findings

In 2005, 14% of the Nation's households, accounting for 16 million households, experienced one or more violent or property victimizations as measured by the NCVS. Major findings included:[23]

- Fewer than 1% of households had members victimized by more than one type of violence.
- About 1 in 320 households were affected by intimate partner violence.
- 4.4% of all households were vandalized.
- 18% of households headed by Hispanics experienced one or more crimes, compared to 13% of non-Hispanics.

- Households in the West were more likely to experience one or more crimes compared to households in other regions.
- 1 in 36 households experienced one or more violent crimes in 2005.
- Fifteen percent of urban households had experienced a property crime, compared to 10% of rural households.
- U.S. households experiencing one or more crimes dropped from 25% in 1994 to 14% in 2005.
- About a quarter of incidents of violent crime occurred at or near the victim's home. Among common locales for violent crimes were on streets other than those near the victim's home (19%), at school (12%), or at a commercial establishment (8%).
- Of victims of violent crime, 22% were involved in some form of leisure activity away from home at the time of their victimization, 22% said they were at home, and another 20% mentioned they were at work or traveling to or from work when the crime occurred

Advantages of NCVS

The advantages of the NCVS data include:[24]

1. It can be used to assess the costs of crime attributable to direct losses, injuries, insurance premiums and crime reduction measures.
2. The survey permits collection of crime data, independent of police agencies and makes it possible to measure crimes reported and unreported to the police.
3. It makes it possible to discover who calls the police and why, what happens when they do (and do not) and whether they are satisfied with the results.
4. It provides more detailed data about crime incidents and victims which can be of particular use in terms of eliciting descriptions of the modus operandi of offenders including the use of weapons, means of access to targets, the efficiency of alarms, and the utility of resistance.

It is clear that these advantages are directly attributable to the nature of the data and its source, the victims themselves.

Limitations of NCVS

The possible sources of NCVS invalidity include the potential for false reporting by respondents:[25]

1. Lying: If people are not trustworthy in talking about their voting behavior, financial position, business practices, sex lives, and the academic progress of their children, why take for granted their reporting about crime? Motives: To gain the sympathy of the interviewer respondents may feel obligated to give the interviewer what they think he is seeking.
2. The questions asked may elicit different recollections from different people.
3. People are unaware of legal definitions and may interpret "trivial grievances" as crime.
4. Respondents may be unwilling to discuss victimizations of an embarrassing nature or crimes which are committed by persons known to the victim.

In addition, the NCVS could fall victim to the following sources of interviewer bias:

1. Although each interviewer follows the same questionnaire, interviewers may still unwittingly cue respondents to answer in a particular way.
2. The interviewer could record answers incorrectly or make up answers to questions which the respondents do not wish to answer.
3. Interviewer self-interest: Keeping their jobs, avoiding work which is unpleasant, pleasing superiors by producing results in keeping with what they think is most advantageous to the organization (i.e., uncovering unreported crime), and self-serving purposes (i.e., altering responses to relieve the tedium of a steady stream of negative answers).

Errors in the coding of the data may also be made.

Conclusions Concerning the NCVS

Obviously, the NCVS is not a foolproof source of crime information. The obvious strength of the NCVS is that it attempts to go directly to the victims of crime and overcome the problems of under or non-reporting. It includes data concerning victims; their personal characteristics, where and when the crime took place, and the nature and extent of the victimization. It also includes information on households touched by crime during the past year. The NCVS thus provides information on criminal victimization on a nationwide basis.

The scope of the NCVS, however, is one of its basic weaknesses. The data presented is representative of the nation as a whole and is not broken down by state or city. The deciding factor in the selection of NCVS over UCR data (or vice versa) should be the needs of the particular study. The determination of their strengths, weaknesses, and differences in terms of the treatment of the data should help the researcher make a choice.

SELF-REPORT STUDIES

The final possible source of crime information is to go directly to the offender. Like the victimization survey, this technique is designed to uncover unreported crime. It also questions the validity of official crime statistics by examining the criminal justice process. System-produced data may have "holes" in it: some persons are arrested and sanctioned while others who commit the same crime are not. Nettler lists the various methods in which self-report studies can be conducted:[26]

1. By asking people to complete anonymous questionnaires.
2. By asking people to complete anonymous questionnaires identified in a circuitous fashion and validated against later interviews or police records.
3. By asking people to confess criminal acts on signed questionnaires validated against police records.
4. By having people complete anonymous questionnaires identified by number and validated against follow-up interviews and the threat of polygraph.
5. By interviewing respondents and validating their responses against official records.

We shall examine a famous study of career criminals, a major source of information on drug abuse in the United States and a sexual victimization survey of prison inmates that features the self report approach.

Petersilia, Greenwood, and Lavin, "Criminal Careers of Habitual Offenders"

Research conducted by Petersilia, Greenwood, and Lavin of the Rand Corporation represents a recent attempt to use the self-report method as a means of uncover crime.[27] Here, the focus of the study was habitual offenders and the key research hypothesis was "How many crimes do habitual offenders actually commit?" The policy implications of this study revolved around the issue of incapacitation, namely "Can crime be prevented by incarcerating habitual offenders for longer periods of time?" The research represents a direct test of the rationale behind habitual offender and mandatory sentencing legislation.

The study focuses upon the criminal careers of 49 inmates from a medium-security California prison. In order to be considered for the study, inmates must have been convicted of armed robbery (indicator of serious criminal conduct) and have served at least one prior prison term (indicator of persistent criminal activity).

Each interviewee was sent a formal notice of the interview and the purpose of the study was explained to them. One inmate was transferred, four did not appear at the interview station and one interview was discarded because the inmate appeared to be "under the influence" at the time of the interview. The researchers utilized a highly-structured questionnaire which collected data on 200 variables. In addition, the questionnaire corresponded to three career periods: (a) juvenile (first offense, incarceration to age 18), (b) Young Adult (from release after first juvenile incarceration through first adult incarceration), and (c) Adult (from release after first adult incarceration to the current prison term). During the interview, only the inmate and the interviewer were present with no correctional officer within hearing distance.

Petersilia has explicitly discussed the method used to attempt to validate the inmate responses.[28] Respondents confirmed each period of incarceration which the researchers recorded from the inmates' official criminal record ("rap sheet") and supplied information on how long each of the incarcerations lasted. Each self-reported arrest or conviction item was validated only if the official record showed an arrest or conviction for the same type of crime during the specific dates identified as the beginning and end of each crime period. In short, the rap sheet was used as a benchmark to gauge the accuracy of the inmates' responses. If they correctly reported the offenses known to the researchers, the assumption was that they would be truthful about the nature and number of offenses for which they were not apprehended. Offenders in the study reported 63 percent of the arrests, 74 percent of the convictions, and 88 percent of the incarcerations contained in their official records.

Other tests of validity were also conducted. For the two adult career periods, the offenders reported roughly half of their official arrests and convictions. The theory that, if the respondent wants to present himself in the best light, he will underreport the most stigmatizing offenses was not supported. In fact, just the opposite pattern was discovered by the researchers. The offenses which were less serious (i.e., grand larceny, auto theft) were less accurately reported. It was also found that the inmates, apparently due to their desire to appear "rehabilitated," underreported those offenses which occurred in the time period closest to the interview. Overall, the respondents reported approximately 50 percent of their adult and 75 percent of their juvenile arrests and convictions.

Selected Findings

As a group, the 49 respondents admitted that they were responsible for over 10,500 crimes. The top three categories were drug sales (3,620), burglary (2,331), and auto theft (1,492). Since the average criminal career was about 20 years long and half of this time was spent in prison, the average respondent committed 20 crimes every year they were on the street. It was also reported that the number of self-reported offenses committed per month of street crime noticeably declined as the group grew older. Even in the later stages of their careers, these offenders averaged only a few thousand dollars per year for their crimes.

Only 25 percent of the group said that they had trouble adjusting to prison life. However, with advancing age and more frequent incarceration, their main source of difficulty was not the other inmates but their own feelings and the growing realization that life is short and the desire to be on the outside living it. The inmates strongly felt that what they needed most upon release was someone who cared and employment. Drugs and alcohol were found to play a prominent role in the offenders' lives. The offenders who had problems handling both had the highest offense rates.

This report is noteworthy for the manner in which it states the policy implications of the research. These conclusions are of particular importance to the criminal justice researcher in that he/she is interested in providing, through research, information upon which policy can be built. With regard to rehabilitation, these inmates felt that prison programs did not provide a strong inducement for them to go straight. They stated that they would prefer job training programs and it was also clear that, by their own admission, they could benefit from drug/alcohol treatment programs. In terms of the deterrent effect of punishment, it was clear that the inmates did not fit the definition of the rational criminal and that they were unconcerned about the possibility of apprehension. Over half of the inmates said that "nothing" could have deterred their return to crime following release from prison. In fact, those who served longer sentences did not have shorter periods of street crime after release and until the next incarceration.

Finally regarding incapacitation, if it were enacted as a policy, the research indicated that the greatest effect in crime prevention would come from imprisoning the younger, more active offenders, since individual offense rates appeared to decline substantially with age. Unfortunately, it is very difficult, if not impossible, to develop an accurate method of predicting criminal behavior and identifying this crime-prone group.

Monitoring the Future: National Results on Adolescent Drug Use

Via grant support from the National Institute of Drug Abuse, this long term study of adolescents, college students and adults through age 45 in the U.S. has been conducted by the University of Michigan's Institute for Social Research since 1975. The 2005 edition of this survey contacted nearly 50,000 eighth, tenth and twelfth grade students in over 400 secondary schools nationwide. The respondents were asked about their attitudes about and use of illicit drugs. The research also tracks trends in illicit drug use over time.

The survey asks whether the respondents have used certain illicit drugs in the past twelve months. Concerning the adolescent sample, the following findings were reported in the survey:[29]

- Exactly half of American secondary school students surveyed had tried an illicit drug by the time they near high school graduation.
- A number of specific drugs showed continuing declines this year in at least one grade. These include marijuana, LSD, ecstasy, amphetamines, methamphetamines, steroids, androstenedione, alcohol and cigarettes.
- Gradual declines in use were noted for marijuana (by far the most prevalent of the illicit drugs), LSD, and Ecstasy. After rapidly gaining in popularity from about 1998 through 2001, ecstasy showed a sharp turnaround in use.
- Amphetamine use showed some continuing decline in 2005 in the upper grades but not in 8th grade.
- Methamphetamine use showed a rather steady decline in all three grades.
- Tranquilizer use increased steadily for nearly a decade, from 1992 to about 2000 among 10th and 12th graders, before declining. Thus, the decade-long upward march in tranquilizer use in the upper grades has ended, and some modest downward trending has been occurring.
- Three so-called "club drugs" – ketamine, Rohypnol, and GHB – have each shown a pattern of declining use that for the most part continued into 2005. They have all shown considerable proportional declines since their recent peaks, with all three having an annual prevalence rate well under 2%.
- Anabolic steroid use reached recent peak levels by 2000 in 8th and 10th grades and by 2002 in 12th grade. Androstenedione and creatine, two other substances used to build strength and muscle mass, also have declined appreciably in use in recent years at all three grade levels.
- Drugs that showed practically no change at all in 2005 were cocaine, crack, and heroin. In each case, annual prevalence rates are below where they were at their recent peaks, but no further decline occurred at any grade level for these drugs.
- Cocaine and crack use held generally steady in 2004 and 2005 at levels somewhat below recent peaks and far below the levels attained in the mid-1980s among 12th graders. The annual prevalence for powder cocaine is 1.7% in 8th grade, 3.0% in 10th grade, and 4.5% in 12th grade, while the annual prevalence for crack cocaine is between 1.4% and 1.9% in all three grades.

• Heroin use finally fell below its recent peak levels in all three grades by 2001. Since then use has held quite steady, including use with and without a needle. Annual prevalence is now slightly below 1.0% in all three grades.

• Narcotics other than heroin, taken as a class, are reported only for 12th graders. After increasing substantially in use since the early 1990s, this class of drugs has appeared to level in use over the past few years. Still, the annual prevalence rate stands at 9.0%. Vicodin, an important drug in this class, held steady in all three grades this year. The prevalence rates for Vicodin at each of the three grades range between 2.6% among 8th graders to 9.5% among 12th graders.

• Ice, or crystal methamphetamine, use has held quite steady for the past two years among 12th graders, the only ones asked about such use. Its annual prevalence is now 2.3%.

Despite these encouraging downward trends in illicit drug use, the authors of the report caution that there is still a problem with "generational forgetting." Many drugs make a comeback because succeeding generations of youth are unaware of the adverse consequences of their continued use.

Sexual Victimization in State and Federal Prisons Reported By Inmates, 2007

Research conducted by Bureau of Justice Statistics attempted to determine the incidence of sexual violence in state and Federal prisons as required by the Rape Elimination Act of 2003. A random sample of inmates (from not less than 10 percent of prison facilities) was drawn and computer assisted self interviews were conducted. Following audio instructions, the inmate survey respondents responded to a touch screen, audio computer assisted questionnaire. The assumption was that inmates would be more likely to respond and give a more complete account of their victimization under this format.

About 24,000 inmates participated in the survey and 1,109 reported one or more incidents of sexual victimization. Central findings included the following:[30]

• About 2.1% of the inmates reported an incident involving another inmate. 2.9 percent reported an incident involving staff.

- Inmates at ten institutions reported total sexual victimization rates of 15 to 10 percent.
- Overall, the sexual victimization rate nationwide was estimated at 141/1000 inmates in State and Federal institutions.
- 14 facilities had nonconsensual sex rates of 300 or more incidents per 1000 inmates.

This example demonstrates the utility of the self report method. Mechanisms such as this survey help us study a serious subject that would otherwise go unknown.

Advantages of Self-Report Studies

The crucial advantage of self-report studies is that the research is again uncovering unreported crime by going directly to an original source, the offender. In our drug use example, official figures could only show how many people were arrested for drug sales or possession. These figures would exclude illicit drug users who were never caught and for those who were, only those times when they were caught. The prison sexual victimization rate would be largely unknown without the self report study. In other words, self-report studies also help illuminate the dark figure of crime.

Limitations of Self-Report Studies

The most common problem surrounding self-report studies is an obvious one – the determination of validity of the findings. How do you know that the research subjects are telling the truth?

One problem is exaggeration. The respondents may also gain some perverse pleasure out of conning the researcher, thus demonstrating that they, not the researcher, are the true expert on crime. A related problem is underreporting of crime. In our drug use example, this is especially pertinent. Perhaps these juveniles were afraid to state how often they had used illicit drugs. Either way, the researcher is at the mercy of the respondents.

One of the strongest critics of this method, Nettler has concluded that the examination of the reliability and validity of measures of crime based on confessions does not encourage substitution of self-reports for official statistics.[31] Yet, it is apparent that the self-report technique offers the researcher another method of discovering information about crime. The method allows active participation in the research process in a way not possible when the researcher is dependent upon data produced by others (police records, or program officials). Researchers should recognize the value of such an all-purpose tool is dependent upon the skill with which it is applied to the task at hand.[32]

TRIANGULATION

Triangulation refers to the use of several different research methods to measure a phenomenon. Triangulation is also concerned with **convergent-discriminant validation**. Using different methods to measure crime (UCR, NCVS, and self report) should yield the same findings (convergence) while measures of different things with the same measure should yield different results (discrimination). Triangulation thus offers a way to validate the accuracy and reliability of different criminal justice data sources.

For example, comparisons of UCR and NCVS data have indicated that they share common strengths and weaknesses as measures of criminality. Hindelang reported that there was a close proximity between UCR data and an earlier victimization study in terms of the frequency in the occurrence of index crimes.[33] Decker discovered that there were positive correlations between the two data sources with regard to the index offenses and concluded that the official measures of crime provided a relatively good indicator of the distribution of Part I crimes as measured by victim surveys.[34] Other researchers found that correspondence between these two crime measures did not always occur.[35]

Of course, the main problem when attempting to triangulate UCR and NCVS data is to obtain data sets from the same jurisdiction, for the same time period which also are concerned with the same crimes. It may be necessary to conduct a victimization survey on a smaller scale within a particular area and then make the comparison to UCR information.[36]

However, triangulation is not limited to a comparison of UCR and NCVS results. It can be used any time there are multiple data sources which can be used to measure a phenomenon. For example, Baldus, Pulaski, and Woodworth used triangulation to determine an accurate method to ascertain the proportionality of Georgia's death penalty statute. Their research was based upon the fact that the Georgia State Supreme Court is required by law to conduct a review of all death sentences in order to determine whether the sentence is excessive or disproportionate when compared to the sentence imposed in similar cases, considering both the crime and the defendant. The authors attempted to determine the best method of making this determination. They opted for a triangulation approach using three different methods for identifying similar cases for comparative purposes while cross-checking the results of each method.[37] In this manner, triangulation can help to solve the reliability and/or validity problem by identifying and considering the use of multiple data sets or multiple methods of measurement.

CONCLUSION

The criminal justice researcher faces serious problems when attempting to measure crime. The validity and reliability of the indicators selected are of paramount concern. This chapter has raised some of the critical issues surrounding the use of the most common sources of crime information (UCR, NCVS, and self-report studies). They all have their particular strengths and weaknesses, and it is important to remember that the choice of crime measures can affect both the course and results of the study. Unfortunately, none of these measures is error-free. We must recognize the limitations of each, attempt to deal with them, and in some way attempt to improve them.

KEY TERMS

Validity
Face validity
Content validity
Reliability
Uniform Crime Reports
Index Crimes
Crime Rate
Unfounding
Crime clock

National Incident Based Reporting System (NIBRS)
National Crime Victimization Survey
Forgetting (memory decay)
Telescoping
Bounding technique
Households touched by crime
Triangulation

REVIEW QUESTIONS

1. What is the definition of validity and how does it apply to the indicators discussed in this chapter? Perform the same exercise with reliability.

2. Read the following hypothetical example and describe how it would be classified in the Uniform Crime Reports and under the National Crime Victimization Survey. What would the differences be and how well would the classification describe what actually happened?

> A young couple living in the household of the young woman's parents in Stanford, Connecticut, go to New York City on December 31 to celebrate New Year's Eve. They park their car in a lot on the east side of Manhattan and have a leisurely dinner at a nearby restaurant.
>
> After dinner when they return to their car, they are accosted by five young males just outside the parking lot and are taken into an adjacent alley way, at approximately 11:00 P.M.
>
> One of the youths threatens the couple with a revolver, and the other four take turns raping the woman. When the woman resists, one of the youths assaults her with a knife, and then he also assaults the man.
>
> Following the acts of rape, the youths take the woman's purse and the man's wallet and they appear to flee.
>
> It is now 1:00 A.M., January 1. The couple have to travel several blocks to report the incident to the police. When they finally return to the parking lot with a police officer at 3:00 A.M., they discover that their automobile is missing.
>
> A week later, three young males are stopped by the police in Newark, NJ, driving the couple's car through a red stoplight and they are arrested.

3. Go on the World Wide Web and find recent results for the Uniform Crime Reports, National Crime Victimization Survey and Monitoring the Future. How have the findings for each changed compared to those reported in this chapter?

4. Go to the latest National Crime Victimization Survey report on the World Wide Web and find the rate of rape victimization and compare that to the rate presented in prison sexual victimization study.

REFERENCES

1. Nettler, G. (1984). *Explaining crime.* New York: McGraw-Hill.
2. Skogan, W.G. (1975). Measurement problems in official and survey crime rates. *Journal of Criminal Justice,* 3:17–31.
3. Nettler, *Measuring crime.*
4. Skogan, Measurement problems.
5. Federal Bureau of Investigation, *Uniform Crime Reports,* http://www.fbi.gov/ucr/ucr.htm
6. Zolbe, P.A. (1981). *The role of the uniform crime reporting program as a data source for criminological research: Promise and limitations.* Paper presented at the Annual Meeting of the American Society of Criminology, Washington, D.C.
7. Wolfgang, M.E. (1963). Uniform crime reports: A critical appraisal. *University of Pennsylvania Law Review,* 3:708–738.
8. Crime in the United States, 2005, http://www.fbi.gov/ucr/05cius/data/table_01.html#overview
9. Seidman, D. and Couzens, M. (1974). Getting the crime rate down: Political pressures and crime reporting. *Law and Society Review,* 8:456–493.
10. McClintock, F.H. (1977). The dark figure of crime. In Radzinowicz, L., and Wolfgang, M.E. (Eds.), *Crime and justice, Volume I. The criminal in society.* New York: Basic Books, pp. 126-139.
11. Kleinman, P.H., and Lukoff, I.F. (1981). Official crime data: Lag in recording time as a threat to validity. *Criminology,* 19:449–454.
12. Quinney, R. (1977). What do crime rates mean? In Radzinowicz, L. and Wolfgang, M. E. (Eds.), *Crime and justice, Volume I. The criminal in society.* New York: Basic Books, pp. 107-111.
13. Ferracuti, F., Hernandez, R.P., and Wolfgang, M.E. (1962). A study of police errors in crime classification. *Journal of Criminal Law, Criminology and Police Science,* 53:113–119.
14. Seidman and Couzens, Getting the crime rate down.
15. Wolfgang, Uniform Crime Reports.
16. Ibid.
17. *Crime Clock, Crime in the United States,* 2005 http://www.fbi.gov/ucr/05cius/about/crime_clock.html
18. Zolbe, The role of UCR.
19. Federal Bureau of Investigation, *Synopsis of crime in schools and colleges – A study of national incident based reporting system (NIBRS) Data* http://www.fbi.gov/ucr/schoolviolence.pdf
20. Fienberg, S.E. (1980). Victimization and the national crime survey: Problems of design and analysis. In Feinberg, S.E., and Reiss, A.J. Jr. (Eds.), *Indicators of crime*

and criminal justice: Quantitative studies. Washington D.C.: U.S. Government Printing Office, pp. 33–40.

21. Garofalo, J., and Hindelang, M.J. (1977). An introduction to the National Crime Survey. Washington, D.C.: U.S. Department of Justice.

22. Gottfredson, M.R., and Hindelang, M.J. (1977). A consideration of telescoping and memory decay biases in victimization surveys. *Journal of Criminal Justice*, 5, 205–216.

23. National Crime Victimization Survey. *Crime and the nation's households, 2005* http://www.ojp.usdoj.gov/bjs/pub/ascii/cnh05.txt

24. Skogan, W.G. (1981). *Issues in the measurement of victimization.* Washington, D.C.: U.S. Government Printing Office.

25. Levine, J.P. (1976). The potential for crime overreporting in criminal victimization surveys. *Criminology*, 14:307–330.

26. Nettler, G. (1984). Explaining crime. New York: McGraw-Hill.

27. Petersilia, J., Greenwood, P.W., and Lavin, M. (1977). *The criminal careers of habitual felons.* Santa Monica, CA: The Rand Corporation.

28. Petersilia, J. (1978). *Validity of criminality data derived from personal interviews.* In Wellford, C. (Ed.), Quantitative studies in criminology. Beverly Hills, CA: Sage, pp. 30–47.

29. Johnston, L.D., O'Malley, P.M., Bachman, J.G., and Schulenberg, J.E. (2006). *Monitoring the future - National results on adolescent drug use: Overview of key findings, 2005.* (NIH Publication No. 06-5882). Bethesda, MD: National Institute on Drug Abuse.

30. Beck, A.J., and Harrison, P.M. (2007). *Sexual victimizations in state and federal prisons reported by inmates, 2007.* Washington, D.C.: Bureau of Justice Statistics.

31. Nettler, *Explaining crime.*

32. Hirschi, T., Hindelang, M.J., and Weis, J.G. (1980). *The status of self-report measures.* In Klein, M.W., and Teilmann, K.S. (Eds.), *Handbook of criminal justice evaluation.* Beverly Hills, CA, Sage, pp. 473–488.

33. Hindelang, M.J. (1974). The uniform crime reports revisited. *Journal of Criminal Justice*, 2, 1–17.

34. Decker, S.H. (1977). Official crime rates and victim surveys: An empirical comparison. *Journal of Criminal Justice*, 5, 47–54.

35. Booth, A.J., David, R., and Choldin, H.M. (1977). Correlates of city crime rates: Victimization surveys versus official statistics. *Social Problems*, 25, 187–197; Eck, J.E. and Riccio, L.J. (1979). Relationship between reported crime rates and victimization survey results: An empirical and analytical study. *Journal of Criminal Justice*, 7: 293–308; Schneider, A.L. (1981). Differences between survey and police information about crime. In Lehnen, R.G., and Skogan, W.G. (Eds.), *The National Crime Survey: Working papers, Volume I - Current and historical perspectives.* Washington, D.C.: U.S. Government Printing Office, pp. 39–46; Gove, W.R., Hughes, M., and Geerken, M. (1985). Are Uniform Crime Reports a valid indicator of the index crimes? An affirmative answer with minor qualifications, *Criminology*, 23, 453.

36. Bursik, R.J. and Grasmick, H.G. (1993). The use of multiple indicators to estimate crime trends in American cities. *Journal of Criminal Justice*, 21, p. 511.

37. Baldus, D.C., Pulaski, C.A. Jr., Woodworth, G., and Kyle, F.D. (1983). Identifying comparatively excessive sentences of death: A quantitative approach. *Stanford Law Review*, 33, 1–76.

Chapter Five

ELEMENTS OF RESEARCH DESIGN

CHAPTER OVERVIEW

This chapter features an introduction to research design – the plan or blueprint for a complete research project. The research design outlines: the questions to be studied, the number and nature of the variables under study, how the data will be obtained, and how it will be analyzed. It contains the strategy for the investigation – how the analysis will address the research questions. The aim of the research design is to isolate the impact of the independent variable(s) (the program, policy, theory) that is under study. In that way, the researcher insures that conclusions drawn from the research are the result of the effect of the independent variable upon the dependent variable and not due to other factors.

TYPES OF RESEARCH DESIGN

There are several types of designs used in criminal justice research. Here, we begin with the basis for all research designs, the classical experiment, and then consider its progeny – the quasi experimental and non-experimental designs. In addition, we will consider the problems that can plague any type of design – threats to internal and external validity.

The Classical Experiment

The **classical experiment** is the basis for all other types of research designs. It outlines the comparisons that must be made to reach a conclusion about research hypotheses. The classical experiment is considered to be the most powerful research design. The classical experiment:

- Attempts to discover the cause and effect relationship between dependent and independent variables in a controlled setting.
- Attempts to measure specific effects of variables within specific contexts by "screening out" undesirable influences upon the research and maintain the focus upon the research variables under consideration – whether the independent variable (X) has a causal relationship to the dependent variable (Y).
- Involves a comparison between groups (Experimental and Control) of individuals and variables (independent and dependent).

Measurement of the dependent variable is taken at two points in time – Pre and Post Tests. The pre-test establishes the value of the dependent variable before exposure to the treatment (the independent variable). The post-test determines the value of the dependent variable after exposure to the treatment. Figure 5.1 presents a diagram of the classical experiment.

Figure 5.1 The Classical Experiment

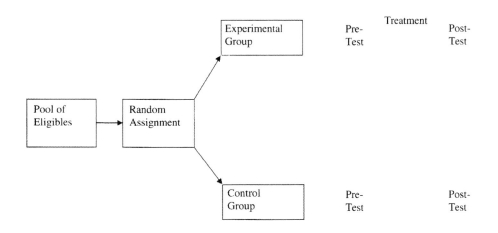

The magic of the classical experiment is random assignment of the subjects under study. **Random assignment** means that each subject under study has an equal chance of being assigned to the experimental group and being exposed to the treatment. It also means the selection of one individual for the experimental group does not affect the chance that any other individual will be selected. It insures that the experimental and control groups are alike and comparable. To reach a conclusion about the effect of the independent variable, you want to isolate that difference. The other difference you want to have between these two groups is that the experimental group "gets it" (the independent variable/treatment) and the control group does not.

A major strength of random assignment is that it makes the groups alike, even on those differences that are impossible to measure. For example, one of the keys to effective treatment of drug or alcohol abuse is amenability to treatment. Put simply, the abuser must be ready to change and accept treatment.[1] The pretest on the dependent variable will reveal if the groups are alike. Thus, the comparability of the experimental and control groups can be checked. With random assignment, the researcher is also assured that difficult-to-measure variables like amenability to treatment will also be spread between the two groups under consideration.

Again, random assignment assures the similarity of the experimental and control groups. Without it, the experimental and control groups may differ on attributes which the experimenter is unable to measure or consider their impact. With random assignment, this is not a problem. With it, every member of the population has an equal chance of being selected, therefore, members with certain distinguishing characteristics (i.e. they are more "crime prone") will, if selected, probably be counterbalanced in the long run by the selection of other members with the "opposite" quality.[2] The only difference between the two groups is the one that the experimenter desires – the **experimental group** is exposed to the treatment but the control group is not. Any difference between the two groups on the posttest (dependent variable) is presumed to be the result of the treatment (independent variable). The treatment is the program or project itself while the control is the absence of treatment or one in which traditional or customary treatment is delivered to the subjects.[3]

The **control group** isolates the effects of the independent variable upon the dependent variable. If the two groups have different results or outcomes, the assumption is that it is a legitimate effect of the treatment and that it is not due to other differences between the members of the experimental and control groups. The classical experiment measures the impact of a treatment by applying it to the experimental group while withholding it from the identical control group and then measuring what happens. If the treatment has an effect, it should only appear in the performance of the experimental group and not the control group.

Of course, the control group performs a vital function in experimentation. Without a control group, we would have no basis of comparison and any conclusion about the effect of the treatment would be less conclusive. Note that the term "control group" is only used when a classical experiment is described. As we shall see, groups constructed in ways other than random assignment have a different name.

In criminal justice, the treatment can take many forms. It can be a special form of policing (a stakeout or crackdown on drug sales). It can be the impact of a sentence like home incarceration or electronic monitoring. It could be treatment in the medical sense – counseling for drug abusers or perpetrators of domestic violence. It could be a curfew for juveniles. In other words, any policy or program aimed at crime prevention. The elements that are randomly assigned can be people, neighborhoods, cities, or even states. As stated in Chapter One, criminological theory guides the design by specifying why the treatment should have an effect and if that effect should take a specific direction. Theory provides the basis for an expectation that the policy or program under consideration will be effective – that it will help to prevent crime.

For example, suppose you wished to determine the effect of drug testing upon drug abuse rates among probationers and parolees.[4] A classical experimental design would look something like this:

- Experimental Group (Constructed via random assignment of subjects).
  - o Determine the level of drug abuse (Pre-test).
  - o Conduct random drug testing (Treatment).
  - o Determine the level of drug abuse (Post-test).
- Control Group (Constructed via random assignment of subjects).
  - o Determine the level of drug abuse (Pre-test).
  - o Do Nothing (No Treatment).
  - o Determine the level of drug abuse (Post-test).

On the Pre-test, the positive rate for drug testing between the members of the Experimental and Control groups should be close to equal. However, if the process of drug testing has a deterrent effect upon drug abuse, the members of the Experimental group should have a lower positive drug test rate on the Post-test than the members of the Control group who were not exposed to drug testing.

The classical experiment in criminal justice research has been widely used in criminal justice research.[5] To show how the classical experiment can be applied in criminal justice research, let us review two examples – the Provo Experiment and experiments on the impact of mandatory arrest in domestic violence cases.

The Provo Experiment

The Provo Experiment was designed to treat delinquents through the establishment of a social climate that would give these boys the opportunity to experience alternatives to delinquent behavior. The boys would also be given the opportunity to declare publicly their belief (or disbelief) that they could benefit from a change in values. The treatment (established in 1956) was a halfway house (Pinehills) where boys would spend a part of each day. They still lived at home and were otherwise free in the community. The assignment to the Pinehills facility (the treatment) gave these boys new responsibilities.[6] It stressed peer group decision-making. Status and recognition was granted to individuals for their successful participation in the program and for their willingness to help others. It was specifically designed to help those habitual delinquents whose persistence made them candidates for the reformatory.

When conducting an experiment, it is important to focus on the **pool of eligibles** – those individuals that the program is designed to serve. The pool of eligibles for the Provo Experiment included boys, aged 15–17, who were identified as habitual offenders. Highly disturbed, psychotic boys were not assigned to the program and no more than 20 boys were assigned at once.

Figure 5.2 outlines the original research design for the Provo Experiment. The initial design was constructed with the idea that all the groups could be drawn randomly from a common population of habitual offenders in Utah County (pool of eligibles). The design would provide a means by which two groups of boys who receive the treatment (experimental group) would be compared with boys in two control groups: (1) a control group of offenders who were placed on probation at the time of sentencing and (2) a control group of boys who were sentenced to the Utah State Industrial School.

Figure 5.2. The Provo Experiment

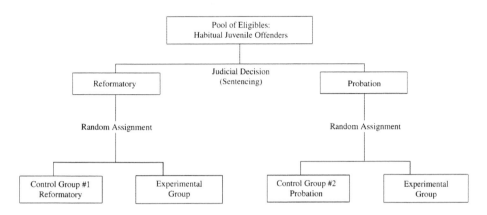

The key issue here was to use random assignment while not interfering with the judicial process. The judge was instructed to hear the case and decide whether to sentence the juvenile offender to probation or incarceration as though Pinehills did not exist. Thus, the experiment did not interfere with the usual operations of the juvenile court because the random assignment to the experimental (Pinehills) and control (Reformatory or Probation) groups was done after the sentence was pronounced by the judge. The researchers in charge of the experiment felt that this procedure was adopted by the judge in the hope that that in the long run, his contributions to the research would enable judicial decisions to be based ultimately on a more realistic evaluation of treatment programs available.[7]

However, as is typically the case with criminal justice research, the classical experiment proved difficult to implement.[8] First of all, habitual offenders comprised only 15 percent of all cases which came before the court. Thus, the pool of eligibles was not always large enough to fill two experimental and two control groups. Second, Judge Paxman was never inclined to send boys to the reformatory, so that control group was not adequately filled. Therefore, it became necessary to select a random sample of boys from the reformatory and to determine if (and on what characteristics) they differed from the established experimental and control groups. This adjustment was made and no significant difference between groups was revealed. Thus, as we shall see, the Provo Experiment was actually a combination of an experimental and a quasi-experimental design.

Research on the Provo Experiment was conducted and the following results were reported. The measure of recidivism (the dependent variable – rearrest and reincarceration) used in the study was the filing of an arrest report six months after release. In the experimental group, it was discovered that 73 percent of the boys assigned to and 84 percent of the boys who had completed Pinehills had not been arrested. None of the experimental group recidivists had been incarcerated. For the probation control group, the success rate for boys who were assigned to regular probation was 73 percent and 77 percent for those who had completed probation. Therefore, the difference in outcome between the experimental and probation control groups was not substantial. Empey and Rabow reported that this lack of results may have been due to the fact that the probation department and the community adopted a daily work program and other facilities as aids to the experiment and the probation department. Finally, the second control group of incarcerated offenders (selected from the reformatory) generated a 58 percent rearrest rate. Half of the incarcerated recidivists had been arrested two or more times during the six month period. Although the classical experimental design broke down for this group, it must be remembered that a comparison of all the groups indicated that they were substantially similar.

Experiments on the Impact of Mandatory Arrest in Domestic Violence Cases

Arrest may have diverse effects upon different types of crime. For example, Lawrence Sherman has conducted several studies of the impact of arrest in domestic violence cases. In the first study, suspects in Minneapolis were randomly assigned to one of three potential responses by the police: (1) arrest, (2) threat of arrest (with the suspect leaving the home) and (3) a "talking to" by the police (with the suspect left at the scene).[9] Here, the first group (arrest) was the experimental group while the second (threat of arrest) and third ("talking to") were the control groups. The aim of the experiment was to determine which of the three methods produced the lowest level of domestic violence in these households in the future.[10]

The results of the Minneapolis domestic violence experiment supported the use of arrest in domestic violence cases as a way to protect the victim. The suspects who were arrested had the lowest rate of recidivism among the three groups. Arrest appeared to have a specific deterrent effect upon domestic violence.[11]

This study had a dramatic impact upon policing in domestic violence cases. Although the authors were careful to recommend against the passage of mandatory arrest laws until further research was conducted, the results of the Minneapolis experiment contributed to the passage of such laws in 15 states by 1991.[12]

The relevance of the findings of the Minneapolis experiment, particularly the value of mandatory arrest in the protection of domestic violence victims was tested in other sites when the study was **replicated** (repeated with the same methodology in a different location). When the replications were conducted in Omaha,[13] Charlotte,[14] and Milwaukee, the results were not the same as Minneapolis. Arresting domestic violence suspects in both Omaha and Charlotte was no more effective than other methods of handling the case (e.g., citation or advisement).

In Milwaukee, Sherman and his colleagues specifically examined the impact of arrest upon domestic violence cases in poverty ghetto areas. In this experiment, suspects were randomly assigned the same potential police responses as in the Minneapolis experiment. Their interviews with victims in such cases revealed that arrest had a short-term deterrent effect. In the end, there was no difference in outcome among the three sanctions (arrest with a night's stay in jail, arrest with release after about three hours, a warning by police). The authors concluded that short term arrest may even cause harm by increasing anger at society without increasing the fear of rearrest. Thus, "a little jail time can be worse than none."

The Milwaukee experiment also determined that suspects with a "stake in conformity" were more likely to be deterred by arrest. Persons with "nothing to lose" were not deterred in domestic violence cases. They found that unmarried, unemployed and black subjects were more likely to become involved in domestic violence again. The authors believe that the results confirm that the effectiveness of arrest is domestic violence cases is dependent upon informal controls (e.g., employment, marriage) upon the subjects.[16]

In Metro-Dade (FL), evidence of the influence of social bonds was also present. Arrest had a significant deterrent effect upon employed suspects. It had the opposite effect upon unemployed suspects. Pate and Hamilton felt that these results highlighted the interrelationship between formal and informal sanctions.[17] Policies should take into account that arrest seems to deter only those who have something to lose (e.g., a job).

Berk and his associates analyzed the findings of these domestic violence experiments plus a fourth in Colorado Springs. They found that arrest appeared to do little to either increase or decrease the likelihood of repeat offending in domestic violence cases. In all four locations, arrest seemed to have a deterrent effect upon employed suspects and also increased the risk of future violence for the unemployed. Marital status seemed to have little or no effect. These authors caution us not to consider these findings too literally. For example, employment may be a measure of exposure — employed subjects are less likely to be at home and thus have less interaction with the victim. They also note that the findings do not suggest that arrest should be dropped as a policy option. The results of all four experiments should be viewed with caution.

On the basis of these results, it is difficult to determine the effect of arrest in domestic violence cases. Other social variables (e.g. "a stake in conformity" – family, job, education) may be as effective as a formal arrest policy by the police.

Problems in the Use of a Classical Experiment

Despite its strengths, there are several problems with the use of an experimental design. First, both ethical and legal issues surround the use of the classical experiment in criminal justice research (see Chapter Three). For example, the use of a control group implies that some persons (perhaps offenders) will be deprived of the presumed benefits of a program. Of course, the catch here is that, without sound research, the benefits of a program cannot be accurately ascertained. Also, the number of slots available in a program is typically limited and assignments made fail to guarantee equal access to all persons who need or could benefit from treatment. In our previous drug testing example, not all probationers and parolees could be tested. As Baunach (1980) has pointed out, this problem is not insurmountable. If the benefits of the program (treatment) are unknown, the control group offenders are not being deprived. Once the effectiveness of the program is determined, control group offenders can be admitted.[19]

Second, the classical experiment has the potential to encroach upon the decision-making authority of criminal justice agents. The clear solution here, as the Provo Experiment indicated, is to use random assignment after a decision is made. Surely, experimenters cannot expect to randomly sentence people to prison or probation. Modifications can be adopted which do not restrict the power of the classical experimental design while protecting the rights of individuals.

Third, there is the major issue of the feasibility of carrying out an experiment in the field.

The random assignment process must be structured to meet both the demands of the classical experiment and the operations of the criminal justice system – in these two examples, sentencing by judges and arrest and other sanctions by police. It requires very close cooperation between the operational agencies and the researchers. Implementing random assignment and maintaining it throughout the process can be problematic. Also, to repeat, the subjects selected for study must be eligible for treatment and the experimental and control groups must be kept separate so that the integrity of the treatment is maintained.[20] After all, exposure to the treatment should be the only difference between the two groups.

The Quasi-Experimental Design

The classical experiment is not the only form of research design. However, it serves as the point of departure for other designs which attempt to approximate its key features. The quasi-experimental design is the mirror image of the classical experiment with one key difference: the absence of random assignment. As previously mentioned, it is not always possible to implement the classical experiment. Yet, it is vital that a group is constructed to compare findings generated by the experimental group. Thus, a **comparison group** is selected using a method other than random assignment to insure that it is comparable to the experimental group.

Our example here is the evaluation of a prison-based treatment program for drug/alcohol abusing inmates.[21] We need to find a group of inmates in the same prison who have the same problem, but who were

never involved in the program in any way. After all, if we selected inmates who were excluded from the program, we would commit
the error of selection bias. Similarly, if we chose inmates who dropped
out of the program, the data would be contaminated because the comparison group would have been exposed to the treatment. What is left?
Adams' suggests screening inmates who were considered for, but **for
reasons of their own**, decided not to take part in the program – a
self-drop group.[22] Before such a group can be considered however,
two important considerations must be checked out. First, the researcher must be certain that such inmates were not thrown out of the
program by project administrators (Beware of selection bias!). Second,
you must be certain that these inmates were never enrolled in or exposed to the treatment (contamination of data problem). It would also
be possible to check for eligible inmates who were simply unaware of
the program. It is also possible to use a variation of the **matching** technique (again the missing element is random assignment). Here, the
experimenter would construct a comparison group which was identical to the experimental group on a number of known variables (i.e.,
age, race, prior record, present offense, education, marital status, etc.).

In any event, since randomization was not utilized, it is necessary to
record relevant personal and socio-demographic information on such
inmates and compares them directly to the experimental group. If differences do exist, it would be necessary to control for them statistically. Remember that the crucial issue here is that the experimental and
comparison groups must be similar. The problem is that, even if you
determine that the two groups are comparable, they may still differ on
some important attribute which was beyond your means to measure.
This is not a problem when random assignment is used, hence the
power of the classical experimental design.

However, since it is not always possible to use random assignment,
the quasi-experiment gives you another possibility to conduct accurate
research. Quite simply, it may not be possible for you to do anything
else and it is especially valuable when performing evaluation research
(see Chapter Eleven).

Other Types of Research Designs

Pre-Experimental Designs. Pre-experimental designs take a variety of forms which emphasize description but typically fail to make a

comparison between the experimental group and another group of subjects. Typically, they are undertaken out of necessity because they, like the quasi-experimental design, offer a feasible alternative to research when the classical experiment is impossible to conduct. The chief problem is that the researcher is then unable to protect the integrity of the research results and clearly state that they reflect the effect of the treatment and not some other force. They are not as reliable as the classical experiment.

The first type of pre-experimental design is the **one-shot case study** or the one group post test design. Here, measurements are obtained for one group after the treatment has been administered. For example, one could determine if a group of police officers became more sensitive to diversity issues after they went through a diversity training program. Their score on an examination would determine if they had learned the principles of diversity covered in the training program.

Probably the most common type of pre-experimental design is the **before-after study** (also known as the "one group pretest-posttest design"). This design is simply the first half of the experimental design. The performance of the experimental group is recorded before and after the treatment is administered. It is the simplest design but, due to the absence of comparison, it fails to document the effectiveness of the treatment. It is commonly used when it is difficult to construct a comparison or control group. For example, let's say that we wish to evaluate the effectiveness of a neighborhood watch program in a particular neighborhood. Under a before and after study, we would measure the burglary rate (number of reported burglaries) before and then after the implementation of the neighborhood watch. Even if the burglary rate declined after the establishment of the neighborhood watch program, we would not be able to make a comparison to another neighborhood that did not have a neighborhood watch. Our only comparison is to our selected neighborhood before and then after the neighborhood watch began.

One way to attempt to provide this comparison is to use the **static group comparison design**. With this design, the number of reported burglaries in a neighborhood that has had a neighborhood watch program would be compared to the number of reported burglaries in another neighborhood that did not have a neighborhood watch program. Here, the weakness is that, before the research is conducted, there is no examination to determine whether the two neighborhoods are comparable. The research conclusion is based upon comparing the impact upon each group to determine the effect of the treatment on one of them.

Cross-Sectional Design. A **cross sectional design** takes measurements of subjects at a single time in their lives. The **case study** is a form of cross sectional design used in criminal justice research. The case can be an individual (a professional criminal), an event (a police strike), or a place (Alcatraz). This type of design is capable of generating great quantities of descriptive information which can be used by policy makers. It is especially valuable in time of rapid change because it allows you to respond immediately to an historical event or a **natural experiment** – i.e., the effect of a judicial order on the operations of a prison or a change in sentencing policy.[23] Follow-up recidivism research on the former Kentucky death row inmates is an example of a natural experiment because their death sentences were commuted by a U.S. Supreme Court decision and they were later released by the parole board.[24]

Longitudinal Design. A **longitudinal design** is similar to the cross sectional design with the key exception that measurements are taken at more than one point in time. One form of longitudinal design is the **time series design**. The time series design is one in which the treatment is introduced during a series of measurements on the dependent variable. All of the measurements are obtained from the same group. For example, a researcher could examine the deterrent effect of an execution by measuring the homicide rate in a state in the months prior to and following an execution. A sharp change in the trend of measurements on the dependent variable (the homicide rate) immediately following the treatment (the execution) is assumed to be attributable to the treatment. Again, the comparison in results is within the experimental group only.

Another form of longitudinal design is a **cohort study**. It examines the behavior of a particular group over time. Cohorts are groups constructed by the researcher that share some common experience (i.e., involvement in the same program, graduating from the police academy in the same year). Their performance over time is then recorded. Wolfgang, Figlio, and Sellin (1972) tracked the delinquency records of a birth cohort of boys born in 1945 who lived in Philadelphia from their tenth to eighteenth birthdays. They discovered that 35 percent of the boys had some type of contact with the police and that about 50 percent of the juveniles who commit an offense are likely to commit another.[25]

Regardless of the type of design, there are several threats to validity that can affect the results of the study.

THREATS TO INTERNAL VALIDITY

Internal validity refers to ways in which the process of experimentation may affect the research results. In other words, the researcher is then uncertain if the outcomes generated by the research are a result of the treatment or the way in which the experiment was conducted. In effect, the experiment becomes a treatment in itself.

Cook and Campbell identified the following sources of internal validity:[26]

1. **History**: events, in addition to the treatment, may occur between the pre and post tests which are beyond the control of the experimenter. For example, Vito, Longmire, and Kenney (1984) reported that, during their evaluation of a police burglary suppression program, the state of California passed legislation requiring a mandatory prison sentence for burglary.[26] As a result, the researchers were uncertain if the number of reported burglaries recorded during the project were affected by the new methods of police operations or due to the new law. Often, the only thing which researchers can do when an historical event occurs in the middle of their experiment is report that it occurred and let the findings be interpreted accordingly.

2. **Maturation** refers to the processes operating within research subjects as a function of the passage of time, including growing older, growing hungrier or becoming more tired. Boredom could also be a problem which could affect the behavior of the research subjects. For example, Vito and Wilson (1988) conducted a long term follow up of former death row inmates in Kentucky whose sentence had been commuted to life in prison as a result of the *Furman* v. *Georgia* (1972) decision. Was their on parole behavior due to the commutation of their death sentence or due to aging?[28]

3. **Testing** concerns the effect of taking a test upon the scores of a second testing. If the same instrument is used for the pre and post test, the subjects in the control group may be able to tease out what the instrument is designed to measure (i.e., fear of crime) and try to answer "the right way" rather than express their own true feelings.

4. **Instrumentation**. If, upon repeated use, an instrument yields the same results, it is considered to be reliable. But what would happen if your instrument was altered somehow between the pre and post tests? If there is some alteration in your instrument, the research results would be affected.

5. **Statistical Regression** is especially problematic when research subjects have been selected on the basis of their extreme scores or attributes. "Regression toward the Mean" is a statistical phenomenon which operates in nature. Any extreme attribute tends to be balanced out over time. The problem, therefore, is that extreme subjects tend to improve over time regardless of the treatment. Their behavior or performance goes to the average level for the group of subjects under study. For example, in his book, *The Future of Imprisonment*, Morris (1974) proposed a new prison model which he would like to test using the "toughest group of inmates." Morris encouraged the use of a classical experimental design to assign such inmates to his model institution. Clearly, statistical regression could be a threat to his proposed experiment. If these inmates are so "bad" to begin with, their behavior may simply regress toward the mean. If they did improve, it would be difficult to say that the benefits were due to the new prison design.[29]

6. **Experimental Mortality** has to do with the loss of subjects from your experimental and control groups. If large numbers of subjects "drop out" for whatever reason, the groups may change so much that they are no longer comparable. Thus, the major strength of randomization is violated. Researchers conducting recidivism studies have particular problems with mortality since parolees are often mobile and do not leave forwarding addresses and they often literally die while on supervision.[30]

7. **Selection Biases**: Remember, the groups must be comparable to begin with. If techniques other than random assignment are used, selection biases may affect the research results. Put simply,

you do not wish to compare apples to oranges. Researchers or program officials should not put all the "best risks" in the experimental group and then compare them to a group of poor risks.

8. **Interactions of the Above Problems**. To make matters worse, it is possible that your research can be affected by combinations of the problems just mentioned. The design proposed by Morris (1974) could not only be subject to problems due to statistical regression, but also due to maturation. And what would happen to the research results if a riot or escape occurred during the study (History)?

9. **Causal Time Order**. If somehow the time order between the treatment and the measure of the dependent variable (post-test) is fouled up, it is obvious that the causal relationship between variables is no longer being tested.

10. **Diffusion or Imitation of Treatment**. If the respondents in the control group can communicate with the members of the experimental group, they each may discover information intended for the other group. Put simply, the physical closeness of the two groups may render them equal by exposing them both to the treatment. The Provo Experiment was plagued by this problem since both the experimental and control (probation) groups were supervised by the same probation office.

11. **Compensatory Equalization of Treatments**. When the experimental treatment provides goods or services generally believed to be desirable, the experimenter (or administrators in charge of a project) may be sympathetic toward the control group and provide them with some compensatory benefit, such as special attention. Of course, this special attention would thus become another form of treatment and the original design would suffer.

12. **Compensatory Rivalry by Respondents Receiving Less Desirable Treatments**. When the assignment of persons to experimental or control groups is made public (as is frequently required by ethical and legal considerations), competition may be generated. In particular, the control group (the natural underdog) may be motivated to perform at the highest possible level.

13. **Resentful Demoralization of Respondents Receiving Less Desirable Treatments**. This potential response is very much related to rivalry. The control group may become demoralized

about the conditions of the research and thus perform more poorly than the experimental group or get angry and revolt.

Other internal validity questions of special interest to criminal justice researchers have been identified by Adams:[31]

14. **Masking**. Experimental treatments may have opposite effects upon different kinds of subjects. Vito (1982) has suggested that it is simply illogical to assume that all members of the experimental group were amenable to or served equally by a correctional treatment program. Unless some measure of the effectiveness of the treatment among the experimental subjects is included in the study, masking could cloud the findings by failing to make such differentiations in the experimental group.[32]

15. **Contamination of Data**. If the subjects in the control group become exposed to the treatment, their post-program performance may be affected. This may have been one of the problems regarding the controversial Kansas City Preventive Patrol Experiment.[33] The treatment in this experiment was proactive police patrolling – a test of deterrence theory. The experimental neighborhoods received proactive patrolling, the reactive (control) areas underwent traditional patrolling (police responding to incoming calls for service and patrolling only the perimeter of the beat or an adjacent proactive beat), while officers in the control sections were to patrol as they normally would. The problem was that the 15 neighborhoods in the study were adjacent to one another. Was the treatment clearly isolated or did the neighborhoods, in effect, all receive the same type of patrol?

16. **"Erosion" of the Treatment Effect**. The gradual or abrupt disappearance of performance superiority shown by the experimental group in the early months after treatment may decrease or simply wear off. This problem could be especially pronounced if the researcher is following the performance of the experimental subjects over a long period of time.

These problems are not insurmountable. They have been presented because the researcher must be aware of them in order to combat them. Some can be dealt with through the use of randomization and the classical experimental design (i.e., selection bias and statistical regression). Others can be handled by careful monitoring of the conduct of the research. It is vital that the experimental and control groups are kept separate and that the integrity of the treatment is maintained. Exposure of the control group to the treatment must be avoided at all costs. It is clear that when the subjects in both groups are aware that an experiment is being conducted, the researcher must take some steps to see that compensation, rivalry, and demoralization do not occur.

THREATS TO EXTERNAL VALIDITY

The threats to **external validity** are concerned with the generalizability of the research findings. **Generalizability** simply means that the results of the study are applicable to other persons in other settings. If the research findings apply in other places, they are more significant. The key question is: Did something happen during the conduct of our experiment which makes it so unique that our findings have no meaning to the outside world? The answer to this question often resides in the manner in which the original population of subjects (or "pool of eligibles") was selected. Sampling techniques will be discussed in the next chapter which can help to solve some of the following problems.

Cook and Campbell[34] identified the following threats to external validity:

1. **The Reactive Effects of Testing**. The pre-test could increase or decrease the sensitivity (or awareness) of the respondents to the treatment so they are no longer like their counterparts in the outside world.

2. **The Interactive Effect of Selection Bias**. If your research group is not representative of the general population, your findings will not be generalizable. This is one of the problems with the Minneapolis domestic violence experiment. The findings from the one city were not upheld in later studies in different cities.

3. **The Reactive Effects of Experimental Arrangements**. This problem occurs when the subjects of the experiment become aware of their status. This phenomenon has been termed the **Hawthorne Effect** and it was experienced by researchers attempting to determine the effect of changes in working conditions on employee satisfaction and productivity.

Research by Roethlisberger and Dickson (1939) in the "bank wiring room" of the Western Electric Works in Chicago revealed that the ex-perimental group reacted favorably to any change in treatment which the experimenters instituted.[35] They were responding to the attention given to them by the researchers, regardless of the treatment.

One way to combat the Hawthorne Effect is to utilize a double blind experiment in which neither the experimenters nor the research subjects know when the treatment is being adminis-tered. This technique is especially valuable in medical experi-ments. For example, Allen and his colleagues (1976) tested the drug imipramine pamoate on an experimental group of incar-cerated sociopaths to determine if the drug could alter their behavior. The drug was given to experimental and control group subjects in orange juice at the prison treatment center. No one on the project in the institution and none of the subjects knew whether the drug or the orange juice placebo was being admin-istered. In this fashion, the researchers could determine if any differences in behavior were due to the drug, not due to any "coaching" by the ex-perimenters. It was discovered that the sociopathic prisoners who received the drug felt and performed better than their counterparts in the control group.[36]

4. **Multiple-Treatment Interference**. This can be a problem when more than one treatment is applied to the same respon-dents. Here, it would be difficult to separate the effects of the dif-ferent treatments and the research results would be muddled.

Figure 5.3. The Solomon Four Group Design

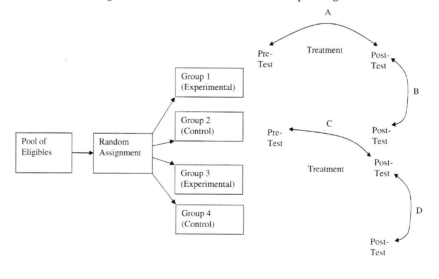

One way to combat problems of external validity is the **Solomon Four Group Design** (see Figure 5.3). This design is a combination of the classical experiment (Groups 1 and 2) and what is termed the **post-test only control group design** (Groups 3 and 4).

An evaluation of the DARE (Drug Abuse Resistance Education) program in Colorado Springs, Colorado utilized a Solomon Four Group Design to assess the effectiveness of the program.[37] The curriculum was designed to serve students in one semester during their last year of elementary school. As a new group of students entered DARE, students in half the schools were assigned to it and students in the remaining schools were assigned to the control group. In addition, students in half the DARE classes (the experimental group) and half of the classes in the control group were randomly assigned to receive a pretest that measured attitudes toward the self, family, teachers, police, their peer group, and risky behaviors regarding alcohol, tobacco, and other drugs. At the end of the semester, all students were administered a post test that was identical to the pretest.

As the Table demonstrates, the study followed a Solomon Four Group Design. In terms of Figure 5.3, this design followed an experimental group (Group 1) and a control group (Group 2) that were both pre and post tested. It also included a second experimental (Group 3) and control (Group 4) group that did not receive a pretest. In this manner, the Solomon design helps to control any interaction between testing and the stimulus by attempting to isolate the impact of the pretest ("Testing") as well as the impact of maturation on the posttest. It also provides a greater number of comparisons (A through D in Figure 5.3) than the classical experiment. The results of the DARE experiment revealed that most experimental group respondents had positive self-esteem and negative attitudes toward the use of alcohol, tobacco, and drugs. The self-esteem and bonds to family, police, and teachers gains recorded by the experimental group significantly decreased over time – an example of the erosion of a treatment effect. Contrary to the desired effect of the DARE curriculum, there was also no difference in resistance to peer pressure and endorsement of risky behaviors between the groups. In terms of examining the effect of testing, the research showed that groups that had taken a pretest (Groups 1 and 2) differed from those who only had a post test (Groups 3 and 4) in resistance to peer group pressure but this difference was attributed to DARE involvement. It is clear that this complex design helped to isolate and evaluate the effectiveness of the DARE treatment.

CONCLUSION

This chapter reviewed the basic elements of research design - the blueprint for research. A number of key points were made. First of all, the researcher should attempt to use the soundest possible design. When random assignment cannot be conducted, several alternatives to the classical experiment do exist. The researcher must be aware of and plan to combat threats to internal and external validity to protect the accuracy of the research findings. Finally, it should be clear that sound research does not occur by accident. Careful planning of the conduct of the research is required. Of course, you wish to use the strongest and most reliable design available, but your choices are often limited by forces beyond your control. As a result, researchers often compromise as far as they can without jeopardizing the quality of the research.

KEY TERMS

Classical experiment
Random assignment
Experimental and control groups
Pool of eligibles
Replicated
Quasi-experimental design
Comparison group
Matching
One Shot Case Study
Before-after study
Static group comparison design
Cross sectional design
Case Study (Natural Experiment)
Longitudinal Design
Cohort study
Time Series Design
Internal validity
History
Maturation
Testing

Instrumentation
Statistical Regression
Experimental Mortality
Selection Biases
Interactions of Problems
Causal Time Order
External validity
Generalizability
Diffusion or Imitation of Treatment
Compensatory Equalization of Treatments
Compensatory Rivalry by Respondents Receiving Less Desirable Treatments
Resentful Demoralization of Respondents Receiving Less Desirable Treatments
Masking
Contamination of Data
Erosion of the Treatment Effect
Reactive Effects of Testing
Interactive Effect of Selection Bias
Reactive Effect of Experimental Arrangements
Double blind experiment
Multiple Treatment Inference
Solomon Four Group Design

REVIEW QUESTIONS

1. What are the key features of the classical experiment?
2. What are the problems surrounding its use?
3. Review and discuss the threats to internal and external validity.
4. Design a quasi-experiment to evaluate the impact of an educational program for prison inmates.

REFERENCES

1. Baunach, P.J. (1980). Random assignment in criminal justice research: Some ethical and legal issues. *Criminology*, 17:435–444.
2. See Kerlinger, F.N. (1973). *Foundations of behavioral research.* New York: Holt, Rinehart and Winston.

3. Boruch, R.F. (1998). Randomized controlled experiments for evaluation and planning. In Bickman, L., and Rog, D.J. *Handbook of applied social research methods.* Thousand Oaks, CA: Sage, pp. 176–177.

4. See: Vito, G.F. (1998). What works in drug testing and monitoring. *The International Community Corrections Association Journal,* 8:22–34.

5. Farrington, D.R. (1983). Randomized experiments in crime and justice. In Tonry, M., and Morris, N. (Eds.): *Crime and justice: An annual review of research.* Chicago: University of Chicago Press, pp. 257–308; Dennis, M.L. (1990). Assessing the validity of randomized field experiments: An example from drug abuse treatment research. *Evaluation Review,* 14:347–373.

6. Empey, L.T., and Rabow, J. (1971). The Provo experiment: Theory and design. In Radzinowicz, L., and Wolfgang, M.E. (Eds.): *Crime and justice, Volume III. - The criminal in confinement.* New York: Basic Books, pp. 266–271.

7. See also: Wood, M.T. (1979). Random assignment to treatment groups: A strategy for judicial research. *Criminology,* 17:230–241.

8. See Finckenauer, James O.: *Scared straight! and the panacea phenomenon.* Englewood Cliffs, NJ: Prentice-Hall, 1982.

9. Sherman, L.W. and Smith, D.A. with Schmidt, J.D and Rogan, D.P. (1992). Crime, punishment, and stake in conformity: Legal and informal control of domestic violence. *American Sociological Review,* 57:680.

10. Boruch, Randomized controlled experiments, p. 167.

11. Sherman, L.W. and Berk, R.A. (1984). The specific deterrent effects of arrest for domestic violence. *American Sociological Review,* 49:261–272; Berk, R.A., and Sherman, L.W. (1988). Police responses to family violence incidents: An analysis of an experimental design with incomplete randomization. *Journal of the American Statistical Association,* 83:70–76.

12. Sherman and Smith, et al., p. 680.

13. Dunford, F.W., Huizinga, D., and Elliott, D.S. (1990). The Omaha domestic violence experiment. *Criminology,* 28:183–206.

14. Hirschel, J.D., Hutchison, I.W., and Dean, C.W. (1992). The failure of arrest to deter spouse abuse. *Journal of Research in Crime and Delinquency,* 29:7–33.

15. Sherman, L.W., Schmidt, J.D., Rogan, D.P. et al. (1991). From initial deterrence to long-term escalation: Short custody arrest for poverty ghetto domestic violence. *Criminology,* 29:846.

16. Sherman, L.W., Schmidt, J.D., and Rogan, D.P. (1992). *Policing domestic violence: Experiments and dilemmas.* New York: Free Press.

17. Pate, A.M. and Hamilton, E.E. (1992). Formal and informal deterrents to domestic violence: The Date County spouse assault experiment. *American Sociological Review,* 57:691–697.

18. Berk, R.A., Campbell, A., Klap, R. et al. (1992). The deterrent effect of arrest in incidents of domestic violence: A Bayesian analysis of four field experiments. *American Sociological Review,* 57:698–708.

19. Baunach, Random assignment.

20. Boruch, Randomized controlled experiments, p. 178; Petersilia, J. (1989). Implementing randomized experiments: Lessons from BJA's intensive supervision project. *Evaluation Review,* 13:435–458.

21. Vito, Does it work?
22. Adams, *Corrections.*
23. Travis III, L.F. (1983). The case study in criminal justice research: Applications to policy analysis. *Criminal Justice Review,* 8:46–51.
24. Vito and Wilson, Back from the dead.
25. Wolfgang, M.E., Figlio, R.M., and Sellin, T. (1972). *Delinquency in a birth cohort.* Chicago: The University of Chicago Press.
26. Cook, T.D., and Campbell, D.T. (1979). *Quasi-experimentation: Design and analysis issues for field settings.* Boston: Houghton Mifflin.
27. Vito, G.F., Longmire, D.R., and Kenney, J.P. (1984). Burglary suppression: A program analysis. *Journal of Contemporary Criminal Justice,* 2: 11–14.
28. Vito, G.F., and Wilson, D.G. (1988). Back From the dead: Tracking the progress of Kentucky's Furman-commuted death row population. *Justice Quarterly,* 5:101–112.
29. Morris, N. (1974). *The future of imprisonment.* Chicago: The University of Chicago Press.
30. Maltz, M.D. (1984). *Recidivism.* Orlando, FL: Academic Press.
31. Adams, S. (1975). *Evaluative research in corrections.* Washington, D.C.: U.S. Department of justice.
32. Vito, G F. (1982). Does it work? Problems in the evaluation of a correctional treatment program. *Journal of Offender Counseling, Services and Rehabilitation,* 7: 5–22.
33. Kelling, G.L., Pate, T., Dieckman, D., and Brown, C.E. (1974). *The Kansas City preventive patrol experiment: A summary report.* Washington, D.C.: Police Foundation.
34. Cook and Campbell, *Quasi-Experimentation.*
35. Roethlisberger, F.J. and Dixon, W.J. (1939). *Management and the worker.* Cambridge, MA: Harvard University Press.
36. Allen, H.E., Dinitz, S., Foster, T.W., Goldman, H., and Lindner, L.A. (1976). Sociopathy: An experiment in internal environmental control. *American Behavioral Scientist,* 20:215–226.
37. Dukes, R.L., Ullman, J.B., and Stein, J.A. (1995). An evaluation of D.A.R.E. (Drug Abuse Resistance Education), using a Solomon Four-Group design with latent variables. *Evaluation Review,* 19:409–435.

Chapter Six

PRINCIPLES OF SAMPLING

CHAPTER OVERVIEW

In this chapter, the fundamentals of sampling are discussed. Whether or not you realize it, people are involved in sampling everyday. Probably the most common example is when you "sample" some part of a song from iTunes, you are hearing one piece of the whole song. You assume that the rest of the song is similar to the sample that you heard. Similarly, when you ask someone their opinion, or when you make a statement about some group based on your knowledge of a member of that group, you are in fact using the principles of sampling. The selection of a sample is one of the most important functions in the research process. Whether a researcher is surveying an entire population, or selecting individuals to observe or interview, the way in which a sample is chosen helps determine the usefulness of the study. In this chapter, the principles of sampling are examined; sampling is defined, and some of the more common types of samples found in criminal justice research are described.

OVERVIEW OF SAMPLING

Sampling involves the selection of a proportion of the population, or a sample, in an attempt to draw a conclusion about the population on the basis of the analysis of the sample that is selected. Sampling in social science has its origins in political polling. Every election the American media inundates the airwaves with polls and predictions about political candidates. Polling has become so sophisticated that major news networks have predicted the winners before some states have ended their voting. But, how accurate are such polls? Pollsters have the opportunity to check the accuracy of their polls through Election Day results. And, although polls have become increasingly accurate, errors are still possible. Consider the 2000 presidential election where the media announced that the electoral votes of Florida were won by Al Gore, only to find out there was an error![1] In this case, the media were not aware of the differences in time zones across the population; that is, the Florida Panhandle region (which is largely politically conservative) is in the Central time zone and the polls there would close one hour later than the polls in Central and South Florida (which is largely politically liberal). Thus, the prediction prior to the polls closing in the Florida Panhandle created the error.

Perhaps the best known example, however, of a **sampling error**, was the *Literary Digest's* prediction that Alfred Landon would beat Franklin D. Roosevelt in the 1936 presidential election.[2] The error came even after polling an incredible two million people! The *Digest* had accurately predicted the previous four presidential elections, so what went wrong? The **sampling frame** used by the *Digest* included individuals from the telephone directories and automobile registrations from that time.[3] A sampling frame is the actual list of sampling units from which a sample is selected or drawn. Under normal circumstances, one might argue that there is nothing wrong with this choice of sampling frame; however, consider the time period. The country was in the midst of the Great Depression in 1936, and only the more affluent in the population had phones and cars. As a result, the *Digest's* sample contained a disproportionate number of Republicans and well-to-do individuals, and excluded the poor, who predominately voted for FDR.[4]

The above example represents a common pitfall of sampling, a **non-representative sample**. A sample is non-representative if the population from which it is drawn does not closely approximate the characteristics of the entire population. In other words, if iTunes presents you with one part of the song which has a different rhythm or and tempo than the remainder of the song then you might make an error in deciding that the entire song is worth (or not worth) downloading. Think about the *Literary Digest's* sampling frame in today's world; could this sampling frame be used to successfully (validly) predict the 2008 or 2012 president? While you think about this question, consider whether the sampling frame of telephone directories and automobile registrations is inclusive and representative of the US voting population today.

While political polling is probably the most common form of sampling, the criminal justice researcher has made considerable use of this technique. Public attitudes about crime, punishment, the death penalty, and numerous other criminal justice topics abound. The *Sourcebook of Criminal Justice Statistics*[5] lists over 150 different topics that address public attitudes toward crime. These range from questions concerning the media's coverage of crime stories, to ratings of police honesty and ethics. Sampling is not only commonplace, but necessary to study virtually all areas of social science, including crime and criminal behavior. The **sample elements** are not always about people. Sample elements may include families, gangs, and organizations. Elements may also include all examples of **units of analysis** (as presented in Chapter One); for example, news stories, arrest reports, halfway houses, and probation departments are also example of sample elements.

As it relates to **when to sample**, the researcher should consider whether the data may be obtained more accurately, faster, and cheaper. She should also consider whether a sample "will do," that is, whether or not the entire population is needed to address the research questions. Consider for a moment that in 2005 there were over 7 million individuals under correctional supervision in America, with 1.4 million incarcerated in prisons.[6] If an individual wanted to measure all prisoners' prior criminal record or their attitudes toward punishment, how would he do it and what would he need to consider? In this example, it would not only be tremendously expensive to collect data on all prisoners, but it would take a considerable amount of time, and could actually be less accurate than if the researcher drew a sample. Additionally, a data collection effort of such magnitude would require extensive record-keeping and a large number of staff. Furthermore, the chances of errors and inconsistency would increase because of the numbers and time involved. Due to the constraints of time and money, it is generally impossible and certainly not necessary, to collect data from an entire population; this is when a sample may be constructed.

No matter how a sample is selected, there are two possible sources of error: (1) **probability error** or chance error; and (2) **systematic**

bias which occurs from selecting the sample from only one portion of the population. Probability or chance error occurs when a non-representative sample is selected *despite* the researcher following all of the prescribed steps and precautions in selecting a sample. In Chapter Nine, we discuss field research methodology. The nature of field observation often does not lend itself to collecting or observing a sample that is representative of the population in study; when this happens systematic bias may occur. Suppose that you wanted to study probationer recidivism rates and developed your sampling list from two counties in Kentucky; your sample might accurately reflect probationers in those counties, but it would not necessarily represent all probationers in Kentucky, let alone the entire country.

One example of systematic bias is the new form of telephone or text polling in which television viewers call or text their votes about a show they are watching. As one television executive noted, "It looks like a poll, it sounds like a poll, but it isn't a poll."[7] Indeed, even though the results are often presented as scientific, they are not. The results of such tallies only represent the people who self-selected to cast a vote and are neither randomly selected nor selected through some methodological process. The danger with sampling bias is evident when the results are presented as representative of a population. When this occurs, the public is misled, and officials that make policy decisions are misinformed, potentially resulting in ungrounded decisions. In the criminal justice arena, particularly heinous crimes are often used as a means of representing more general crime rates or crime trends. Again, the problem with this is that "personal" and violent crimes make up a relatively small percentage of the complete crime picture.[8]

The size of the sample to be drawn depends largely on the type of research being conducted and the nature of the population being studied. In quantitative studies, the larger the **sample size** the better. This is because certain types of statistical analysis require a minimum number of cases (e.g., at least 30 cases for correlations) and subgroup analysis requires more cases. For example, suppose you have a sample size of 100 criminal justice seniors and you want to study whether they are more or less likely to go on to graduate school after graduation. The sample size is perfect for a prediction based on the entire sample; however, what if you want to predict by sex, or by sex and race, or by sex, race, and grade point average? The more subgroups you add for statistical analysis, the fewer cases (individuals) in each group. Thus, it is important for a researcher to know what types of **subgroup** analysis he might use *prior* to drawing the sample.

Sample size is also dependent on the nature of the **population**. If the population is easy to reach and is a reasonable size, then the researcher may consider using the entire population for the study. If not, then the researcher must consider whether the individuals are the same (i.e., **homogeneous**) or different (i.e., **heterogeneous**) across the major variables she is studying. Furthermore, if the population under study is hard to reach or at risk, then it is important that the researcher increase the sample size to avoid any potential non contacts or individuals who choose not to participate. Finally, sample size is also dependent on the length of time of the study. In longitudinal studies that extend for a number of years, sample size should be increased to control for **attrition**.

TYPES OF SAMPLES

There are two types of sampling methods, **probability sampling** and **non-probability sampling**. In probability sampling, there is some form of **randomization** used when selecting the sample. This means that each element in the population has an equally likely chance at being selected. Because some element of randomization is utilized, the researcher is able to avoid systematic bias in sample selection. Additionally, probability sampling allows for precise statistical descriptions of large populations as well as estimates of sampling error. Limitations in probability sampling method relate, mainly, to its limited use in social sciences, more specifically in criminal justice. For example, consider whether a judge would allow random selection of individuals convicted of the same crime, to a sentence of prison or to mediation; oftentimes, mandatory sentencing will not allow for such judicial discretion, never mind the fact that randomly assigning individuals to such disparate sentences might be questioned.

Non-probability sampling method does not include any use of randomization in the selection of the sample. Thus, potential limitations include selection bias, lack of generalizability, and lack of statistical error estimates. Additionally, non-probability sampling cannot guarantee that the sample observed or selected is representative of the research population. However, with all the potential limitations, non-probability sampling is often used in social science research because the samples are often quicker and easier to draw, the researcher does not have to have complete knowledge of the population being studied, and, again, sometimes randomization is not possible in sample selection.

Probability Samples

Simple Random Samples are often generated using a table of random numbers or through computer generation. With simple random sampling, each population member is assigned a unique number and is selected randomly to get the desired sample size. Theoretically, this gives each member of the population an equally likely chance of being selected. Simple random sampling is the basis of experimental research as discussed in Chapter Five, where the experimental and control groups are assigned randomly. Probably the most common examples of simple random sampling are state lotteries or Bingo games in which numbered balls are selected at random, and each have an equal chance of being selected.

One problem with the simple random sample is that it is not always possible to develop a complete list of the population. Indeed, the larger the population, the more difficult this task becomes. If for example, one wanted to draw a random sample of probationers from the entire population of probationers in the United States it would be very difficult, if not virtually impossible, to generate a complete list of the entire population. One advantage of the simple random sample is the attempt at controlling for systematic bias, specifically, selection bias. Consider, for example, that a market researcher thinks he will approach individuals entering a store without bias. That is, the researcher believes he will approach each individually no matter what they look like or act like; the reality is that there may be some individuals who he does not approach for some reason (e.g., the individual is talking on the phone; the individual is accompanied by a screaming child, etc.). These characteristics influence the researcher's decision on whether or not to approach an individual; thus, the likelihood that each individual entering will be approached is not equal.

One technique that has been widely used by researchers is random digit dialing, where telephone numbers are randomly dialed as a means of randomly selecting participants for a study. In the first edition of this text, we stated, "Due to the fact that over 95 percent of the population in the United States have a telephone, this technique is highly reliable and is considered a form of simple random sampling."[9] Although random digit dialing is still used today, researchers must consider how representativ this technique is with the explosion of cell phone use, as well as the number of individuals who no longer have land lines, but only use cell phones. Furthermore, the federal Telephone Consumer Protection Act does not allow for computerized or random digit dialing calls to cell phones.[10]

Systematic Samples are a second type of probability sample. In systematic sampling, the researcher again obtains a list of all elements in the population. The list should be in no special order (e.g., alphabetical or numeric order) so that selection bias is avoided. The starting point in the list where the sample elements are selected is generated or selected at random. From this point, the researcher selects every "nth" or "kth" element from the list until the desired sample size is drawn. Systematic samples are useful when the researcher has access to a list of all members of a population.

A third type of probability sample is the **stratified sample**. With stratified sampling, the population is divided into strata or groups based on some criteria (e.g., class rank, sex, race, crime type), and a random sample is selected within each group proportionate to the size of that segment in the population. The most common characteristics used for stratification are variables related to the nature of the study. One benefit of stratified samples is that they do not require a complete list of all the members of the population, but rather some knowledge of the proportions of the population according to some characteristic.

By first dividing the sample based on some variable, there is greater likelihood of representativeness of the population and sampling error may be reduced. Remember, all samples have a source of random error. By producing more homogeneous subsets of the population you reduce the error in the variables selected for stratification to near zero. In other words, with a simple random sample you have the chance of selecting a disproportionate number of males, or whites, or violent offenders and so forth. With stratified sampling you would eliminate this error for those variables selected for stratification.

Cluster samples are also a type of probability sample. The use of cluster sampling involves dividing the population into clusters such as census tracts, sections, blocks, or neighborhoods and then selecting a random sample within each cluster. Cluster sampling is useful when it is impossible to develop a complete listing of the population under study. However, as is often the case, the population elements may already be grouped into subpopulations, and a list of those groups may exist. Consider, for example, if you wanted to conduct a study about fear of crime in your city with the population being "all individuals living in the city between October 1, 2007 and September 30, 2008." The proposed study fits the description above in that it is probably impossible to develop a complete listing of the population, especially since a simple resident list or county driver license list will not completely identify all individuals living in the city. Using this example, a sample may be drawn by first dividing the city into city blocks (clusters) and then selecting the blocks at random. At this point, still, a list of all individuals living in the city may still not be available, but the researcher has the ability to generate such a list by going door-to-door in the selected blocks.

Similarly, in a research project where one wanted to survey all inmates currently incarcerated in state prison systems, it would be difficult to establish a list of the entire inmate population. The researcher could, however, identify all the prisons in the country (i.e., the prisons represent clusters). The researcher could then take a sample of prisons and obtain a list of inmates for the identified prisons. Cluster sampling is particularly useful when interviews are being conducted since it greatly reduces time and costs.

Non-Probability Sampling

There are situations when it is impossible or undesirable or there is no need to use random selection or probability sampling. When this occurs, the researcher must choose between a non-probability sample and scrapping the study altogether. In the field of criminal justice, random samples are oftentimes difficult to obtain due to the state of criminal justice information and data, costs, and human subjects research restrictions. There are also situations where a sampling frame simply cannot be developed. If, for example, you wanted to study juvenile gangs it is impossible to obtain, or even to create a list of juvenile gang members. You would be forced to use a non-probability sample. Of course, this is better than no sample at all! The most common types of non-probability samples include availability/convenience, judgment/purposive, quota, snowball, and self-drop.

The **availability or convenience sample** involves selecting a group of individuals who are "available" for the study. This is particularly relevant when the researcher is faced with the decision to either go with individuals who are available or abandon the study. Have you ever been stopped while shopping at a mall and asked to complete a questionnaire? This is an example of an availability or convenience sample. It is a sample selected based on who is available or convenient to the researcher at a given time. In criminal justice, delinquency studies are often conducted from readily available (incarcerated) delinquents. Many researchers would not scrap a study because of their inability to acquire or construct a random sample, but given the limitations of the sample it is important to remember that the generalization of the results are usually limited to the group under study.

A **judgment or purposive sample** involves taking a group which, based on the researcher's knowledge of the population, seems to be representative of all members of the population. Judgment samples are particularly useful if a researcher is studying a group that is fragmented and difficult to identify. For example, if one is interested in studying motorcycle gang members, he might have to settle for a certain group or gang, who, in the researcher's judgment represented a good crosssection of motorcycle gang members. Judgment samples are fairly common in field research, where the researcher chooses subjects because the subjects seem to represent the population under study. For example, if a researcher was studying the Ku Klux Klan it is highly doubtful that she could establish a sampling frame; instead, she might focus her efforts on one state chapter and attempt to study that group. Again, judgment or purposive samples are selected based on the researcher's own judgment about the purpose of the study.

Selecting a sample so that it is representative of the larger population based on some criteria is an example of **quota sampling**. It is a form of non-probability stratified sampling in which cases are selected according to a characteristic proportionate to the population under study. If, for example, the target population for a study was a sample of prisoners in a particular state, the researcher would need to determine the proportions that were male and female (by sex) or across other **independent variables** or descriptors. As with the other non-probability samples described above, there is no random selection involved in quota sampling. Once the researcher establishes the quotas for each category, she would then select adequate numbers to fill the quotas.

Snowmen usually start with a snowball that is rolled until it becomes large enough to form the body of a snowman. **Snowball sampling** derives its name from the process. Let's say that you are interested in studying professional thieves, and you find a suitable candidate. After you have interviewed this person you would ask for the name or an introduction to another professional thief, and so on until you had a suitable sample. Snowball samples are best used when a researcher is trying to study a hard to reach population.[11] For example, in his study on prostitution, Bryan obtained a sample of call girls by using a snowball sampling technique.[12] Most of the call girls studied were provided through other prostitutes.[13]

Lockwood also used this technique in selecting a sample of inmates that had been the target of sexual aggression in prison.[14] Prison staff charged with handling inmate crises referred 34 targets of aggressors for the study.[15] Both of these examples represent hard to reach groups that are not readily available or accessible for study. By using a snowball sample, Bryan and Lockwood were able to gather valuable information about two relatively under-researched areas of deviant behavior.

Self drop samples are created by individuals choosing to participate or be part of a sample. That is, the sample is constructed without researcher influence or participation. Self drop samples are used in situations or environments where participation must be voluntary and/or includes special populations. Oftentimes, researchers conducting studies in prisons, especially when attempting to evaluate the effectiveness of a program, will utilize self drop samples.

Probably the most recognized type of self drop sample, however, involves you and other citizens. Have you ever completed a "How are we doing?" customer satisfaction card at a restaurant? What about dialed that number on the back of an 18-wheeler and let the person on the other end know "how the driver's driving is"? Each is an example of gaining feedback from individuals who take the initiative and *choose* to participate; this is a self drop sample. Because participants volunteer or show initiative to participate in the study through self drop, there exist some inherent dangers in the type of sample one achieves as well as the findings and conclusions that are drawn.

In all types of samples, it is important to remember that the usefulness of a sample is directly related to its ability to provide information about and a description of the population from which it was drawn.

Probability samples are designed to eliminate or reduce selection bias; however, there are situations in which non-probability samples are justified or even necessary. Thus, it is important for researchers to use their research questions, as well as questions of cost, needs, and outcomes, to determine whether it is necessary to collect information from an entire population or if a probability or non-probability sample will be beneficial.

SAMPLING IN CRIMINAL JUSTICE: SOME EXAMPLES

This section provides several examples of samples used in actual criminal justice research. Each of these studies involved the identification of a sample or respondents in order to address different research questions. The types of sample used, as well as the selection of the cases, are highlighted.

Police Manager Perspectives

In their studies on police manager perspectives of Compstat (Computerized Statistics)[16] and of *Reinventing Government*[17] ideas reflected in community policing[18, 19] Vito et al., used a non-probability sample that was part judgment/purposive and part availability/convenience. They describe their sampling technique as follows:[20]

> Although not a probability sample, this group of police administrators does represent 35 agencies from as far north as Alaska and as far south as Florida. Twenty-one students came from local police agencies with a mean size of 316 officers (range = 12–1,022) and serving an average population of 137,976 residents (range = 22,000–364,040). Nine students were working for county law enforcement agencies with an average size of 639 officers (range = 124–1,700), serving an average population of 561,670 citizens (range = 104,605–1 million). Five students were from state law enforcement agencies, with an average size of 1,946 officers. In terms of police organizational rank, there were 16 sergeants, 13 lieutenants, 3 captains, and 2 corporals among the respondents. The use of this convenience sample can be questioned. These officers were volunteers – motivated administrators who were attending the [Southern Police Institute] SPI to further their careers in police management. Therefore, they may not be perfectly representative of the corps of police middle managers across the United States. However, it would be impossible to conduct a survey of police administrators who have read these texts in any other fashion. A sampling frame of such police administrators simply would not be available.

Although this was not a probability sample, it did permit the researchers to gauge the views of police middle managers from a selection of police agencies. Although it lacks generalizability, it provides a basis for future research, and a rough indicator of police managers' perception of government reform initiatives that may have utility in law enforcement.

Criminal Victimization in the United States

Beginning in 1972, the Law Enforcement Assistance Administration and the Bureau of the Census began a national victimization study based on a stratified multistage cluster sample[21] survey, part of the National Crime Survey, which involved a very expensive and complicated sampling procedure that used as its basis for the sampling frame housing units of virtually all types. The sampling units for the first stage of the sample were counties, groups of counties or large metropolitan areas.[22] These units were divided into strata by grouping the primary sampling units with similar demographic characteristics as determined by the census.

From each stratum, one area was selected for the sample. The remaining stages of sampling were designed to ensure a self-weighting probability sample of housing units within each of the selected areas.[23] This was followed by the selection of clusters of approximately four housing units each from within each enumeration district. A total of approximately 69,000 housing units were designated for the sample.[24] For the field interviews, the sample was divided into six groups, each of which contained housing units whose occupants were to be interviewed every six months over a three year period. A total of 57,000 of the 69,000 households were subsequently surveyed. All told, 96 percent of the eligible households, or some 123,000 persons, participated in the survey.[25]

Even as elaborate as this sample was, it excluded Armed Forces personnel living in military barracks and institutionalized persons, such as prisoners. Naturally, it also excluded all homeless individuals since by definition they do not have a housing unit.

Wardens' Perceptions of Inmate Fear of Sexual Assault

In their study to examine wardens' perceptions of inmate fear of sexual assault and what factors significantly affect warden's perceptions within their institutions, Tewksbury and Hensley used a random sample of wardens in state correctional institutions:[26]

> Anonymous surveys were distributed to a random sample of 378 wardens of male prisons in the United States in 2001. In addition, because of the low number of female prisons, all wardens of these facilities were surveyed (63 wardens).Wardens supervising federal correctional facilities, privatized correctional facilities, prerelease centers, juvenile detention facilities, and jails were excluded from the study. . . . Each warden received a questionnaire along with a cover letter and stamped, self-addressed envelope. The cover letter described the research project and provided important instructions and information to the respondent.

The use of an anonymous survey, in addition to not requiring the respondent to sign an informed consent form and including a reminder mailing allowed for a greater potential in response rate, thus increasing the sample size. In fact, the authors were successful in yielding a 51.2% response rate.[27]

Guns and Crime

In their study of felons and their firearms, Wright and Rossi illustrate the compromises that are often involved in sampling an incarcerated population.[28] The purpose of their research was to survey incarcerated felons in state prisons about how and why they purchased, carried, and used guns. A cluster sample was chosen since prisoners are located in clusters (prisons). First they chose states, then prisons within states, and finally, prisoners within prisons.[29] They originally wanted to select states based on the density of private gun ownership, and the stringency of state firearms regulation. They also wanted a reasonable geographical spread.

One problem was the willingness of states to participate, and as a result they only approached states where they had reason to believe the state would cooperate. Once the states were identified they hoped to survey inmates at maximum-security institutions, but in most cases they were not permitted to do so. In fact, in nearly every instance, the decision as to which prison they would be allowed to study was made by the correctional officials. In the prisons themselves, new restrictions were imposed on which men they could interview. Inmates in protective custody, in disciplinary confinement, in psychiatric wards, or on death row were excluded. The researchers also decided against including certain offenders in the sampling frame. These included misdemeanants, women, and offenders that had been incarcerated prior to a certain date. Once the sampling frame was completed, they either surveyed all inmates in the institution (if the eligible population was less than 400), or they drew a simple random sample from the prison census list.

The Wright and Rossi study is a good example of where a combination of sampling techniques was used, and where constraints imposed by the environment led to compromise and modification. Despite the departure from their original sampling plan, their research represents a major study of weapon behavior on the part of convicted felons.

CONCLUSION

This chapter reviewed the basics of sampling and how it can be applied to criminal justice research. Sampling can take on many forms, ranging from simple random sampling where every member of the population is given an equal chance of being selected, to availability samples where the researcher selects whoever is accessible at one moment.

Despite the constraints and problems of sampling within the criminal justice field, many important and groundbreaking research projects have been conducted using less than ideal sampling procedures. Thus, it is important to understand that the research findings should only be generalized to the sampling frame from which the sample was selected.

KEY TERMS

Sampling
Sampling Error
Sampling Frame
Non-representative Sample
Sample Elements
Units of Analysis
When to Sample
Probability Error

Systematic Bias
Sample Size
Subgroup Analysis
Population
Homogeneous
Heterogeneous
Attrition
Probability Sampling
Non-probability Sampling
Randomization
Simple Random Sample
Systematic Sample
Stratified Sample
Cluster Sample
Availability or Convenience Sample
Judgment or Purposive Sample
Quota Sample
Independent Variables
Snowball Sample
Self Drop Sample

REVIEW QUESTIONS

1. What is sampling? Why is it important?
2. Define and provide examples of: (1) sampling frame; (2) sampling error; (3) variable for stratification; (4) representativeness; and (5) population.
3. What is/are the difference(s) between probability and non-probability samples?
4. Discuss the pros and cons of: (1) simple random sampling; (2) cluster sampling; (3) quota sampling; and (4) self drop sampling.
5. Describe a judgment or purposive sample. Discuss how you, a researcher, would select such a sample.
6. List at least four (4) situations in which a non-probability sample would be appropriate.
7. What is/are the key(s) to drawing a sample?
8. Discuss whether it is possible to control for selection bias in a non-probability sample?

9. The following describes what type of sample: "The researcher divides the state of Florida into area codes (i.e., 850, 904, 407, 321, etc.) and then randomly selects from each of the codes until she gets the desired sample size."

10. The following describes what type of sample: "The researcher is interested in learning students' opinion of the food service on campus. He sits outside the university's main cafeteria at lunch time and asks each individual entering to participate in a short questionnaire."

REFERENCES

1. Cable News Network, How we got here: A timeline of the Florida recount, (12/13/2000), http://archives.cnn.com/2000/ALLPOLITICS/stories/12/13/got.here/index.html.
2. Babbie, E. (1973). *Survey research methods*, Belmont, CA: Wadsworth.
3. Ibid.
4. Ibid.
5. Pastore, A.L. and Kathleen M. eds., *Sourcebook of criminal justice statistics, 31st Edition 2003* [Online], http://www.albany.edu/sourcebook/.
6. Bureau of Justice Statistics. (2005). *National Prisoner Statistics* (Washington, D.C.: U.S. Department of Justice).
7. Belkin, L. (7/8/1987). TV phone polls provoke controversy, *Cincinnati Enquirer*, p. E–8.
8. Federal Bureau of Investigation, *Crime in the United States*, 2006 (Washington, D.C.: U.S. Department of Justice 09/2007), http://www.fbi.gov/ucr/cius2006/.
9. Tuchfarber, A.J., Klecka, W.R., Bardes, B.A., and Oldendick, R.W. (1976). Reducing the cost of victim surveys, in Skogan, W.G. ed., *Sample surveys of the victims of crime*, Cambridge: Ballinger, 207–221.
10. Cell Phones and Political Surveys: Part I, (7/3/2007), http://www.pollster.com/blogs/cell_phones_and_political_surv.php.
11. Goodman, L.A. (1969). Snowball sampling, *Annals of Mathematical Statistics*, 32:148–170.
12. Bryan, J.H. (1965). Apprenticeships in prostitution, *Social Problems*, 12:287–297.
13. Ibid.
14. Lockwood, D. (1980). *Prison sexual violence*. New York: Elsevier.
15. Ibid.
16. Vito, G.F., Walsh, W.F., and Kunselman, J.C. (2005). COMPSTAT: The Managerial Perspective, *International Journal of Police Science and Management*, 7:187–196.
17. Osborne, D., and Gaebler, T. (1982). *Reinventing government: How the entrepreneurial spirit is transforming the public sector from schoolhouse to state house, city hall to*

Pentagon. Reading, MA: Addison-Wesley.

18. Vito, G.F., and Kunselman, J.C. (2000). Reinventing government: The views of police middle managers, *Police Quarterly*, 3:315–330.

19. Vito, G.F., Walsh, W.F., and Kunselman, J.C. (2005). Community policing: The middle manager's perspective, *Police Quarterly*, 8:490–511.

20. Vito and Kunselman, Reinventing government: The views of police middle managers.

21. Bureau of Justice Statistics. (1982). *Criminal victimization in the United States, 1980*, Washington, D.C.: U.S. Department of Justice.

22. Ibid.

23. Ibid.

24. Ibid.

25. Ibid.

26. Hensley, C. and Tewksbury, R. (2005). Wardens' perceptions of inmate fear of sexual assault: A research note, *The Prison Journal*, 85:198–203.

27. Ibid.

28. Wright, J.D., and Rossi, P.H. (1975). *Armed and considered dangerous: A survey of felons and their firearms.* New York: Aldine De Gruyter.

29. Ibid.

Chapter Seven

SURVEY RESEARCH

CHAPTER OVERVIEW

Survey research is generally conducted in an attempt to describe a population. A survey can take on many forms, ranging from a mailed questionnaire, to an online feedback form to a personal interview (see Chapter Ten). In today's world of marketing research and public opinion polls, virtually every individual has completed a survey of some type. Indeed, the expansion of consumer and marketing research as well as the ease and the convenience of the Internet and email has made surveys a very popular and widely used way of gathering information. This chapter examines several forms of survey research, and the ways in which surveys are applied in the field of criminal justice. The chapter also highlights principles of good question writing and the steps of survey research.

INTRODUCTION TO SURVEY RESEARCH

Surveys are used to measure attitudes, beliefs, behaviors, knowledge, and just about any other phenomena an individual might be interested in studying. **Survey research** is the best method to use to collect original data for the purpose of describing a population that may be too large to observe directly. Usually survey research is used to describe a population rather than determining why something exists. One might argue, however, that one of the benefits of survey research is that it has the flexibility to be used with any type of study

135

– **descriptive**, as well as **exploratory**, **explanatory**, and **applied** (see Chapter One). This is one of the many benefits of survey research.

A second benefit of survey research is that it can, and often does involve large samples. This is a major advantage of surveys and is often made possible today through email and the Internet. A third benefit of surveys is their flexibility which allows for them to be used in either a **cross-sectional** or **longitudinal** design; recall, this means that a survey could focus on citizen attitudes at one point in time or could measure their attitudes over some period of time. One example of a longitudinal survey is the **National Crime Victimization Survey (NCVS)**.[1] The NCVS includes a representative sample of over 77,000 households each year and:

> is the primary source of information . . . on the frequency, characteristics and consequences of criminal victimization in the United States. The survey enables [the Bureau of Justice Statistics] BJS to estimate the likelihood of victimization by rape, sexual assault, robbery, assault, theft, household burglary, and motor vehicle theft for the population as a whole as well as for segments of the population such as women, the elderly, members of various racial groups, city dwellers, or other groups. The NCVS provides the largest national forum for victims to describe the impact of crime and characteristics of violent offenders.[2]

Note above the different segments of the population included in the NCVS. Again, this is one of the benefits of surveys. Other examples of longitudinal surveys include public opinion polls about crime or other subjects that are taken on a regular basis. Additional benefits highlighted later in the chapter include the options for administering surveys, unlimited options to address research questions (e.g., again, look at the breadth in the NCVS coverage of types of victimization), and the low costs associated with some forms of survey administration.

Surveys are not without their drawbacks, however. Some of the more prevalent weaknesses of survey research include the following:[3]

1. Standardization can be a problem. This is especially true when superficial questions are used in an attempt to deal with complex issues.

2. Survey research cannot deal with the context of social life. There will be no feel for the thinking or logic involved, or the social context.

3. Direct observations can modify as field conditions warrant, but survey designs stay unchanged.
4. Artificiality tends to be a problem, and the respondent may not have thought about a question until they were asked.
5. Surveys cannot measure social action, they only collect self-reports or recollections of the past.

Additionally, surveys sometimes tend to be weak on validity and strong on reliability. An awareness of these problems can help to partially offset them. Additionally, researchers often use surveys to complement another method of collecting data in an attempt to compensate for these shortcomings and/or build in an opportunity for **triangulation**.

PRINCIPLE TYPES OF SURVEYS

There are a number of ways in which surveys are administered: (1) Self-Administered; (2) Mail and Email; (3) Face-to-Face Interviews (see Chapter Ten); and (4) Telephone Interviews (see Chapter Ten). This chapter highlights self-administered questionnaires, mail, and email questionnaires.

Self-Administered Questionnaires

The self-administered questionnaire generally takes two forms, those that are handed-out to a group of respondents, and those that are mailed or emailed. A survey that is administered to a group of respondents gathered in one place is common when a researcher has a captive audience, such as a prison population. In the Vito and Kaitsa[4] study of an institutional drug and alcohol program, questionnaires were administered to inmates who volunteered with the inducement of a pack of cigarettes. Similarly, Wright and Rossi's[5] study of firearms involved interviewing inmates within the institution. The researchers agreed to pay overtime to the correctional officers that supervised the inmates, and contribute $100 to the prison library.[6] Self-administered studies are often used in market research. How many times have you been asked to complete a questionnaire in a supermarket or in the parking lot of a shopping center?

Mail and Email Surveys

Mail and email surveys are the most typical self-administered form of data collection. Generally, postal service mail involves a questionnaire along with a letter or explanation and a return envelope mailed to the respondent. Historically, the mail questionnaire's popularity probably stemmed from it being able to be administered quickly and for relatively low cost. It also afforded researchers a wide range of coverage for cost; that is, it cost researchers the same to mail a letter across town than it did to mail a letter across the United States! One might argue that, with the advent of the Internet and email, mail surveys are no longer cost-effective or timely. In fact, a study by Salo and his colleagues found the cost was less than $10 for email surveys, while the U.S. Mail equivalent surveys totaled $580.[7]

One benefit that remains, however, with the use of mail surveys is that respondents may be more willing to reveal personal information with a mail questionnaire than they would be in a face-to-face interview. The nature of the mail (and email) surveys may help the respondent feel more at ease in answering sensitive questions since privacy is virtually assured. A second major advantage of the mail and email survey is that they afford a wide geographic range of coverage. A national mail survey will cost about the same as a local one, and it may also be more representative. Consider the cost savings of an email or Internet based survey; the cost will depend on the type of survey software used (if applicable) and the personnel used to tackle the mailings, but will essentially be low cost. Meanwhile, email and Internet surveys include the additional potential to have an international sample.

Mail and email questionnaires are suitable for situations in which a respondent might need to check for or gather information to complete the survey. This provides greater uniformity in the manner in which the questions are posed, and they afford a simple means of continued reporting over time, i.e., longitudinal surveys. Both mail and email surveys also eliminate interviewer bias since there are no interviewers involved.

Despite the wide range of coverage and the low cost (compared to interviews), mail and email questionnaires have some inherent problems. Perhaps the most prevalent problem is the response rate. Generally those that fail to respond to mail or email surveys fall into one of two categories: those that have not yet responded and those that refuse to respond. If a potential participant refuses to cooperate, the researcher should honor that request. Since this is usually a small percentage, **oversampling** may compensate for this problem. The more common non-response falls into the "have not yet responded" group.

A number of strategies have been employed to increase **response rates** for both mail and email surveys including follow-up letters, offering copies of results, appeals to altruism, endorsements from well-known individuals or organizations, remuneration, short instruments, certified mailings, and telephone follow-ups. One question that is often asked is "what is a sufficient response rate?" Unfortunately, there is no correct answer. Response rates will vary greatly from survey to survey depending on a number of actors including the type of sample surveyed, the follow-up method, length and complexity of the instrument, and whether it is mailed or emailed. Generally, a 40 percent response rate is considered very good, 60 percent excellent, and over that, the researcher is doing exceptionally well. For example, Moon and Marsolais[8] conducted a survey of citizens in one Kentucky county concerning their attitudes about the sheriff's office, which resulted in a 55 percent response rate. They used a variation of the Dillman[9] method:[10]

> A pre-notice letter from the [County] Sheriff's Office was mailed to all residents selected for the study. One week later each member of the sample was sent a copy of the questionnaire, a cover letter explaining the purpose of the study, and [a] business reply envelope. In order to avoid bias and encourage more truthful responses, participants sent their completed questionnaire directly to [the authors]. Three weeks after the initial mailing, a second copy of the questionnaire, a new cover letter, and an additional business reply envelope were sent to those individuals who had not yet responded to the initial mailing.

This technique is an effective way to increase the response rate, however, it does increase the costs, since another mailing must be conducted.

The problem with a low response rate is that there is no way of knowing whether or not those that did not respond differ from those that did. Related to this problem is the issue of bias. Mail and email surveys generally miss a certain segment of the population. This includes individuals without mailing addresses, i.e., the homeless, and the lower educated and illiterate. The result may be a homogenous sample. Therefore, the real issue is not the response rate, but the randomness of the sample. In the Salo[11] study above, the total response rate was 25% (across both the postal service mail and email).[12]

> [However,] [t]here was a significantly greater response by U.S. mail 307/820 (37.4%) than email 129/82 (15.7%) (p<.05). . . . Conclusion: While email is cheaper and less work intensive, response rates were twofold greater for the U.S. mailed survey.

Mail questionnaires, as with surveys in general, do have the problems of artificiality, standardization, oversimplification, validity, and the inability to measure social actions. There is also the possibility that the respondent will misinterpret or misunderstand the question.

CONDUCTING SURVEY RESEARCH

It is important to mention that regardless of the nature of the survey or the manner in which it is administered, it is always important to conduct a thorough review of the literature. As with conducting any type of research, this helps the researcher develop a **conceptual framework** for the study, and prevents reinventing the wheel. Remember, there is nothing wrong with replicating a previous study, but in doing so the researcher must be aware of the major findings about a topic before he begins to work. Reviews of the literature also provide valuable information about the strengths or weaknesses of a particular method.

Next, decide on the target population. Who is the study about? Once the population is determined, then the researcher must determine the type of respondent and the type of survey administration that will get the questionnaire to the respondent. If the population is large and geographically dispersed, then the researcher has to consider the costs associated with these characteristics. This also impacts the type of survey administration; consider, for example that face-to-face interviews are probably too time consuming with a large population or large sample. In the case where she will draw a sample, she must determine the type and size of the sample (see Chapter Six). The next step involves developing the questionnaire.

Questionnaire Construction

The way in which a questionnaire is organized may affect the **response rate**, so it is important to follow some basic guidelines when constructing a questionnaire. First, begin with easy questions that are interesting, but nonthreatening. For example, if your first question is Have you ever been sexually assaulted? then it is likely that your survey will be over before it begins. Likewise, if you start with boring demographics, such as age, race, education, and so forth, you will likely turn off many of your respondents.

A second important consideration of questionnaire development is the order of the questions. The appearance of one question can affect the answers given to subsequent ones. For example, if you ask a number of questions about heinous or well-publicized crimes and then followed them with a question asking them to list and rank the most pressing problems facing the country, it is very likely that crime would be cited more and given a higher rating than it would have otherwise. It is important that the researcher think about these things when organizing the **question sequence** for the entire questionnaire.

The **layout** of the questionnaire is also important. This includes paying attention to the question sequence above, but also relates to how the questionnaire looks. Is the title of the questionnaire clearly marked? Are there directions for the respondent if it is self-administered? Does is look clean and not crowded on the page? Is it easy to record answers (if applicable)? A questionnaire's layout is especially important when one considers whether or not an individual will make the time to respond to a questionnaire. Potential respondents are much more likely to complete a questionnaire, too, if the questionnaire does not appear like it will take them a long time to complete.

When developing a questionnaire, the researcher must also decide on the **response categories** for individual questions and if the questionnaire will be administered in interview format, then he must also plan a **system for recording answers**. The ability for the researcher to address both of these issues prior to the start of the study will lessen the amount of time it will take the researcher as he analyzes the data. Oftentimes, the researcher will engage in a pilot study to assist in developing both the questions and response categories.

Pilot Study

Prior to getting started on data collection, researchers may also choose to engage in a **pilot study** of the survey. Generally, a pilot study involves testing the survey on a smaller scale. Benefits to conducting a pilot study in preparation for full scale survey research include: (1) initial findings that may be used to secure funding to support your future study; (2) potential suggestions for revisions on delivery strategies and questionnaire development; and (3) determine the feasibility of a larger study. Pilot testing also allows an opportunity for training additional interviewers, if applicable. Of course, this enhances both validity and reliability when using multiple interviewers.

Following the pilot study, the researcher will select a sample and then begin the data collection phase of the research. In the data collection phase, the researcher first locates and contacts potential participants. Once an individual has agreed to participate, the researcher will make the introductory statements about the research and the questionnaire, ask the questions and record the answers, and thank the respondent for his time. Once the researcher has collected all of the data, he will conduct the analysis.

Guidelines for Questions

Developing good questions is essential if you wish to gather accurate, valid, and reliable information. The same points apply to interview situations and will be discussed in Chapter Ten. Remember, if questions are unclear, confusing, or misleading, the result will be responses that are uncomfortable.

The following guidelines should be used when asking questions:[13]

1. Provide a clear introduction of the purpose of the survey.
2. Order the questions to establish a rapport with the respondent.
3. Write clear items.
4. Avoid double-barreled questions.
5. Respondents must be competent to answer the questions.
6. Questions should be relevant.
7. Short items are best.
8. Avoid negative items.
9. Avoid biased questions.
10. Cross-check questions.
11. Pre-test the instrument.
12. The questionnaire should look good.
13. Language should be pitted to the level of the respondent.
14. Use words with the same meaning to everyone, avoiding jargon.
15. Establish a frame of reference.

16. If examining unpleasant feelings, provide an opportunity for a positive response.
17. Phrase questions so that they are not objectionable.
18. Go from general to specific.

Structured questions, also called **closed-ended questions**, provide a list of possible answers for the respondent. The problem is that the list of possible answers may overlook some relevant answers. By using close-ended questions, the researcher is essentially forcing the respondent to select one of the choices offered. One way to avoid this is to include one additional space for "other." Close-ended questionnaires are easier to complete, but the response categories must be **exhaustive** and **mutually exclusive**. Exhaustive means each item has a response category such that each respondent is able to provide the appropriate or "correct" answer. Again, the inclusion of the "other" space allows for all items to be exhaustive. To be mutually exclusive, response categories must not overlap; that is, a respondent is able to answer in one and only one response category.

There exist many advantages to using closed-ended questions for both the respondent and the researcher. A respondent will find closed-ended questionnaires easier and quicker to answer, identify response choices which can clarify question meanings, and respondents are not disadvantaged if they are less articulate and/or illiterate. Benefits to the researcher mainly come after completion of the survey; that is, the answers are easier to compare, easier to code and statistically analyze, and the study is easier to replicate. The biggest disadvantages associated with closed ended questioning are that it forces simplistic answers to complex issues, forces individuals to make choices that they may not have to necessarily make in the real world, and there is a greater potential for data entry errors.

Unstructured questions or **open-ended questions**, when used correctly, allow a respondent to elaborate on his responses. Essay questions are one type of open-ended questions. The researcher utilizes these types of questions in order to provide an opportunity for the respondent to give more detailed answers. Interviewers often use unstructured questions to allow the respondent to answer at length about an issue or topic. Of course, one problem with open-ended questions is that they may result in irrelevant answers. This is particularly a problem with mail questionnaires since there is no interviewer to clarify a question. When used with a mail survey, open-ended questions should be placed at the end of the instrument to insure that the close-ended questions are answered. If the open-ended questions are placed first, the respondents may not complete the survey because it appears to be too complex.

The advantages to using open-ended questions include the possibility for respondents to include an unlimited number of possible responses, provide detail and both qualify and clarify responses, in addition to providing adequate space for complex issues. Furthermore, it provides the respondents with an opportunity to be creative in their responses. Given these possibilities for respondents, it is likely that the researcher may be provided more feedback than he anticipated. Additionally, it may be possible for the researcher to follow the respondent's logic and thinking process from his written responses. The disadvantages of open-ended questions are related to the amount of space and time it takes to review individual responses, making it difficult to compare answers. This also relates to the fact that the researcher must sift through irrelevant responses in an attempt to find buried detail; it also makes coding responses difficulty.

Oftentimes, in an attempt to glean the advantages of each type of questions, a combination of the two types of questions are used. Even if the questionnaire is predominately closed-ended, a researcher may want to provide the respondent an opportunity to provide additional information at the end of the survey by using an open-ended question.

EVALUATING A QUESTIONNAIRE

This section highlights questions to think about as you begin to look at opportunities for survey research either as a researcher or as a consumer of research. The questions below follow the sections of the text above related to types of surveys, format construction generally, and how to write good questions. The questions also assist you in beginning to think about the connection between survey research and the last chapter on sampling. Use the questions below to evaluate the survey presented in Figure 7.1. As you go through the questions, think about what the answer *should* be and if that is the answer that you actually find in the survey. If the survey does not meet your expectations, does it (also) make you (or, worse, an alleged victim of domestic violence) not want to complete it?

Figure 7.1. Domestic Violence Petitioner's Questionnaire[14]

Thank you for your interest in this research project being conducted by Drs. Julie Kunselman and Diane Scott of the University of West Florida. The purpose of this research is to profile domestic violence cases to examine and analyze court processes related to coordinating social services and supervising case progress from the time you file your injunction through disposition. In all cases, the information you provide in this questionnaire will be kept strictly confidential; this means that no one other than the Domestic Violence Case Coordinator will be able to connect your name with the information you provide. Again, we appreciate your assistance and thank you for answering the following questions so that we may better serve you.

Petitioner Information:

1. Date _____   2. Age: _____   3. Sex: □ Male □ Female

5. Race: □ White   □ Black   □ Hispanic   □ Asian   □ Other_____

6. Employment: □ Full time □ Part time   □ Not employed

7. Do you receive any form of Public Assistance? □ Yes   □ No   8. What is your monthly income?_____

9. What is the last year of education that you completed? _____

10. Are you in the military? □ Yes   □ No   If Yes: □ Officer   □ Enlisted

...

Relationship Information:

18. Specify your relationship to the respondent_____

19. Pertaining to the violence that brought you here to file an injunction: a) Was alcohol involved?
                                                                                b) Were drugs involved?

    If Yes to drugs, what drugs? _____

20. Did the respondent use any object that placed you in imminent fear of danger? □ Yes   □ No

    If Yes, what was this object? _____

21. Do you have any pets? □ Yes   □ No

    If Yes, has the respondent demonstrated any abuse towards the pets? □ Yes □ No
    If Yes, has the respondent demonstrated any threats towards the pets? □ Yes □ No

Children Information:

22. Were there any children at home during the domestic   22. □ Yes   □ No
violence?

23. Were *all* child(ren) that were home during the incident of   23. □ Yes   □ No
your relationship?
    If No, what is the relationship of the children to you? _____

24. Has the respondent ever threatened to remove or hide the   24. □ Yes   □ No
children from you?

Injunction Information:

25. Have you ever had any previous injunctions with this person?	25. □ Yes	□ No
26. Have you ever filed an injunction against any one else?	26. □ Yes	□ No
27. Have you ever called/sought help for domestic violence from the police?	27. □ Yes	□ No
28. Have you sought any help from a domestic violence shelter?	28. □ Yes	□ No
29. Do you wish to be given any additional information about counseling?	29. □ Yes	□ No
30. Have you ever made contact with a victim's advocate ?	30. □ Yes	□ No

Format and Construction

1. Are the most important items at the beginning?
2. Are the questions pertaining to demographics at (near) the end?
3. Does it look interesting?
4. Is it a 'good' length?
5. Judge the questions – Review and critique them on the following:
   a. Mixture of open and close ended?
   b. Clear and easy to understand?
   c. Short or lengthy questions?
   d. Are there negative items?
   e. Are there biased items/terms?
6. Discuss positives/negatives of the format/construction of the questionnaire.

Development

1. Is the questionnaire designed for self-administered, face-to-face, or phone interview (CATI)?
2. What would you change? Why?
3. Discuss the benefits of using the proposed survey.

Sample Selection

1. Who is the target population?
2. Discuss the sampling frame.
3. What type of sampling would be appropriate?
4. Discuss sample selection – how will you obtain your type of sample?

Data Analysis

1. What might be five (5) research questions the survey results could answer?
2. How will coding be accomplished?
3. Discuss the positives and negatives associated with doing data analysis of these survey results.

CONCLUSION

Surveys are a common form of gathering information in the criminal justice setting. Surveys can take many forms, including mail and telephone surveys, self-administered questionnaires, and interviews. Questionnaire development can be complex and difficult, and each type of survey brings with it a particular set of strengths and weaknesses. Surveys provide the ability to measure attitudes, factual information, and perceptions of a wide and virtually endless range of social phenomena, including crime.

KEY TERMS

Survey Research
Descriptive Research
Exploratory Research
Explanatory Research
Applied Research
Cross-Sectional Study
Longitudinal Study
National Crime Victimization Survey (NCVS)
Triangulation
Conceptual Framework
Response Rate
Question Sequence
Layout
Response Categories
System for Recording Answers
Pilot Study
Structured or Closed-Ended
Exhaustive
Mutually Exclusive
Unstructured or Open Ended

REVIEW QUESTIONS

1. There are six major steps in survey research as listed below. Suppose you are being hired to study <u>domestic violence</u> and one component of the research will include a survey. Briefly define each survey step listed below.
   a. Decide on the type of survey (survey options?):
   b. Decide on the type of respondent and the population (options of who to study?):

    c. Develop the questionnaire (type of question options?):
    d. Plan for recording answers (options?):
    e. Pilot test the instrument and train interviewers (how?):
    f. Draw a sample (sampling options?):

2. List four (4) principles for good question writing <u>as discussed in class</u>.
3. List two (2) advantages of closed questions <u>as discussed in class</u>.
4. List two (2) *disadvantages* of closed questions <u>as discussed in class</u>.
5 List two (2) advantages of open-ended questions <u>as discussed in class</u>.
6. List two (2) *disadvantages* of open-ended questions <u>as discussed in class</u>.
7. What does it mean for a variable to be exhaustive?
8. What does it mean for a variable to be mutually exclusive?
9. Discuss a process for increasing the response rate in mail or email survey research.
10. Describe the process for including a pilot study in research.

REFERENCES

1. Bureau of Justice Statistics. (2007). *National crime victimization survey.* (Washington, D.C.: U.S. Department of Justice, Office of Justice Programs), http://www.ojp.usdoj.gov/bjs/cvict.htm.
2. Ibid.
3. Babbie, E. (1986). *The practice of social science research,* Belmont, CA: Wadsworth.
4. Vito, G.F. and Kaitsa, G. (1977). *Marion Correctional Institution, drug/alcohol abuse therapeutic community: Project Papillon.* Columbus, OH: Program for the Study of Crime and Delinquency, Ohio State University.
5. Wright, J.D., and Rossi, P.H. (1975). *Armed and considered dangerous: A survey of felons and their firearms,* New York: Aldine De Gruyter.
6. Ibid.
7. Salo, D.F., Shapiro, T., Paige, S., Lebowitz, J., Lavery, R.F. and Symonette, D. (2000). Comparison of survey response rates sent by the U.S. Postal System versus internet email, *Academic Emergency Medicine,* 7:444.
8. Moon, M. and Marsolais, M. (2007). *Boone County satisfaction and safety survey.* Highland Heights, KY: Northern Kentucky University.
9. Dillman, D.A. (1978). *Mail and telephone surveys: The total design method,* New York: John Wiley and Sons.
10. Moon and Marsolais, *Boone County satisfaction and safety survey.*
11. Salo, et al., Comparison of survey response rates.
12. Ibid.

13. Babbie, *The practice of social science research.*
14. Scott, D.L. and J.C. Kunselman. (2007). Using profile analysis for assessing Need in domestic violence courts, *American Journal of Criminal Justice*, 31:81–91. [Adapted survey]

Chapter Eight

SCALING

CHAPTER OVERVIEW

Researchers often attempt to gauge the degree, strength, or amount of a concept under study. For example, they might want to know how much influence lack of a high school education has on one's likelihood of criminal activity, the strength of the relationship between completing a batterer's intervention program and recidivism of a domestic violence offender, or simply the amount of illicit drugs consumed by college students. In order to accomplish any of these tasks in a quantitative fashion, a researcher may quantify a concept using a numerical scale.

In this chapter, the concept of scaling and some common methods of scale construction are introduced. Scaling is also related to concepts such as levels of measurement (discussed below) and **validity** and **reliability** (Chapter Four). Additionally, in this chapter special attention is given to the use of scales developed by researchers to measure the severity of crime as well as client performance while under probation or parole supervision.

Scales are quantitative measures developed to measure a concept or variable; they are a form of **operationalization** (Chapter One) and usually involve the construction of several constructs or questions that are assigned a numerical value. The score on each item is then added together to form a total score value. This single score then serves as an indication of the degree, strength, or amount of the concept under analysis. In this manner, the scale combines several items (which measure different aspects of the concept) into a total score (which represents the total amount of the concept which is present). The researcher then has the option and the flexibility to examine each item on the scale individually and/or to conduct an analysis using the total score value.

CONCEPTS IN SCALING

There are several important issues to be considered in the construction or use of a measurement scale: (1) Face Validity, (2) Unidimensionality, (3) Construct Validity, and (4) Levels of Measurement. First, **face validity** means the items included in the scale are reasonable representatives, after quick glance, of what is being measured, and that they provide some measure of the concept under consideration. For example, in his study of the use of the death penalty in South Carolina, Paternoster[1] developed a basic scale to measure the heinousness of a homicide. He identified four factors which indicated the degree of seriousness or severity of the murder and assigned a value of one point if any of the following factors were present in the case: if the homicide involved strangers, if there were multiple victims, if there were multiple offenders, and if female victims were in evidence.[2] Here, the researcher would review a case and scan for the presence of these factors; resulting in a score ranging from 0 to 4. Note that the items included in the scale do have face validity, that is, they have a "common sense" ring to them. They provide a measure of the features of a homicide that makes it heinous. With this scale, the researcher can analyze and compare homicides on the scale values on the individual items as well as the total score.

A second key feature of a scale is that its items are **unidimensional**. They should measure differing amounts of the same concept under consideration. Again, the Paternoster scale meets this requirement since each item relates to the heinousness of the murder.[3] Unidimensionality is especially important when the researcher intends to combine each item on the scale to form a total score value. After all, if one item on the scale duplicated the concept measured by another item, the total value would be inaccurate. In other words, the researcher would not have the ability to analyze the total score value if unidimensionality was not present.

A third issue is that of internal validation. **Internal validation** means there is a relationship between the scale items and the total score value, and ensures that the scores on each individual item on the scale ranks the cases in terms of the total score value. If the scale has internal validation, then the total score value per respondent will reflect the scoring patterns on the individual items s/he answers. This means there is a consistent and clear pattern between the individual items and the individual's total score. For example, suppose an offender is asked to mark "yes" or "no" to a list of felony property offenses depending on whether she has previously committed the offense. If each "yes" item is scored at "1," then the higher the total score the "more serious" the offender. However, whether the higher total score *in fact* measures more seriousness also depends on external validation.

External validation tests whether there are other indicators or **variables** not included in the scale, but that may have a relationship between other measures included in the study and the items included in the scale. For example, if a researcher was collecting data on cases involving persons convicted of murder, are the items on the scale and the total score related to the decision of (and sentence imposed by) the court in the case? If the scale has both internal and external validation, then the resulting measures are much more accurate in terms of its ability to measure the concept under study and means the scale has **content validity**.

Finally, measuring a variable involves the identification and operationalization of the indicators or attributes of the variable. For example, the indicators of the variable sex are male and female. This variable is discrete or categorical, that is, it has only two different categorical values, specifically, "male" and "female." Categorical variables have non-numeric attributes which means their attributes are usually labels. However, variables measured with response categories representing grouped data (e.g., Number of prior arrests equal 0, 1–5, 6–10, 11–15, etc.) are also categorical variables. Furthermore, the variables "social security number" and "phone number" are also categorical variables even though the responses are numeric; in both cases, the numeric response is representative of a label and, therefore, has no numerical meaning. Other variables, such as prior number of arrests, are **continuous** variables. This means theoretically that the variable has an infinite number of values, for example, "one" through "one million" arrests! In order to operationalize or measure both categorical and continuous variables, a researcher must be familiar with **levels of measurement**: nominal, ordinal, interval, and ratio. The level of measurement for a variable is a critical factor in answering research questions and minimizing threats to validity and reliability.

Variables measured at the **nominal** level of measurement have categories that are different from one another. We do *not* know how much more or less different than another attribute or response category, only that the categories are different. For example, if Alex is a correctional officer in the Midwest and Harry is a correctional officer in the South, then one difference may be drawn: Alex and Harry are correctional officers in different regions of the country. It is not possible to arrange regions in any order, or calculate any distance. Many demographic variables are measured on a nominal scale including sex, race, and marital status.

Variables measured at the **ordinal** level of measurement have attribute categories that differ from each other (just like nominal level) and it is possible to rank order the categories. However, it is still *not* possible to tell how much more or how much less the categories are from one another. This means the attribute categories may be arranged in order of magnitude. Consider the question,

Do you believe it is possible to rehabilitate criminals?

A. In All Cases
 B. Occasionally
 C. Seldom
 D. Never

It is possible to rank order the categories, but the distances between the responses are not quantitatively measurable. Think about your letter grade in this class; it is a categorical variable because: (1) it has a letter which represents the numerical grade in the class and (2) there are only five options: A, B, C, D, and F. It is an example of an ordinal level of measure because it is possible to rank your "A" grade as being higher than your neighbor's "B" grade, while it is not possible to know *how much higher* your grade is than your classmate's grade. For example, your "A" grade could be a 90 and your classmate's grade could be an 89; or, your grade could be higher and his lower. With ordinal level of measurement it is possible to only order the responses. It is not possible to measure or know the exact distance between the attributes. Other examples of variables measured at the ordinal level of measurement include class standing (i.e., Frosh – Senior), offense levels (i.e., felony, misdemeanor, etc.), and felony classes (e.g., 1–4 or A–D).

The third level of measurement is used with continuous variables and is the **interval** level of measurement. The interval level of measurement allows an individual to document differences among responses, rank ordering of responses, and how may units more or less one response or score is from another. An example of a variable measured at the interval level is time. Consider, for example, if a robbery is reported at 9:00 p.m., and a rape is reported at 11:00 p.m. It is possible to determine that (1) the crimes occurred at different times; (2) the rape was reported later than the robbery; (3) the rape was reported 2 hours later than the robbery. Since time does not have an absolute zero point, meaning "0 o'clock" does not mean the absence of time, it is not possible to make any other judgments about the information presented. It might be easier for you to grasp interval level of measurement and an arbitrary zero (i.e., zero measure does not mean an absence of something) by thinking about another variable that is measured at the interval level, temperature. If your outside thermometer reads 0 degrees one day, then it is not telling you that there is no temperature outside, right? Instead, it is telling you it is pretty cold outside!

The **ratio** level of measurement is the highest level of measurement. Variables measured at the ratio level incorporate all of the characteristics of the nominal, ordinal, and interval levels of measurement in addition to having a known zero point. The known zero point is important because it adds a multiplicative trait to the variable, allowing one to determine that score (response) X is so many times score Y. If, for example, a questionnaire asked Alex and Harry to record the number of years of experience each had as a correctional officer: Alex has twelve years of experience and Harry has six. Since this question measures the variable "years of experience" at the ratio level, it is possible to know the following:

1. Alex and Harry have a different number of years of experience.
2. Alex has more years of experience than Harry.
3. Alex has six more years of experience than Harry.
4. Alex has twice as many years of experience than Harry.

Since zero years of experience are possible, it is evident that the variable is measured at the ratio level of measurement. Thus, in this example it is also possible to state that ratio of years of experience between Alex and Harry is 2 to 1.

Consider the difference in the amount of information that a researcher gains from measuring a variable at the ratio level of measurement (if possible). It is possible to measure the variable "years of experience" at all four levels of measurement, but since the most data are gleaned from the ratio level it is important for the researcher to ask the question at that level. *Always measure a variable at the highest level of measurement possible.* This is because it is always possible to move or condense the data to lower levels of measurement, but it is not possible to extrapolate raw data or numerical responses from lower levels of measurement. Again, consider the variable "years of experience" measured at each level of measurement:

1. Nominal: Do you have prior years of experience? [Yes, No]
2. Ordinal: How many years of prior experience do you have? [0, 1-5 years, 6-10 years, 11-15 years, etc.]
3. Interval/Ratio: How many years of prior experience do you have? [In Years]

Because more specific data are gained from the interval/ratio level question, it is possible to complete higher levels of statistical analyses with the variable. It also provides much more information to the researcher about the variable she is measuring. Furthermore, it is possible for the researcher to use her answer from question 3 to also answer questions 1 and 2; however, it is not possible to generate the response to question 3 with the answers to questions 1 and 2. Thus, it is important for a researcher to always measure a variable at the highest level of measurement possible.

TYPES OF SCALES

Scales are not only used in research but also as a guide to decision making throughout the criminal justice system. Measurement scales are used to help guide parole board decision making,[4,5] caseload management in probation and parole supervision,[6] bail release procedures,[7] and classification of inmates in prison.[8,9] Basically, these prediction scales were based upon an analysis of the performance (e.g., recidivism) of a group of subjects (i.e., parolees). For example, the scales indicate the risk factors associated with the behavior under study. Consider, therefore, that parolees who possess the risk factors associated with recidivism would score the highest on such a scale.

The analysis of this type of scaling procedure is beyond the scope of this chapter. Instead, this chapter focuses on the use of scales to measure attitudes or a particular phenomenon (e.g., the severity of crime). For example, Brodsky and Smitherman[10] have compiled some 380 scales which have been used in studies on crime, law, delinquency, and corrections. Thus, it may not be necessary to construct a brand new scale to measure the concept under analysis.

However, the researcher must be aware of the need to address issues of validity and reliability with existing scales. That is, it is important that the existing scale is valid for the researcher current interests and that the scale measures what it was designed to measure. The scale must also be reliable, meaning that upon repeated use, the scale should produce the same or similar results (see Chapter Four). Researchers and criminal justice officials often make the mistake of assuming that, since a scale was effective under one set of circumstances, it has universal application. For example, Wright, Clear, and Dickson[11] have demonstrated that probation and parole supervision instruments (designed to measure both the risk of recidivism posed by and the specific treatment needs of the client) are not universally applicable and that they must be carefully validated in each locale. They tested the Wisconsin scale with a sample of New York City probationers and determined that many of the variables contained in the instrument did not accurately predict risk in that situation.[12] Therefore, existing scales must be utilized with caution.

Likert Scales

Likert scales are commonly associated with attitudinal questionnaires. The format of a Likert scale (named for Rensis Likert[13]) is probably familiar to you if you have responded to such questions even if you do not recognize the name. Basically, individuals are asked to respond to a series of statements and to indicate whether he or she "strongly agrees, agrees, is not sure, disagrees, or strongly disagrees" with the statement in question. In this manner, a Likert scale generally measures the intensity of feeling which the subject demonstrates. The items on the scale should clearly reflect a definable opinion concerning the attitude under study. The items should be ordered in such a way that the total score indicates a high degree of the attitude in question (e.g., support for capital punishment). An example of a Likert scale is presented in Figure 8.1.

Figure 8.1. Likert Scales: Measurement of Conservative
Attitudes toward Crime and Criminals.[14]

Measurement of Conservative Attitudes toward Crime and Criminals

Directions: Answer the following questions and state the extent to which you either agree or disagree with the following statements. Use the following scale to indicate the extent of your agreement:

1 = Strongly Disagree
2 = Disagree
3 = Uncertain
4 = Agree
5 = Strongly Agree

1. Most criminals know exactly what they are doing when they break the law.

2. The main reason why we have so much crime is because young people are not taught to respect authority.

3. Stiff sentences are necessary to show criminals that crime does not pay and to make sure that they don't commit crimes again.

4. Rehabilitating a criminal is just as important as making him/her pay for the crime.

5. The major goal of the criminal justice system should be to protect society from violent crime, communists, and other politically disruptive people.

6. The rich get richer and the poor get prison[a] is a fair way to characterize how our criminal "justice" system works.

7. If we really cared about crime victims, we would make sure that criminals were caught and given harsh punishments.

[a]Reiman, J.H. (1979, 1984). The Rich Get Richer and the Poor Get Prison: Ideology, Class, and Criminal Justice. Needham Heights, MA: Allyn and Bacon.

The purpose of this scale is to measure the extent of agreement with conservative attitudes and policies toward crime and criminals. This scale is a modification of a scale developed by Garrett and Matthews which was utilized in an analysis of the opinions of legislators on criminal justice policy.[15] The range of scale values is from 7 to 35. The higher the score, the more clearly the respondent is expressing a conservative attitude toward crime. However, notice that items 4 and 7 reflect liberal attitudes toward crime.[16] These items serve as checks upon the responses of individuals. Persons who score high on the conservative scale should register a low score on these two scale items. Therefore, when a Likert scale is utilized, it is necessary to conduct an item analysis to determine which individual items correlate the highest with the total score value. The items which correlate in this manner are then selected to form the modified scale which then serves as the basis for analysis. The item analysis is not only applicable to the response check items (i.e., items 4 and 7) but to every item on the scale. Utilized in this fashion, Likert scaling can provide an accurate method of gauging the intensity of attitudes toward a certain phenomenon.

Thurstone Scale

This type of scale is developed using statements that focus on some concept which is judged by individuals. The individuals are asked their opinion about the concept in question and their responses (usually in the form of some type of ranking) are then utilized to form a scale to measure the phenomenon under consideration. Miller[17] notes that the individuals classify a number of statements ranging from most favorable to neutral to most unfavorable. This ranking system (usually consisting of 1–11 groups) has been set by the researcher in such a manner that the intervals between the groups are approximately equal. This is why the Thurstone scale is commonly known as an equal appearing intervals scale. The scale value of a statement included in the new scale is the median value which it has been assigned by the judges. Statements which have a broad spread of values assigned by the judges are dropped from the scale.

One disadvantage of this type of scale construction is that it takes a considerable amount of time, effort, and expense to generate a Thurstone scale. After all, the researcher must create a pool of statements, group them, construct a sampling list of individuals to judge the statements and then survey them, and then analyze the results in order to construct the scale that will actually be used in the research. In short, the construction of a Thurstone scale is a survey research project in and of itself!

Wolfgang, Figlio, Tracy, and Singer[18] conducted a national survey of crime severity to determine public attitudes about the severity of crime. They surveyed some 60,000 persons over the age of 18 in regard to their opinion about crime. This survey was conducted in conjunction with the National Crime Survey in 1977 (see Chapter Four). The procedure was relatively simple. The respondents were given the following description of a crime: "A person steals a bicycle parked on the street" and were told that the seriousness rating for this crime was 10.[19] They were then provided with the descriptions of other crimes and were asked to rate them in comparison to the bicycle theft. Thus, if the respondent considered a crime description to be twice as serious as bicycle theft, then he would rate it as 20. Every respondent ranked 25 crimes and a total number of 204 crime descriptions were reviewed.[20]

A summary of the responses are listed in Figure 8.2 The severity score rankings were compiled from the ratings of the individual judges (respondents) and were developed through a complex weighting procedure. The top ten crime rankings listed in the table reveal that per-

Figure 8.2. How do People Rank the Severity of Crime: The Top Ten Rankings from the National Survey of Crime Severity.[21]

Severity Score	Offense Description
72.1	A person plants a bomb in a public building. The bomb explodes and 20 people are killed.
52.8	A man forcibly rapes a woman. As a result of physical injuries, she dies.
47.8	A parent beats his young child with his fists. As a result, the child dies.
43.9	A person plants a bomb in a public building. The bomb explodes and one person is killed.
43.2	A person robs a victim at gunpoint. The victim struggles and is shot to death.
39.2	A man stabs his wife. As a result, she dies.
39.1	A factory knowingly gets rid of its waste in a way that pollutes the water supply of a city. As a result, 20 people die.
35.7	A person stabs a victim to death.
35.6	A person intentionally injures a victim. As a result, the victim dies.
33.8	A person runs a narcotic ring.

sons have different opinions concerning the severity of crime. Specifically, a severity score of 33.8 (a person runs a narcotics ring) was rated approximately three times more serious than stealing a bicycle off the street (10).[22] These responses were also utilized to develop a scale to measure the severity of a crime which will be considered later.

Guttman Scale

Another commonly used method of scaling was developed by Guttman.[23] It is also known as scalogram analysis or **cumulative scaling** in that it allows the researcher to determine if the attitude (or behavior) in question fits a certain, ordered response pattern. Typically, the items on the scale are placed in such a manner that the overall response pattern can be predicted on the basis of the total score of the individual.

Figure 8.3 presents an example of a Guttman scale. Here, the researchers are interested in conducting a self-report study of criminal behavior (see Chapter 4) and each respondent is asked and has answered the three questions contained in the scale. The items on the scale are cumulative and so affirmative answers to one question also result in positive answers to other questions on the scale. For example, if a person has been incarcerated, that person has also been arrested and convicted. Thus, it is possible to predict the respondents answers based on his or her total score. Consider, further, that an individual scores a "1." Since arrest, conviction, and incarceration are ordered events, it is possible to predict that the individual with a score of 1 has only been arrested.

Figure 8.3 Example of a Guttman Scale: Self-Reported Crime Survey

SELF-REPORTED CRIME SURVEY

QUESTIONS:

Have you ever been:

Scale Score	Incarcerated?	Convicted?	Arrested?
3	Yes	Yes	Yes
2	No	Yes	Yes
1	No	No	Yes
0	No	No	No

Naturally, it is not so easy to construct a Guttman scale. Such an ideal response pattern is not usually present. "Errors" refer to those responses which fail to fit a pattern of predictable responses. Items which fail to fit the pattern should be discarded. For example, if we included the following statement to the hypothetical scale in Figure 8.3: "Have you ever been the victim of a crime?" this statement would be dropped because it is unrelated to the indicators of criminality which were originally included in the scale. Victimization is not related to arrest, conviction, and incarceration.

POTENTIAL USES OF MEASUREMENT SCALES

No matter what the form of the scale, these measurement devices have a number of uses in criminal justice research. This section highlights the uses of two scales: the severity of crime scale developed by Wolfgang, Figlio, Tracy, and Singer[24] and the positive adjustment scale constructed by Allen and Seiter.[25]

Severity of Crime Scale

The severity of crime scale (see Figure 8.4) was developed as a result of the National Survey of Crime Severity and it therefore reflects public sentiment about which crimes are most serious. It also represents a revision of an earlier attempt by Sellin and Wolfgang[27] to construct a crime severity index. The need for such a scale is rather obvious. If a researcher is primarily interested in gauging the severity of an offense, he/she has a few potential sources to make such a determination. For example, one could consider the charge at arrest or conviction. The problem here is that the charge may not adequately reflect the events surrounding the crime (see Chapter Four) due to the fact that police may "overcharge" an individual at arrest and that the conviction offense may be complicated by "plea bargaining." Even the use of the Uniform Crime Report's Crime Index (see Chapter Four) does not solve this potential problem. The crime index offense may not adequately reflect the severity of the crime due to the fact that it: (1) fails to count multiple offenses, (2) does not differentiate between completed and attempted crimes, and (3) does not weigh crimes according to their severity.

A severity scale is one mechanism which can be used to solve these measurement problems. The researcher must have a description of the offense (normally provided in the police report or in the presentence investigation compiled by the probation officer). Using these data, the researcher can then ascertain the severity of the offense committed.

Figure 8.4. Scale of Offense Severity – *The National Survey of Crime Severity.*[26]

Identification Number: _____

Effects of Event   I   T   D   (circle all that apply)

Component Scored	Number of Victims	x	Scale Weight	=	Total
I Injury					
(a) Minor harm	_____		1.47		_____
(b) Treated and discharged	_____		8.53		_____
(c) Hospitalized	_____		11.98		_____
(d) Killed	_____		35.67		_____
II Forcible Sex Acts	_____				_____
III Intimidation	_____				_____
(a) Verbal or physical	_____		4.90		_____
(b) Weapon	_____		5.60		_____
IV Premises forcibly entered	_____		1.50		_____
V Motor vehicle stolen	_____				_____
(a) Recovered	_____		4.46		_____
(b) Not recovered	_____		8.07		_____
VI Property theft/damage	_____		*		_____
			Total Score		_____

---

*log10Y =.26776656 log 10X
  where Y = crime severity weight
       X = total dollar value of theft or damage

The seriousness scoring system listed in Figure 8.4 consists of six basic elements surrounding a criminal event:[28]

1. The number of victims who, during the event, received minor bodily injuries or were treated and discharged, hospitalized, or killed.
2. The number of victims of forcible sexual intercourse.
3. The presence of physical or verbal intimidation or intimidation by a dangerous weapon.
4. The number of premises forcibly entered.
5. The number of motor vehicles stolen and whether the vehicle was or was not recovered.
6. The total dollar amount of property loss during an event through theft and damage.

Specifically, the scale operates in the following manner. First, the criminal event must be classified in terms of the presence of I (injury), T (theft) and D (damage). It is possible to have seven different classifications of an event (I, T, D, IT, ID, TD, and ITD). On the scale scoring sheet, column 1 presents the offense components in the scale, column 2 refers to the number of victims involved, column 3 gives the scale weight for each event (developed via the survey), and column 4 then contains the total score for each given event. The figures in column 4 are then summed to obtain the final score. Although these items seem very straightforward, the researcher must be careful to note that the scale is designed in such a way that a forcible sex act is considered to be always accomplished by intimidation. Therefore, any forcible sex act should also be scored in terms of the type of intimidation used by the assailant. Also, a motor vehicle theft is not included under item 6 since it has already been considered in item 5. Researchers should also note that the scale weight for property theft/damage (item 6) is rather complex and will require some special attention.

This scoring system has a number of potential research applications. The severity of an offense could be applied to such outcome measures as recidivism as well as determining the severity of a criminal career. For example, Wilson[29] utilized the Sellin-Wolfgang scale in her analysis of prisoners who were prosecuted and incarcerated under Kentucky's Persistent Felony Offender (PFO) law. She used the scale to determine the severity of the current offense committed by the PFOs in order to determine the level of violence present. Among her conclusions were that 43 percent of the incarcerated PFOs had recently committed crimes which included some form of threatened or actual violence.[30] This type of application and use of scales in criminological studies may improve decision making in the criminal justice arena.

Positive Adjustment Scale

In Chapter Eleven, the problems in the measurement of recidivism rates are discussed. One of the basic problems with recidivism as an outcome measure is that it is strictly a negative indicator. Due to its very nature, recidivism does not consider any positive behavior which the client engages in. This was precisely the problem faced by Allen and Seiter[31] in their evaluation of halfway house program effectiveness. The basic premise was that the successful adjustment of an offender should not be judged on the basis of his/her criminal behavior alone and that positive (or acceptable) behavior patterns should also be considered. A two part scale was developed which measured criminal behavior (in terms of a scale which corresponded to the Ohio legal code) and a measure of acceptable behavior patterns. Since we have already considered a measure of the severity of behavior, we will focus upon the "positive adjustment" segment of the Seiter scale.

Figure 8.5 lists the elements of the positive adjustment scale. It is designed to provide some quantitative measure of "acceptable living patterns." The indicators are not designed as measures of success; rather they should be considered as an index of adjustment within the community. Its major emphasis is upon work or educational stability but other indicators of self-improvement (i.e., financial responsibility, parole or probation progress, absence of critical incidents or illegal activities) are also included. Therefore, the scale appears to have face validity: the qualities listed in the scale suggest stability, responsibility, maturity, and a general pattern of socially acceptable behavior.

Each item on the scale is weighted equally. Individuals receive one point as they qualify for each criterion. The positive adjustment score is the total number of criterion registered by the individual. The scoring range is from 0 through 10. Of course, the individual items as well as the total score value may be examined by researchers. The positive adjustment scale has been utilized in a number of studies; particularly in the evaluation of intensive supervision (Latessa[33]) and prison drug/alcohol rehabilitation programs (Vito[34]). Its basic strength lies in its attempt to provide a positive measure of performance and a point of comparison to the traditionally negative measure of recidivism.

Figure 8.5 Positive Adjustment Scale[32]

DIRECTIONS:
Assign one point for the attainment of any of the following adjustment criteria.

Employed, enrolled in school, or participating in a training program for more than 50 percent of the follow-up period.

Held any one job (or continued in educational or vocational program) for more than a six month period during the follow-up.

Attained vertical mobility in employment, educational, or vocational programs.

For the last half of the follow-up period, individual was self-supporting and supported any immediate family.

Individual shows stability in residency. Either lived in the same residence for more than six months or moved at the suggestion or with the agreement of the supervising officer

Individual has avoided any critical incidents that show instability, immaturity, or inability to solve problems acceptably.

Attainment of financial stability. This is indicated by the individual living within his means, opening bank accounts or meeting debt payments.

Participation in self-improvement programs. These could be vocational, educational, group counseling, or alcohol or drug maintenance program.

Individual making satisfactory progress through probation period. This could be moving downward in levels of supervision or obtaining final release within the follow-up period.

No illegal activities on any available records during the follow-up period.

CREATING A MEASUREMENT SCALE

Measurement scales provide an excellent opportunity to measure attitudes toward concepts. Scales are especially useful when attempting to measure concepts that might be difficult to quantify, or more simply, difficult to clearly define. Consider concepts that you may use often like "at-risk" or "good student" or "good professor"; it may be difficult for you to succinctly define each of these terms. Instead, it might be useful to brainstorm attributes that represent each of the concepts (e.g., "good" professors are fair). The same is true for concepts in criminal justice. Recall, Figure 8.4 presented a scale for measuring the seriousness of a criminal act. This section discusses the main steps in creating a measurement scale.

As with most research projects, the researcher must determine the focus of the scale he is creating. What is the goal of the study? Why would a scale be beneficial? Once the researcher has answered these questions, he should then determine whether there is an existing scale in the literature that he may use for his research or review as he begins his research. Let's suppose the researcher is interested in studying *attitudes employers have related to convicted felons* and he goes to the library and finds no existing research using scales to measure employer attitudes toward convicted felons. The researcher must create his own scale.

First, he develops statements that address specific issues related to convicted felons. Usually this involves creating from 30 to 100 statements. The following are example statements that may be included in the pool:

> *Convicted felons are good hires for service positions in my company.*
> *Convicted felons have good work ethic.*
> *I would hire a convicted felon to work at my company.*
> *Convicted felons are trustworthy employees.*
> *Hiring convicted felons is important for their reintegration to society.*

Notice that each statement uses the same sentence structure and that they are written in the affirmative; thus, if an individual responds "yes" to each statement then the total score value (if "yes" equals "1") would be cumulative. This means the higher an employer scores on the scale, the more likely it is that the employer would hire a convicted felon to work at her company.

Sometimes individuals will negative code at least one statement as a validity check for respondents. For example, the researcher may throw the following statement into the pool above, "Convicted felons use illicit drugs." When using a negative item for a validity check, it is important that the researcher remember to reverse code (i.e., "no" equals "1") the item so that it will also be added to the cumulative score (when applicable). Once the pilot survey of individuals (employers in this example) respond to the pool of statements, the researcher then analyzes the statements (completes an item analysis) to determine which individual items correlate the highest with the total score value. These items are selected for the scale which serves as the basis for the analysis.

EXAMPLE: RACE, HOMICIDE SEVERITY, AND APPLICATIONS OF THE DEATH PENALTY: A CONSIDERATION OF THE BARNETT SCALE

Keil and Vito[35] used the Barnett scale of homicide severity to analyze the capital sentencing process in Kentucky. Barnett[36] reviewed homicide cases from the Baldus[37] study in Georgia. Barnett's scale considered three elements of a homicide: (1) the certainty that the defendant is a deliberate killer; (2) the status of the victim as stranger versus nonstranger; and (3) the heinousness of the killing. There were three separate category ratings resulting in 18 possible outcomes. The higher the defendant scored the greater the risk of the defendant receiving a death sentence. Barnett was highly successful in predicting a death sentence in Georgia.[38] Moreover, he found that whites were disproportionately the victims of homicide that the scale considered most serious.[39]

The purpose of the Keil and Vito study was to determine if the death penalty was disproportionately imposed on blacks who kill whites in Kentucky. If this was the finding, then the authors would examine:[40]

> . . . whether this result is due to those murders being defined, by law, as more "serious" crimes (i.e., they feature several aggravating circumstances). . . whether this bias is the result of the discretion of prosecutors, juries, or both. . . . and whether racial disparities (if any) are concentrated at certain levels within the range of crime seriousness.

Keil and Vito found that Barnett's index of seriousness did not identify persons sentenced to die in Kentucky as well as it had in Georgia. Furthermore, they found that racial disparities in capital sentencing were not limited to the midrange of seriousness on the scale.[41] The use of the Barnett scale in this research is significant for three reasons:[42]

> The Barnett scale is not only useful in predicting final outcome in the capital sentencing process, but also at intermediate stages, such as the prosecutorial decision to seek the death penalty. The scale does not fully capture all of the dimensions of seriousness that prosecutors and jurors evidently take into account in their death sentencing deliberations.

And, third, though the scale seems to be an excellent predictor of death sentencing, the impact of race in Kentucky as shown in the Keil and Vito study, suggests that the possibility of discrimination must be examined across jurisdictions; that is, one cannot assume that death sentencing operates the same in each state.

CONCLUSION

This chapter provided a basic overview of the major types of measurement scales (Likert, Thurstone, and Guttman) and gave some specific attention to the measurement of crime severity and positive adjustment by clients in rehabilitation programs. The criminal justice researcher must be aware of these different forms and make use of existing scales when it is feasible to do so. The chapter concluded with an example of how to create a scale. The measurement of phenomena in a quantitative manner can facilitate and provide more accurate indicators of performance in the criminal justice system.

KEY TERMS

Validity
Reliability
Scales
Operationalization
Face Validity
Unidimensional
Internal Validation

External Validation
Variables
Content Validity
Attributes
Discrete Variable
Categorical Variable
Continuous Variable
Levels of Measurement
Nominal
Interval
Ordinal
Ratio
Likert Scale
Thurstone Scale
Guttman Scale
Cumulative Scaling

REVIEW QUESTIONS

1. Identify the key features of the Likert, Thurstone, and Guttman scales.
2. What was the purpose of the National Survey of Crime Severity?
3. Use the crime severity scale to compute a score for the following crime incident: A holdup man forces a husband and his wife to get out of their automobile. He shoots the husband, gun whips and rapes the wife (hospitalized) and leaves the automobile (recovered later). The husband dies as a result of the shooting.
4. What are the goals of the Positive Adjustment Scale?
5. Describe the process for creating a Guttman scale to measure attitudes of citizens toward individuals charged with sexual abuse of a child.
6. Suppose you are paid to develop a questionnaire to determine citizen satisfaction of the police. One of your friends suggests that a question be, "Are you satisfied with the police?" How do you respond to your friend to explain to him that there might be a better way to ask that question (i.e., using a higher level of measurement)? What question(s) might you propose instead of his question?

7. Discuss internal and external validation and their relationship to construct validity.

8. Interpret the scores of 14 and 34 in the scale presented in Figure 9.1 which measures the extent of agreement with conservative attitudes and policies toward crime and criminals.

9. Interpret the score of 43.9 in the scale presented in Figure 9.2 which measures individual's perception of crime severity.

REFERENCES

1. Paternoster, R. (1983). Race of the victim and location of crime: The decision to seek the death penalty in South Carolina, *The Journal of Criminal Law and Criminology*, 74:754–785.

2. Ibid.

3. Ibid.

4. Hoffman, P.B. (1983). Screening for risk: A revised salient factor score (SFS/81), *Journal of Criminal Justice*, 2:539–547.

5. Hoffman, P.B. and Adelberg, S. (1980). The salient factor score: A nontechnical overview, *Federal Probation*, 45:185–188.

6. Eaglin, J.B. and Lombard, P.A. (1981). Statistical risk prediction as an aid to probation caseload classification, *Federal Probation*, 45:25–32.

7. Eskridge, C.W. (1983). *Pretrial Release Programming*, New York: Clark Boardman.

8. Buchanan, R.A., Whitlow, K.L., and Austin, J. (1986). National evaluation of objective prison classification systems: The current state of the art, *Crime and Delinquency*, 32:272–290.

9. Kane, T.R. (1986). The validity of prison classification: An introduction to practical considerations and research issues, *Crime and Delinquency*, 32:367–390.

10. Brodsky, S.L. and Smitherman, H.O. (1983). *Handbook of scales for research in crime and delinquency*, New York: Plenum.

11. Wright, K.N., Clear, T.R., and Dickson, P. (1984). Universal applicability of probation risk-assessment instruments: A critique, *Criminology*, 22:113–134.

12. Ibid.

13. Likert, R. (1932). A technique for the measurement of attitudes, *Archives Psychology*, No. 140.

14. Cullen, F.T., Bynum, T.S., Garrett, K. and Greene, J.R. (1985). Legislator ideology and criminal justice policy, in Fairchild, E.S. and Webb, V.J., eds., *The politics of crime and criminal justice*, Beverly Hills, CA: Sage.

15. Ibid.

16. Ibid.

17. Miller, D.C. ed., (1977), *Handbook of research design and social measurement.* New York: McKay.

18. Wolfgang, M.E., Figlio, R.M., Tracy, P.E. and Singer, S.I. (1985). *The national survey of crime severity*, Washington, D.C.: U.S. Government Printing Office.

19. Ibid.
20. Ibid.
21. Ibid.
22. Ibid.
23. Guttman, L.L. (1944). A basis for scaling qualitative data, *American Sociological Review*, 9:139–150.
24. Wolfgang et al., *The national survey*.
25. Allen, H.E., and Seiter, R.P. (1976). The effectiveness of halfway houses: A reappraisal of a reappraisal, *Chitty's Law Journal*, 24:196–200.
26. Wolfgang et al., *The national survey*.
27. Sellin, T., and Wolfgang, M.E. (1964). *The measurement of delinquency*, New York: John Wiley & Sons.
28. Wolfgang et al., *The national survey*.
29. Wilson, D.G. (1985). *Persistent felony offenders in Kentucky: A profile of the institutional population*, Louisville, KY: Criminal Justice Statistical Analysis Center.
30. Ibid.
31. Allen and Seiter, The effectiveness of halfway houses.
32. Ibid.
33. Latessa, E.J. (1980). Intensive diversion unit: An evaluation, in Price, B.R. and Baunach, P.J. eds., *Criminal justice research: New models and findings*, Beverly Hills, CA: Sage.
34. Vito, G.F. (1982). Does it work? Problems in the evaluation of a correctional treatment program, *Journal of Offender Counseling, Services and Rehabilitation*, 7:522.
35. Keil, T.J., and Vito, G.F. (1989). Race, homicide severity, and the application of the death penalty: Consideration of the Barnett scale, *Criminology*, 27:511–536.
36. Barnett, A. (1985). Some distribution patterns for the Georgia death sentence, *U.C. Davis Law Review*, 18:1327–1374.
37. Baldus, D.C., Pulaski, C., and Woodworth, G. (1983). Comparative review of death sentences: An empirical study of the Georgia experience, *Journal of Criminal Law and Criminology*, 74:661–753.
38. Barnett, Some distribution patterns.
39. Ibid.
40. Keil and Vito, Homicide severity.
41. Ibid.
42. Ibid.
43. Ibid.

Chapter Nine

QUALITATIVE RESEARCH: OBSERVATIONAL STUDIES

CHAPTER OVERVIEW

Criminal justice research, like all social research, attempts to answer one or more of three basic questions: "What are the characteristics of a particular event/object?" "Why did something happen?" and "What are the consequences of something that happened?" Each of these three types of questions can be answered in a variety of ways, including using both quantitative data and methods (as has been discussed up to this point in the text) and using qualitative data/methods.

As we have been discussing, quantitative research in criminal justice is usually focused on the causes and consequences of crime and crime related processes and procedures. Quantitative criminal justice research might ask questions such as: What kind and how strong of a relationship exists between the distribution of people of various ages in a community and the rate and types of criminal behavior in that community? What effect does an increased number of inmates in a jail have on the job satisfaction of staff in the jail? What consequences follow from the abolition of plea bargaining? or What affect is there of a program that teaches inner-city children the law on rates of delinquency?

On the other hand, qualitative research is focused not so much on explaining how and why something occurs, but instead is focused on the objectives of exploring, clarifying, and describing the characteristics and experiences of a social phenomenon. Typical questions that qualitative research in criminal justice might ask include: What is the culture of the inmate social system in a particular prison? How do serial killers explain their behavior? How does a parole officer actually supervise his/her clients? How do juveniles in detention experience their day-to-day life while detained?

This chapter introduces the basic methods and purposes of qualitative research in criminal justice. As explained above, there are important differences in the types of questions and approaches that quantitative and qualitative researchers use. However, as will also become clear throughout this chapter, in many ways the differences between quantitative and qualitative research are present only in the "ideal-typical" approach to research. In many research efforts, especially those focused on trying to determine if and how well a program/intervention works, there is often a combination of both qualitative and quantitative methodology and data used. Only in the ideal or the abstract are the two methods completely different.

For example, if you are conducting research in an effort to describe how a parole officer actually supervises his/her clients, you are also interested in offering some explanation for his/her behavior. Likewise, if I am interested in knowing whether a drug treatment program for incarcerated offenders is effective, I would need to look at both quantitative and qualitative data. First, it would be important to measure the participants' drug use after completing the program and being released. However, we would also need to know what parts of the program participants found beneficial, where they saw problems in the materials and process of the program, and how the education and counseling of the program were understood. These would be qualitative questions, whereas the measurement of drug use after release would be use of quantitative data. Our interests here are on both describing the outcome, as well as explaining what contributes to the outcome.

Perhaps, the most important distinction between qualitative and quantitative research is that the research question determines the research design – specifically, the types of data that are needed and the way(s) that we can gather such data. Quantitative research attempts to explain and generalize. Qualitative research seeks indepth, detailed information which, though not always completely generalizable, allows for a deeper understanding of at a minimum those specific persons/events from whom data is collected. Quantitative research generally relies on the experimental, quasiexperimental, and survey research designs. Qualitative research relies primarily on participant observational studies and interviews. Since the case study and survey research have been covered, this chapter will concentrate on the basics of qualitative approaches and forms of participant observation. The next chapter will focus exclusively on qualitative interviewing.

BASICS OF QUALITATIVE RESEARCH

Qualitative research is about obtaining a depth of understanding of particular categories/types of events, persons or experiences. Qualitative researchers are primarily interested in providing understandings of the ways that processes operate, what it is like to be or experience a particular incident or status and/or what are the ways that categories/types of persons interpret and understand some aspect of the criminal justice system.

Quantitative research relies on the ability of researchers to accurately and reliably measure variables. This approach to research centers on statistically describing the number/amount of a variable and identifying if, how and how strongly variables (especially independent and dependent variables) are related to one another. Qualitative research is not focused on measurements, and uses the concept of a "variable" in only a very loose way. When a qualitative researcher talks about her "variables" she is really talking about the concepts and processes that she is interested in. As a qualitative researcher she is not trying to find out how much of the variable is present or how strong is its relationship to another variable, but instead she is interested in providing a thorough description of the concept, and explaining to readers what the concept really means and how it plays a role in a larger process.

As an example, think about what types of research questions might be asked when a police department changes from putting officers in patrol cars and instead has officers riding bicycles. A quantitative researcher might be interested in whether or not there is a change in the number of crimes in the community after the change, the response time for officers going to calls and whether the department saves money by using bicycles instead of cars. A qualitative researcher, however, is likely to be interested in questions such as how the process of patrol did or did not change after officers began riding bicycles. Are some streets and neighborhoods not being patrolled by the officers on bicycles? Are officers actually interacting with citizens more when they are on their bicycles? What do the officers like and dislike about riding bicycles compared to driving cars? How do bicycles limit officers' abilities to do their jobs? Each of the qualitative research questions would necessitate data that discusses a process, not data that is a quantifiable measurement. It may be useful to think of qualitative data as a collection of individual explanations for how something operates or is experienced. This collection of individual case explanations is then the data that is used to identify patterns and themes across the population being studied.

At the core of qualitative research is the attempt to identify and explain patterns and themes in events and persons. Recall that quantitative research focused on identifying and statistically stating/describing relationships between variables. In qualitative research we are interested in finding phenomenon that occur repeatedly (a pattern) and phenomena that are very similar in meaning, structure or format and that are common across a population (a theme). Patterns are regular, repeating appearances of a particular observable event, object or action that are predictable. Themes are a bit broader (or "looser") and include differing events, objects or actions that while not all the same are generally similar and tend to be found in a particular population or in the same general place in some process. For instance, consider a research project where we were studying the reasons that sheriff's deputies on one community chose their job. If, when we interviewed the deputies they consistently told us that they were deputies because their father had been a deputy, this would be a pattern in the data. If we heard various deputies tell us that they "wanted to help the community" or "thought they should give back to the community" or "feel making the community safe is important" we can pretty easily see a theme in the data. Although the actual responses received from the deputies about why they have this job differ, there is a fairly obvious commonality of meaning running through these responses.

The identification of patterns and themes is at the heart of qualitative research. However, the job of the qualitative researcher is not only to find the patterns and themes, but also to summarize and describe these patterns and themes in such a way that the consumer (e.g. reader) of this research is convinced that these patterns and themes are really present in the data. Here is one place where qualitative researchers are at a disadvantage compared with their quantitative peers. The quantitative researcher can simply point to his statistics and prove that two variables are related, and that the relationship is strong and consistent. The qualitative researcher does not have anything concrete (like a statistical test) to point to as proof that the patterns and themes he has identified as true and real. This is where the qualitative researcher needs to draw on the data, and use it to build an argument that convinces the reader that his interpretations of the data are accurate.

Qualitative research reports are presentations and descriptions of patterns and themes done in such a way as to be a convincing argument. The point of the qualitative research report is to convince the reader that identified patterns and themes are in the data. This is done by stating the pattern/theme, and showing it through the use of the data itself. Qualitative research reports need to support the arguments being made about the presence of a pattern or theme by showing examples of them. Remember that among the foci of qualitative research are explaining what something means or what an experience is like. When we are working with data that is less than exact such as this, it becomes critically important to show the reader what the data is, as a way of supporting our claims about what the themes or meanings of the data are. Brief examples of events and persons observed, or quotes from those who are interviewed are used to illustrate the patterns and themes that the qualitative researcher is arguing are present.

It is important to remember that the data cannot and does not speak for itself, and simply presenting the data is not what qualitative research is about. It is the responsibility of the researcher to do the thinking work, and to actually find and explain the patterns, themes and meanings of the data. To make this explanation as thorough as possible it is important to show examples. But, examples are just that, they are selected pieces of the data that bring life and thoroughness to an explanation, they are not the analysis itself.

PARTICIPANT OBSERVATION

It . . . is my belief that any group of persons – prisoners, primitives, pilots, or patients – develop a life of their own that becomes meaningful, reasonable, and normal once you get close to it, and that a good way to learn about any of these worlds is to submit oneself in the company of the members to the daily round of petty contingencies to which they are subject.[1]

Participant observation is the data collection method which gathers the most detailed and descriptive information about places, groups and social environments. It is often called field research, because the researcher literally goes to the setting or people that he is studying and he spends time there observing, and sometimes actually participating as a member of the social setting being studied. The activity that is always involved is **observation**. And, depending on the type of setting, characteristics of the researcher, nature of activity in the setting and the research questions being investigated, the researcher may or may not be involved in **participant observation**.

The goal of observational based research is to identify some aspect of behavior or relationships between persons/events without the filtering of interpretation from those persons involved in what is being studied. The observational researcher places herself in the setting where she can collect data about her research question and watches and records what happens. She does this so as to see things in their natural state, without the value-laden interpretations that are likely to be obtained by asking people (either those involved in the setting being studied or others) what is going on. A very simplistic analogy here is to think about some of the fieldtrips you may have taken when in elementary school. The goal of a fieldtrip is to take students to a place so they can see for themselves what that place is like. Taking inner-city children to a farm, so they can see, smell, hear and touch farm animals provides the children with a very different experience than having a farmer come to the inner-city school with pictures of his animals. Many educators would argue that the fieldtrip provides the students with a deeper and more complete understanding of what a farm is like than would be possible in any other way. The fieldtrip is the equivalent of the data collection process for the student/researchers.

The goal of participant observation research may be to complete an **ethnographic** analysis of a social setting. When a qualitative researcher is doing ethnographic work (and producing a research report known as an ethnography), he is seeking to provide a thorough understanding of how a particular social environment operates. This means identifying and describing the culture, the roles of persons in the setting, what types of persons fulfill which roles, what the typical (and deviant) types of activities are in the setting, what setting participants value and see as important, how relationships are formed in the setting, and which persons and roles have relationships with which other persons and roles. The ethnographic research product is the most comprehensive description of an entire setting and all of the cultural, structural and processual workings of the particular setting (or organization) being studied.

Ethnographic studies not only provide understandings of how a social setting operates and what is valued by individuals in the setting, but so too can ethnographies provide much deeper understandings of how a wide variety of factors influence what happens in a particular setting and with particular persons. A good example of this is seen in Mark Fleisher's book *Beggars and Thieves.*[2] This ethnography looks at the lives and daily activities of a largely homeless population of petty criminals and alcoholics/drug addicts in downtown Seattle. Fleisher spent numerous months in the field and talked in depth with 194 individuals during the course of his study. He also simply spent dozens of hours hanging out in popular downtown locations frequented by street people, simply watching and feeling what was going on in the area. What he discovered is that these individuals are almost all from abusive and/or substance-using homes, a common theme is to have been raised either by uncaring and distant parents or outside of families and that most of the programs and interventions designed to not only keep these individuals away from crime but to also help them train for and find jobs, get an education and/or move toward respectable lives fail to target the issues and values that both bring people to street life and keep them there. The holistic understanding that Fleisher brings to his work shows that the problems of and for street persons involved in petty crime are not isolated nor restricted to only their small subculture, but rather the problems are far-reaching, complex and involve multiple social institutions.

Observational research approaches, including ethnography, and the specific methodological approaches used to collect and analyze data are borne out of the science of anthropology. Margaret Mead's pioneering work during the 1930s when she studied three separate cultures in New Guinea is an example of participant observation.[3] She actually traveled to New Guinea and lived within these cultures. Even earlier, in the 1800s, Max Weber advanced his ideas on what he called **interpretive understanding** (Verstehen). Verstehen is subjective understanding of an activity which is identical or similar to the understanding of the actor(s) under study. Weber believed that this was only possible if the researcher could place himself/herself in the place of the individual under study and view the behavior from the actor's perspective. The concept of interpretive understanding is central to participant observation. The assumption is that only people who are actually involved in some behavior can truly understand it. Therefore, the social scientist must try to see and interpret the world as much as possible from the perspective of the actor. Participant observation: (1) requires direct contact with the individuals under study, (2) requires that the researcher go into the social setting of the individuals under study, and (3) takes place in social settings that are relatively natural and normal for the subjects under study.[4] These strategies get the researcher into the natural environment of a group or the natural environment of the activities under study. The researcher is in direct contact with the research subjects. This method of study increases the researcher's empathy with his/her subjects and enhances his/her ability to adopt their perspective and understanding. This method of research is that which most directly involves people and is therefore also the most intimate. Some of these social and moral questions will become evident as we discuss the various types of participant observation and the advantages and disadvantages of each.

Roles and Approaches to Data Collection

Not all observational research endeavors are actually carried out in the same way. There are a multitude of ways that researchers can approach the settings and people that they will be observing. There are also many different ways that observational researchers may or may not interact with the settings they study. And, perhaps most importantly, there are a range of ways to approach the issue of whether the researcher informs those that are being observed and studied that he is in fact observing and studying them.

In this section the five ideal types of roles available for observational researchers will be discussed. Each of these will be defined, the types of research questions and settings for which each is best suited will be discussed, and the advantages and disadvantages for the researcher and the understanding of the setting being studied will also be addressed. This range of roles encompasses both whether or not the researcher is a participant in what is being studied and whether or not the researcher informs those being studied that they are the subjects of research.

Complete Participant

The first form of participant observation is the **complete partici-pant** or, what is sometimes called the unknown observer. In simple terms, in this role the researcher is a member of the setting being stud-ied, participates fully like any other setting member and does not tell others that she is a researcher. This method of data collection places the researcher in a role similar to that of spy or undercover detective. The investigator takes on a role in the group under study and pretends to be a true member while secretly studying the members of the group. For example, a researcher might take a job as a correctional counselor at a state prison for the purpose of studying correctional offi-cers. Similarly, a researcher might join a police force or a juvenile gang to study and understand these groups.

Complete participation as a strategy may be the best way to learn the details of the life and behavior of a group. The researcher is pre-sent, sees what regular group members see and do, and there are no attempts made by the group/setting members to hide what they do or to do things so they will be seen in a positive way. The researcher, dis-guised as a member of the group, is privy to the information of an accepted member of the group an insider. Consequently, she or he can learn about aspects of group life that might otherwise be missed. Recall the discussion of the Hawthorn Effect discussed earlier in the text. This is the idea that when people know they are being watched (e.g., studied) they act differently than if they do not know they are being watched. Essentially, we do not act the same when someone is watching us as when we do not know we are being observed. You can easily think of many instances in your life when the mere fact that someone was present and watching you lead you to change your behavior, at least a little bit. As a complete participant, researchers do not need to be concerned with the Hawthorne effect, because those they are watching/studying do not know it, and therefore do not act differently than they normally do.

One classic criminological study shows the value of a complete par-ticipant role very well. In his book *Asylums*, Erving Goffman describes in intimate detail the "underlife" of a total institution. His very de-tailed, vividly descriptive work on the behaviors of mental patients and staff is based on data gathered while a complete participant in the role of assistant to the athletic director at St. Elizabeth's Hospital. If he had been known as a researcher, his access to information may have been limited since many of the activities he observed were contrary to the rules and formal requirements of the institution.

The disadvantages of complete participation are mainly issues of morality and objectivity. When the results of this type of research are presented, typically the names of the subjects, the place of observation and any identifying criteria of the subjects, place, and group are with-held. However, the question of the morality of studying a group of people without their knowledge or permission still remains. Some social scientists believe that participant observation may injure sub-jects in ways that cannot be anticipated nor compensated for after the fact. When a researcher is not familiar with the group upon entry, the risk of unintended harm is great. Even the rationale of risking harm to subjects for social and scientific benefit is problematic since the sub-jects have not consented to be studied.

Complete participation may also be similar to entrapment. When the investigator finally leaves the group and/or reveals his/her identi-ty, members of the group may feel like they have been setup or mis-led by the researcher. They may have bitter feelings because of this deception and feel that the investigator is a traitor. These ethical ques-tions can only be addressed by researchers themselves, using a set of professional ethics and standards that are objective in nature.

However, there is also an argument to be made that **covert re-search** (that which is done without disclosing the research to those being studied) is sometimes necessary and the only way to study some populations and activities.[5] Miller has argued that there are some types of persons/groups – active criminals, persons in high powered posi-tions and those with extremely high levels of suspicion (paranoia?) of outsiders – who can only be accurately studied via covert and com-plete participation approaches. However, this is not the only reason to justify such an approach. Additionally, Miller argues that many, if not most, criminal justice system actors and clients are unlikely to be com-pletely truthful and fully enact their regular activities if a researcher is present. Therefore, to get a complete and accurate picture of some types of settings it is necessary to overcome active resistance and de-ception from those being studied by studying them without their knowledge. The ethical questions are clear and common, however, and Miller does acknowledge them.

The means and end rule, of course, requires the subjective interpretation of plausible harm to subjects, what exactly constitutes benefit, and who will be beneficiaries. To assess the balance between these elements it is necessary that they be highly specified, a requirement that is not easily met. The means and end formula is thus ambiguous and the choice to use a covert technique must be carefully deliberated. Certainly, deceptive observation carries ethical baggage less common to other qualitative methods, yet its ethicality is negotiable through detailed purpose and design.[6]

In addition to the ethical issues raised by complete participation, there are other disadvantages. First, the role in the group that is played by the researcher naturally restricts his or her activity and so limits his or her ability to move about freely and observe. After all, as a participating member of the group the researcher has a role to fulfill, and in most settings not every role or participant can and does participate in all aspects and activities of the setting. For example, a complete observer who secretly assumes the role of a police officer is not free to move about the police station observing interactions and interviewing police officers and suspects. Instead, he or she must perform the regular occupational duties of a police officer which necessarily restrict his or her mobility and the specific types of police activities which can be observed. Similarly, as an accepted yet disguised member of a group, a researcher is limited to questioning only those matters appropriate to the role he or she is playing. Too many questions about matters outside the role or about matters that should be known to group members who assume the role will raise suspicion.

All of this is not to say that these difficulties and challenges disappear when a different – or opposite – role and approach are used in observational research. As will be discussed later in this chapter, a complete observer is also limited in his or her ability to immediately record observations. The complete participant usually cannot carry tape recorders, video equipment, or even openly write down notes to record the daily life of the group; this is very rarely part of the set of normal activities of a group or social setting. The result is that the actual process of collecting and recording data for the complete participant is heavily dependent on the ability to memorize large amounts of detailed information (so it can later be recorded). Complete participants may also be so self conscious about revealing their true identity that their ability to perform their role and collect data is hampered.

One of the dangers and problems of complete participation has long been known by anthropologists, and that is the danger of "**going na-**

tive." This term refers to complete participants who actually do become true and committed members of the groups and settings that they study. In this instance the researcher becomes so involved in their role and so committed to the group and subjects under study that they lose their abilities to be objective observers. While such a researcher may continue to observe and record information, once they have gone native they are essentially studying themselves. And, to study one's self is to not be objective; many social scientists would argue that it is simply not possible to view yourself (and the world that you care about) in an objective way.

Potential Participant

A variation on the complete participant role is that of the **potential participant**.[7] The idea of the potential participant is that the researcher is present in a setting where they are collecting observational data, and they present themselves as if they are true participants. However, rather than engaging in the full range of activities of the setting, the researcher basically hangs around and is seen and perceived by others as a person who belongs. The primary advantage of the potential participant role is that questions of ethics can be avoided (or at least seriously minimized) when the researcher is present where illegal, immoral or unethical activities occur, but the researcher does not engage in such acts. Rather, the researcher is present and acts as if he might or at a later time will participate, but just does not do so at the present time. In this way the potential participant needs to have all of the skills of fitting in that the complete participant has, but he need not engage in activities that he believes are wrong or harmful.

The potential participant role may be best suited for studies of drug using subcultures, sexual activities, criminal acts, and anything that would impair the researcher's abilities to observe and record notes. Take for instance the case of a researcher attempting to study crack houses. If the researcher took on a complete participant role he might find it difficult to concentrate on watching others and remembering and taking notes on what he observed. However, if he can enter the setting and hang out and present himself as a crack user, others present are likely to assume he is supposed to be there, and they will go about their natural routines.

Participant as Observer

The **participant as observer** is similar to the complete participant and potential participant role yet significantly different since the subjects know the researcher's true identity and purpose. This means that the researcher has greater freedom to move about in the setting and collect data both formally and informally. Because the people being studied know that they are being studied the researcher does not need to be concerned with hiding her activities as a researcher. She does, however, have to be concerned with those she is studying acting differently in front of her than they would if either she were not present or they did not know she was a researcher.

One of the authors of this text did a participant-as-observer study of a plainclothes urban police department unit that targeted drug and vice offenses. The researcher was known to all six members of the unit (and all other officers in the precinct where the study was conducted) as a researcher, yet he was also welcomed to the unit "as just another one of us." The research process involved the researcher working shifts with the unit (usually four days per week), and doing essentially all of the tasks that the unit officers did. Because he was not a sworn officer, the researcher did not carry a firearm, was not permitted to drive police department vehicles and possessed no official authority or power. However, each day the researcher was paired with a unit member as a partner, accompanied the officers on surveillance, serving of search warrants, going to court, making arrests, booking arrestees into jail, going to precinct and departmental meetings, doing background research on suspects and completing paperwork. Within legal bounds, the researcher did everything that the officers did.

As a researcher he carried a small (3" x 5") notebook and pen, and recorded notes throughout the day. In the first couple of weeks of spending time with the unit the notetaking activities occasionally drew attention to the researcher, and officers would comment, such as "You're writing all of this down?" or "Oh, that's right, you're here to analyze us." After about three weeks in the field, the comments from officers ceased, and when anything about note taking was mentioned it was either to ask the researcher for details from an event that happened earlier (so, the researcher served as a resource for the officers) or an officer would mention, "Hey doc, aren't you going to write all of this down?"

The participant as observer role did have the Hawthorne Effect occurring, but only until the officers being studied became used to the researcher's presence and came to take his presence as natural. The fact that the researcher was considered "just another one of us" was made clear when he would be asked why he was not at work on particular days, rather than why he was present on particular days (as was the case at the start of the project).

The project ran smoothly and the researcher was able to not only observe the officers in their daily routines, but because he was known as a researcher, he had opportunities to ask questions that might stand out as odd if he were not known as a researcher. Questions such as: "Why do you always search the front seat of the car first?" or "Why are we spending the first hour of the shift in this neighborhood?" provided insight into what was happening and why it was happening. However, such questions might draw unwanted attention to the researcher if he were truly trying to be undercover and function as a complete participant.

Another reason for adopting a participant as observer role is that sometimes becoming a complete participant would require such a major investment of time and other resources that the costs of doing a project would be too great. In the case of the author studying the police unit, it might have been possible for the author to go through the application and hiring process, get hired as an officer, go through the four month training academy and eventually get assigned to the unit he wanted to study. But, this would be such a huge investment of time and resources, that it would not be feasible. Alternatively the researcher could have negotiated with the police chief to enter the department under the guise of transferring from an out of town department and then be assigned to the unit. However, this would either require the researcher to complete the police academy (so as to be able to be a fully functioning officer) or to fake it and thereby put himself, the other officers and members of the community at risk. Again, these costs are too great for the research.

Clearly, there are times when the situation of the setting and group being studied, and perhaps the characteristics of the researcher her/himself influence the decision about what type of role the observational researcher needs to adopt. The research questions being investigated also limit, or sometimes are limited by, the role adopted as well. In some instances the questions that are to be studied necessitate either significantly more or less freedom to question multiple and varied group members, and are not so dependent on either interaction with group members or lengthy periods of observation. In these instances it would be most appropriate to enter the field in one of our last two roles for observational researchers.

Observer as Participant

The **observer as participant** role for data collection utilizes more formal observation techniques than the previous three methods. More specifically, the observer as participant role relies most heavily on interviews with people in the settings being studied, rather than simply observing and watching them. The observation and interaction are more formal and structured.

The limited contact with the subjects has the benefit of reducing the chances of going native and losing objectivity. An additional advantage is that this role promotes notes being taken and behaviors recorded openly. This means that details may be more easily retained. Even when a researcher is functioning in the participant as observer role note taking is limited simply by the need to be participating in the actions of the setting/group. Here, when functioning in an observer as participant role the activities as a researcher are primary, and therefore they can (and usually do) take most of the researcher's time and attention. This promotes more careful and comprehensive note taking, which in turn is likely to lead to a more detailed final research product.

The observer as participant role for data collection does have disadvantages as well, however. The greatest disadvantages are that the researcher does not benefit from the biggest advantages of truly participating in the setting being studied – there are greater opportunities to misunderstand what is really going on, due to the researcher not experiencing the setting themselves as a participant. Also, the persons being studied may not accurately understand the role that of the researcher. When someone is "studying" you, you may not understand what social science research is about and what the goals are. People are often suspicious of being studied and may actively work to present themselves in ways that make them look good (recall the Hawthorne Effect!).

Numerous examples are available about researchers whom are misidentified or misunderstood by those whom they study. One of the authors spent time studying a jail based education program, and as part of the project attended class sessions, and spent time in the jail with the staff and inmates. Also included in the project were interviews with a sample of the inmates in the program. For most of the interviews the first few minutes were spent trying to explain to the inmates why they were being interviewed, and what would be done with the information they provided. Most inmates thought that the researcher was from the government (usually assumed to be the federal government) who was at the program to investigate it and try to shut the program down. Another example is seen in the work of Peter Lewis who studied (e.g. interviewed) inmates on death row in Florida.[8] When he began his interviews, one of his first subjects was a child molester who was detested by all other inmates on death row. Since Lewis was introducing himself to each inmate individually at the beginning of the interview, none of the inmates knew who he was. Because of his dress and the restriction of access to death row for most outsiders, the inmates assumed he was an attorney who was attempting to help the child molester. The day after his interview with the child molester when he returned to death row to conduct another interview, the death row inmates were very angry with him. They cursed, spit, threw things at him, and generally caused quite a commotion until they were told about his true status and intentions. Many field researchers have similar (although often less extreme) examples of misconceptions held by their subjects. If they are clarified in time, their effect can be eliminated. If not, they can ruin an otherwise sound research project. The limited time the observer spends with the group and, the limited members she/he has contact with can reduce acceptance by the group and so that the atmosphere in which the interviews are conducted may be uneasy and the responses of the subjects less open.

Complete Observer

This method of data collection completely removes the researcher from direct interaction with his or her subjects. When functioning as a **complete observer**, usually the researcher attempts to observe the group in ways so that they will not know they are being observed or studied. For example, observing the behavior of sex offenders in a therapy group through a oneway mirror or systematically eavesdropping on the counseling sessions through hidden tape recorders might be two strategies. Another method is that used by Dabney, Hollinger and Dugan who used a covert camera system in a suburban retail drug store to identify persons who steal.[9] The project relied on video taping by fourteen hidden closed circuit video cameras to be able to see an entire 7,500 square foot retail store over a period of more than 1,000 hours. The video recordings were then watched and coded by the researchers, to identify demographics and actual behavioral patterns of individuals that were observed to steal. The project showed that 8.5% of all persons who entered the store during the study period stole at least one item Most interesting, the demographic profile of the persons who were identified as shoplifting were significantly different that those previously reported from research based on police data or self-report surveys or interviews.

The advantages to this form of data collection are that it has the least probability of the researcher "going native" and the least probability of influencing the subjects' behaviors through the presence of an observer. However, with these advantages which come from greater distance from, and limited interaction with, individuals under study come disadvantages.

A first disadvantage is that greater distance from the subjects decreases the researcher's ability to completely understand the social life he or she is studying. Statements and behaviors may be misperceived and misunderstood and the researcher has no mechanism for direct clarification. Similarly, the ethical issue of subject consent is also present, especially when clandestine methods of observation such as hidden microphones and video and recording equipment are utilized. However, in some types of settings, such as that described above in the Dabney study, there is not an ethical question when what is being observed/studied is in a completely open and public setting. Activities done in public and open places are fair game for observation, by anybody, not just researchers.

SELECTING A SETTING AND GAINING ENTREE INTO THE SETTING

One aspect of the observational research process that tends to get very little attention, and that most people (especially beginning researchers) seem to take for granted is how the specific location for an observational study is selected. In some ways this is logical, and there may not be much specific that can be said, or taught, about how to select where you actually do your research. This is probably because the best means to select a setting and gain permission to enter the setting are determined by the specific situation, and the specific individuals involved. However, there are some general guidelines which can be followed in an effort to enhance the success of the selection and entree process.

Locating the Setting

Selecting the setting in which a researcher collects qualitative data is an important and difficult task. First, the researcher must know some general characteristics of the subjects and the setting. Second, a consideration of whether a particular setting is appropriate for a project needs to consider two primary criterion:

1. **Feasibility**: Does the site provide data that can be collected within the researcher's resource limitations (time, money, skills)? Does the location provide access to data (types of persons, enough activity, etc.) that will be necessary to pursue the study's research question?
2. **Structural Issues**: Does the site provide the researcher with available data collection opportunities which are feasible? Are there things about the setting that can either facilitate observing what occurs, or that would inhibit the ability to see what happens? Are there opportunities to move in the setting, or will the researcher need to be stationary (and perhaps limit what they can/will see)? Is the setting safe for the researcher?

Information on the setting may be gathered through a variety of means: surveying documents and newspapers, phone calls, inperson interviews, or on site assessments. At times, it may be necessary to assess several settings before finding the appropriate or at least the most appropriate location. The most productive and informative way to assess a setting is to actually go and visit it. Doing a "dry run" visit, where you survey the location, think about what you would be doing if you were actually there collecting data, and more or less checking out the physical and social setting will tell you much more about whether a setting may or may not be a good location for a research endeavor than any other type of investigation.

The setting from which the respondents are selected and the setting in which the observation takes place will greatly influence the quality of the collected data as well as the specific data collection techniques used by the researcher.

Gaining Entree

The selection of a setting will usually entail obtaining permission from someone in authority to enter the setting and conduct the research. The perfect setting may be found, but if permission to enter cannot be obtained, the setting must be reselected. Several general guidelines can be followed to obtain entree.

1. In most instances, it is important, if not completely necessary, to obtain permission from someone in authority to enter a setting. Determining who is the appropriate person to contact and negotiate access with may require some investigation of it's own. It is important to think about whether the person from whom you request permission to do an observational study will be one of the persons you actually observe, and if so, this will therefore limit the type of role you use to collect your data. In some instances, as discussed earlier, covert observational data collection may be done, but this should be considered the exception, not the norm.
2. Direct contact with the person of authority or contact with a lower level individual who can approach the top authority are both frequently used tactics. Which one an investigator elects to use will depend on the situation, and more specifically the approachability and availability of those in control.
3. Honesty in describing research objectives and methods is important. The researcher should identify himself or herself along with the sponsoring agency or organizational affiliation. The research objectives and methodology should be clearly and honestly outlined.

An important point that must be remembered is that permission for entree into a field setting will depend upon the value which those in authority place on the research project. Said differently, any type of gatekeeper is more likely to work with you and grant you permission for your study if they see either real value that can come from the research and/or some direct benefit for them (or their organization/group). Therefore, outlining the benefits that could follow from the project for the organization, offers to include areas of interest to those in authority, and a willingness to provide feedback in the form of research findings are strategies which may make entree easier and which should not significantly affect the objectivity of the study.

RECORDING AND ANALYZING DATA

While participant observation may be similar to the interpretive procedures we make use of as we go about our everyday lives there is one major difference. The researcher who elects to use qualitative methodology not only goes about her day interpreting what she sees, hears, smells, senses and experiences, but she also has to have a means and system for recording and analyzing the information she collects. Rather than relying on memory and informal interpretation, the researcher has to formally record her observations (hopefully in an organized and logical way) and subsequently engage in a process to methodically analyze the information which had been collected.

Collecting the Data: What to Look For

The actual process of collecting data in an observational study is the time spent at the field research site watching and recording data. One common experience for almost all first time observers is that when they get to the field research site they either feel that there is nothing notable occurring and worth recording, or that there is so much to see and record that they feel overwhelmed. Both experiences are problematic, but both can also be overcome fairly easily.

The experience of feeling that there's nothing notable and worth noting or recording is almost always a result of a field researcher choosing to do a study in a setting with which they are very familiar. When looking around a place or group of people that you already know well and feel comfortable with, it is only natural that nothing stands out to you. Everything is normal, after all, in our daily lives we are used to the typical places we spend time – our homes, school, place of work, favorite parks, etc. This means that in all probability we really are not even seeing all of what is there. To overcome this feeling, it is necessary to approach familiar settings from the perspective of someone else. Think about what a person from a foreign culture would notice, or what an elderly person would notice, or what would stand out to a small child (and what would they have questions about). Taking the perspective of someone that is not used to the setting can allow the observational researcher to see things that they might not otherwise see from their own perspective.

More common, however, is the experience of going to a setting or into a group of persons with whom one is not familiar and feeling overwhelmed by everything that is present. When observational researchers have this experience it is necessary to begin looking at the field research site and focusing on specific aspects of the setting, people and actions there. There are ten basic categories of observable elements to any field research setting that should each be focused on when collecting data. These categories are:

1. Structural aspects of the environment
2. Descriptions of people present
3. Environmental involvements of those present
4. Spatial distributions of people and objects
5. Verbal behaviors
6. Tie bonds
7. Entrances and exits
8. Body language
9. Auto-involvements
10. Artifacts.

Structural aspects of the environment refers to the physical layout of the setting where observations are being done. Is this an indoor or outdoor location? How large is the setting, what are the boundaries? What is the lighting like? Is the setting clean or dirty? What is in the setting, is there furniture, are there places where people can sit, if outdoors what is the ground like? When observing and taking notes on the structural aspects of the environment the researcher is essentially de-scribing the stage upon which the action of the people present occurs. Where the setting is and what is in the setting physically establishes possibilities for what can occur, and may also inhibit or prohibit other forms of action.

Descriptions of the people present is a focus on how many people are present and what their demographic characteristics are, as well as their general appearance. If there are only two people in the entire setting this is quite different than if there are 100. A setting composed of only persons under the age of 12 will likely be extremely different than a group of only elderly persons. Whether a setting is exclusively or primarily composed of African-Americans, Latino/as or Asians is likely relevant to what occurs in the setting. Observational researchers not only want to know how many people are present and what their general characteristics are, but also evaluative descriptions of the persons present. Does everyone present look like a magazine cover model? Does only one person present have on clean clothes and shoes? Overall, the observational researcher needs to be able to describe who is present and how many persons of what general categories of persons populate the field research site.

Environmental involvements of those present refers to how the people who are present do and do not interact with the structural aspects of the environment. This means paying attention to issues such as whether or not people use the physical objects in the setting. At a party, do people actually sit on the furniture? Is the television always on, and if so do people seem to actually pay attention to it? On your eighth visit to the field setting is there a bowl of candy on the table that has not yet been touched? These types of issues can be useful to inform the researcher about norms and values of thee people in the setting, as well as what behaviors may or may not be considered deviant in the setting.

Spatial distribution of people and objects refers to where people are in the setting. Where do the men and women tend to congregate? Are there apparent pathways that people tend to use to move about in the setting? At a party, does everyone seem to spend their time in the kitchen, near the bar or just outside the bathroom door?

Verbal behavior of all persons is important to pay attention to, although in many settings it may be difficult to hear, and to hear all that everyone has to say. More important than documenting everything that everyone has to say is to identify what is talked about, and how people refer to things. If an observer's field research site is an office, yet no one ever talks about the work being done, but only about what they did the previous evening, this is important for understanding the culture of the setting. How do people talk to one another? Do people yell between their cubicles and offices? Are people polite with one another, or do people scream and swear at one another? When observing verbal behavior the important aspects to observe are the general conversational topics and the style of talking to one another.

Tie bonds are the connections and relationships between persons present in the setting. Not only is it valuable to know the number and types of persons who are present, but who interacts with whom? In an office setting, do the men and women interact and talk with one another, or do they separate into two distinct groups? Are there interactions between supervisors and those they supervise? Do they seem to interact on a friendly level, or just to give directions? When people interact, are their interactions one-way communications, or true dialogues? Tie bonds tell us about the distribution of power and values in a setting, as well as help us to understand if and how groups exist within the population of a setting.

Entrances and exits are important because in many settings they can tell us whether people are familiar with a setting, excited or anxious about being at the setting, and sometimes if they know other people in the setting. How do people come and go? When do they arrive and leave? Do people come and go alone, or with others?

Body language is the way that we use – both consciously and subconsciously – our bodies to communicate both in addition to and in the place of verbal communication. When someone is talking, do they look at the person(s) with whom they are talking? When a supervisor talks to someone she supervises, does the other person fidget, look away and cross their arms? Or, does the supervisee sit up straight, smile and look the supervisor directly in the eyes? At a party, do people gesture when talking to others, or do they sit in the corner and avoid eye contact? What type of posture do people have? What do people do with their hands while talking, or listening, or simply sitting. Many psychologists have long argued that nonverbal communication (body language) is often a more powerful form of communication than actual words. The observational researcher needs to be attuned to how people say things, and what they communicate in all forms of communication.

Auto-involvements are the actions we all do and about which we are generally not aware. These are things like twirling one's hair, biting one's nails, bouncing your legs/feet while sitting and talking to others, etc. Auto-involvements are one way that we can begin to get insights into how comfortable or nervous people are in particular settings and interactions. Although these are not the definitive pieces of information about people and their nervousness/comfort level, they are one piece of information, and often information about which the observed do not realize they are using to communicate to others.

Artifacts are the physical objects that are present in an environment and that people have on or with them. Artifacts include things like jewelry (wedding rings, having eight earrings in each ear), things we carry (a backpack or a designer purse), small objects used to decorate a setting (family pictures, posters from concerts or comic books on someone's desk) and even the unintended objects found in a setting (trash on the floor, graffiti on the walls, the backseat of a car filled to the roof with fast food wrappers). Artifacts can tell us about how a setting is used, what types of activities people do in particular places, what people value, and perhaps things about what people do when in other settings. Artifacts are everywhere in a field research setting, and they are typically one of the later points of focus for observational researchers.

Field Notes: Two Steps to Launch the Analysis

Once a researcher is aware of what to be observing in a field research setting it is necessary to think about how they will go from simply seeing/observing things to creating a record of what they see. Perhaps the biggest challenge in recording observations – taking notes – is figuring out how to get down as much as possible (since taking notes on everything really is not possible). Think about how you have handled the situation when you are in a classroom with a professor who talks very fast and rushes through information without any breaks or in-depth examples or side notes to allow you time to catch up on note taking. What can you do? Some students (and some observational researchers) find that splitting the note taking task between two or more persons can help. This way you are more certain to get down more of what is said (observed). However, this also introduces the risk of not being able to understand someone else's notes, and having people hear or see things differently, and interpret things differently.

A more productive approach for both students and observational researchers is developing a true system of notes. This means not writing everything down in full sentences, spelling everything out and getting every detail down. A true system of note taking is somewhat like learning shorthand. Notes should be just that, jottings of short words, phrases or symbols that have meaning and can later be translated and expanded into more complete, detailed explanations of what was said or observed.

Raw Field Notes

Raw field notes are the actual writings of things observed that the researcher does while in the field research setting and doing observations. In most settings, and always when researchers are using a complete participant, potential participant or participant as observer role, it is necessary and important to take notes in ways that will not be noticed by others in the setting. (If the researcher is a complete observer or observer as participant note taking can be done openly, so long as it does not become distracting for the researcher to continue to observe or the other setting participants to go about their regular activities.) Taking notes surreptitiously can be tricky, and will usually require some creative thinking. What one writes notes on needs to be small enough to not be seen by others and that can be hidden in a pocket, etc. and not seen. What one uses to write notes may need to be creatively thought about also; in some settings a regular pen might be too big to go unnoticed by others, a pencil can break and become useless, and so on.

It is also necessary to think about how and when notes are taken. If the researcher is not able to take notes openly, where will they do so? A common solution is to take a break and go into a private location, such as a restroom. However, after about the seventh time of heading into the restroom, others might become suspicious of what the researcher is doing. So, finding a place and a time where notes can be taken can be tricky. This also means that notes usually have to be taken very quickly, which means that the system of words, short phrases and symbols is even more important.

Regardless of how the researcher creatively solves the problem of when, where and how to take notes, the notes that are taken need to include a variety of issues and ideas. There are the ten general categories of types of things to be observing while in the field that were discussed above, and notes taken while observing should include reports on all of these factors. Additionally, the notes from the field should include the following types of information:

- A chronological description of events occurring in the setting
- Reflections on earlier visits to the field research site; this is the

researcher noting when things seen today are similar or different from that seen previously

- Analytic notes; these types of notes do not usually appear until the researcher has made numerous visits to the field research site and they are suggestions the researcher makes to himself about what observed events and processes may mean. Another way to think of this is that when the observer thinks they are beginning to notice a pattern or a theme, this should be noted in the notes

- Methods notes; these are simply messages and reminders the researcher writes to himself about what is and is not working well in the observing process. Is the researcher discovers that sitting in a particular place allows for especially good or especially bad views of what is occurring in the setting, these are important things to know and remember for future visits to the field research setting.

Most important, however, about the process of taking notes as an observational researcher is that the notes that one takes while actually doing observations are at the same time short but also include as much information as possible. The notes that are actually taken while in the field need to be thought of as simply jottings that will serve to spur the memory of the researcher later, and provide the foundation for developing more detailed notes.

Developed Field Notes

Developed field notes are the complete, detailed notes that the observational researcher writes from the raw field notes after leaving the field research site. Whereas raw field notes are jottings and very short, true notes about what is observed, the developed field notes take those ideas and expand on them, transforming the ideas into complete thoughts. Developed field notes use full words, often full sentences, and are the actual data that will be used to do the analysis (these are the text that will be used to identify and make arguments about the presence of patterns and themes in the actions and culture of the field site being studied).

Developed field notes should be written as soon as possible after the researcher leaves the field; this is important so that details are not lost from memory. Also, if the developed field notes are written the same day that the observation was done the raw field notes are very likely to still make sense and truly be a memory trigger for the researcher.

Generally speaking, developed field notes should be about four to five times longer than the raw field notes. Because the developed field notes are expanding on what is discussed and going into much more detail than the raw field notes, there is much more to be included in them. Although it can be tiring and tedious to expand raw field notes into developed field notes, having as much information and detail included in them is important for the final step of the process, the actual analysis of the data.

Analyzing the Data

The analysis of observational data is the process of identifying patterns and themes in the data. As discussed at the start of this chapter, qualitative research in general is about identifying patterns and themes and then constructing an argument to convince your reader that the patterns and themes you claim are in the data are in fact there. In order to do this it is necessary to have an organized and logical approach to working with data, so as to be able to distill the data down to the point where the researcher doing the analysis can look only at data (e.g. observations) about particular issues, concepts, processes, events or structures (whatever is called for by the research question) and see where patterns and themes are present.

Working with qualitative data can be exciting, invigorating and overwhelming. The actual data that is analyzed in observational studies are the developed field notes described above. These notes are the data, and they are what the researcher uses to sort through all that has been observed to find instances of particular variables. The attractive side of observational data is that it provides detailed, colorful, specific, experiential data about a wide range of events, people and structures. However, just as the process of collecting data and recording fieldnotes is a very time consuming, laborious, and admittedly occasionally frustrating experience, so can the analytic process be a long, tedious and sometimes frustrating experience. The simple fact that observational studies produce a wealth of information, all of which is in the form of typed notes and can be overwhelming to some researchers. When first sitting down to begin the analytic process the feeling is much like sitting down to study for a final exam in a course where you have taken pages upon pages of notes during every class session. It can seem that there is so much material to be reviewed and categorized and interpreted that the process may never be completed. This is why it is critically important to have a process and a plan for reducing the data to a manageable quantity.

Analyzing observational data means working with the developed field notes and culling through them to locate all instances or mentions of particular events, persons, or whatever the research question is about. This is the process known as **data reduction**. Once a note about the concept of interest is found it needs to be moved to a list of all notes about that concept. In this first step of the analysis the researcher works through the collection of developed field notes to find all mentions of a particular concept and then create a list of all of these notes.

The second step of the analysis process is to take the list of all mentions of the particular concept and re-order the list. The re-ordering is done so as to put all same or very similar mentions of the concept together. This allows the researcher to see what was more common in the observations, and essentially begin to identify patterns and themes.

The re-ordered list of selected notes about the concept being focused on is worked with again to put the flow of ideas into an order (describing a process if that is the focus of the analysis) or groups of similar events/objects/persons (if the goal is to identify types in the observations) or similarities in events and reactions to events (if the goal is to identify the culture and values of the setting). Regardless of what the specific focus is, the process is focused on reducing the large amount of data down to a logical, categorized and small-enough-to-be-manageable listing that essentially serves as the outline for what the study's findings and conclusions are.

Remember that the goal is to find patterns and themes in the data. The specific ways that the researcher develops to reduce the data from an overwhelming pile of developed field notes into an ordered list of types or steps in a process will vary according to the ways that the researcher herself finds makes sense to her. The goal and general process is the same though: the data is reduced to a manageable and orderly collection of notes about focused concepts and processes.

CONCLUSION

Qualitative data gathered through observation can provide insightful and very detailed information about human behavior, including actions of criminal justice system organizations and actors. However simplistic participant observation may seem at first glance, or however similar it may seem to be to observational strategies we use in our everyday life, it is a complicated and timely methodology which requires a great deal of organization as well as discretion on the part of the researcher. Because participant observation has not been used extensively in criminal justice research there are few specific guidelines for an investigator to follow. Additionally, as has been ex-plained above, sometimes the specific actions of the researcher are not as important as the researcher keeping the goal in mind, and finding a creative way to get to that goal.

KEY TERMS

Observation
Participant Observation
Complete Participant
Covert Research
"Going Native"
Potential Participant
Participant as Observer
Observer as Participant
Complete Observer
Raw Field Notes
Developed Field Notes
Data Reduction

REVIEW QUESTIONS

1. How does qualitative research differ from quantitative research in terms of the overall goals of each approach?
2. What is a qualitative researcher trying to identify in data that is analyzed?

3. What is participant observation? How is it related to the concept of interpretive understanding?
4. What ethical concerns have been raised about complete participation?
5. What is "going native"? Why is this considered a problem for qualitative researchers?
6. Keeping the advantages and disadvantages of each form of participation in mind, what would be a criminal justice field site appropriate for each type of role?
7. Assume you would like to be an observer as participant in your local police department. What strategies and guidelines would you use to gain entree and make your research arrangements?
8. What are the key elements of field notes? What are the important types of observations that should be included in field notes?

REFERENCES

1. Goffman, E. (1961). *Asylums.* Garden City, New York: Anchor Books.
2. Fleisher, M. S. (1995). *Beggars and thieves: Lives of urban street criminals.* Madison: University of Wisconsin Press.
3. Mead, M. (1935). *Sex and temperament in three primitive societies.* New York: Morrow.
4. Goffman, E. (1961). *Asylums.* Garden City, New York: Anchor Books.
5. Miller, J.M. (1995). Covert participant observation: Reconsidering the least used method. *Journal of Contemporary Criminal Justice*, 11, 97–105.
6. Ibid, p. 103.
7. Tewksbury, R. (2001). Acting like an insider: Studying hidden environments as a potential participant. Pp. 4–12 in J.M. Miller and R. Tewksbury, *Extreme methods: Innovative approaches to social science research.* Boston: Allyn and Bacon.
8. Lewis, P.W., and Peoples, K.D. (1978). *The Supreme Court and the criminal process – Cases and comments.* Philadelphia: W.B. Saunders.
9. Dabney, D.A., Hollinger, R.C. and Dugan, L. (2004). Who actually steals? A study of covertly observed shoplifters. *Justice Quarterly*, 21(4):693–725.
10. Van Maanen, J. (1979). Reclaiming qualitative methods for organizational research: A preface. *Administrative Science Quarterly*, 24: 520–526.

Chapter Ten

QUALITATIVE INTERVIEWS

CHAPTER OVERVIEW

Interviewing is a central skill for both persons who work in the criminal justice system and for qualitative researchers in criminal justice. Interviews are used by police officers, attorneys, court officials, correctional officers, probation and parole officers and myriad other people who work in criminal justice as a basic way to learn about clients, to know how well various parts of the criminal justice system is working at processing and treating offenders, and both what has happened and what is feared/anticipated to happen in the future. Researchers use interviews to address questions about how people, whether they be staff and administrators of criminal justice agencies, offenders, victims or the general public experience the actions of the system or perceive the system and how it operates. Interviews are used to gain in-depth understandings of how individuals experience criminal justice and how attitudes, values and behaviors are shaped by and in turn shape criminal justice system experiences.

The assumption behind using qualitative interviews as a research methodology is that those involved in a social setting have the best information about that setting and can be tapped as an important source of information. Through interviewing a researcher can discover information that cannot be observed by attempting to discover what is on an individual's mind. Interviews as a research methodology are about understanding the **subjective perspective** of the persons.

The benefits that interviews provide to providing deeper understandings are seen clearly in Robert Johnson's book, *Death Work: A*

Study of the Modern Execution Process.[1] The book is a detailed look at the process of conducting executions and the people who work in corrections who carry out executions. Johnson conducted interviews with both corrections staff and inmates on death row so as to identify the social, psychological and social psychological effects that living and working in such an environment has on individuals. He looks at how everyday life on death row impacts those who are there everyday, as well as how the more unique events of actual executions bring significant changes to the daily activities and lives of staff and inmates. Johnson brings readers face to face with both the inmates that are waiting to be executed (and fighting in the courts to avoid being executed) and the staff who work with, get to know, and have to balance personal and professional interests and responsibilities in preparing for and carrying out executions. The words of both inmates and staff are presented throughout the book to show the true feelings of both populations on death row. These words are often chilling, and definitely show the death row experience to be very complex, emotional and full of contradictions.

Because interviews provide data that highlights the subjective experience of research subjects, the types of research questions that are appropriate for a qualitative interview methodology are different than the types of research questions that are pursued with other data collection approaches. Qualitative interviews are appropriate for asking questions that seek to uncover how people experience certain events or statuses. Interviews can be useful for uncovering information about events and behaviors, but only if the researcher is trying to understand how individuals go about doing and conducting particular behaviors. Additionally, understanding attitudes and values that people have can also be effectively studied with interviews. Finally, researchers can also use qualitative interviews to study how individuals progress through a process or procedure.

Interviews are not appropriate data collection methodologies for questions about why things happen, or what the causes of any types of behaviors are. Interviews are also not the correct methodology to use for trying to determine how many times something occurs, how certain behaviors or events are distributed in a population or what the consequences of a particular behavior or event is.

TYPES OF INTERVIEWS

When a researcher talks about doing a qualitative interview, there is a range of types of conversations to which he may be referring. Interviews vary widely in their degree of formality, their degree of structure and even in the number of persons being interviewed. In this section the four basic approaches to interviewing, structured interviewed, semi-structured interviews, unstructured interviews, and elite interviews will be discussed. Focus group interviews, where a researcher gathers information from a small group of persons at one time, will be discussed later in this chapter.

Structured Interviews

A **structured interview** is the most formal and most rigid approach to interviewing. Sometimes structured interviews are referred to as "verbal questionnaires" because the idea is that every person interviewed for a project is asked the exact same questions, in the exact same order, in the exact same ways. In this way structured interviews are the most similar form of interview to quantitative research in that they seek to get comparable data from every respondent who is interviewed.

Structured interviews, in contrast to all of the other forms of qualitative interviews may use some close-ended questions. Structured interviews are also likely to have the most questions that are asked. Because the format is to have all interviewees answer the same questions, it may be possible to look at the data using descriptive statistics. If this is a goal of the project then using closed-ended questions may be desirable.

Regardless of the fact that the structured interview uses a standardized pattern of questions for all persons interviewed for a study, it is still important for the interviewer to strive to develop **rapport** with the people he is interviewing. Rapport simply means developing a sense of a relationship and a connection with the individual. When someone is comfortable with the person who is asking them questions they are more likely to provide more complete answers, to be honest and to invest more time and energy into providing the researcher with the information that he needs for his research project.

A Structured Interview Guide

Elderly Jail Inmates and The Incarceration Experience

How old are you?

Are you married, single and never married, divorced or separated, or a widow/widower?

Do you have any children?

    If yes, how many and how are they?

What is the highest level of education you completed?

With whom do you live when you are not in jail?

How many total times have you been in jail?

How many total times have you been in prison?

When did you come to jail this time?

    What are the charges against you?

    Have you been convicted, or are you awaiting trial?

Describe what a typical day is like for you in jail.

Do you participate in any programs?

    If yes, which programs?

On a typical day in this jail, with whom do you spend your time and talk?

    Which of these people do you spend the most time with? Why?

How do you think your experience as an older inmate in jail compares to that of the younger inmates?

How do the correctional officers treat you here?

    Do you feel that you are treated with respect?

    What differences do you see in how you are treated by the male and female staff?

Do you feel safe in this jail?

If you had a choice, would you prefer to be in a special housing unit for only older inmates? Why or why not?

Semi-Structured Interviews

Semi-structured interviews are a combination of the researcher asking a set series of questions to an interviewee and the interaction being a conversation. Whereas the structured interview involves the researcher asking a pre-determined list of questions, in the same order and (presumably) in the same way to everyone that is interviewed for a project, this is not the way that semi-structured interviews are conducted. Instead, the semi-structured interview is premised on the idea that interviews should be comfortable situations in which the person(s) being interviewed has the opportunity to explain the things they are being asked about in their own words, and in the way that they are most comfortable.

The semi-structured interview attempts to strike a balance between the interview being a formal event where the interviewer fires questions at the interviewee who then provides fairly short and direct answers and a loose, wandering but very comfortable and "natural" conversation. The semi-structured interview does put a priority on obtaining answers to a set of questions the researcher pre-determines to be important, but getting these answers is done in a way that allows the interviewee to feel that they are actually talking with, not responding to, someone who is interested in them and their experience.

A Semi-Structured Interview Guide

Prisons Wardens' Job Stress

How long have you worked in corrections, and in what jobs?
How is being warden different than your previous jobs in corrections?
How is the job of warden similar and different than what you expected it to be?
What are your goals for your prison?
   How are you working to achieve these goals?
Describe what you do in a typical day
   Approximately what percent of your days fit this typical scenario?
What are the biggest challenges of the job of warden?
What do you find are the rewards of being a warden?
What qualities are important for being successful in your job?
   Why?
What aspects of your job cause you the most stress?
   Why?
What advice would you give to someone about to take over your job?
   Why?

Unstructured Interviews

Unstructured interviews when done well look very much like a regular conversation. An unstructured interview involves the researcher having a conversation with an interviewee and simply making sure that the conversation includes a set of specific topics. The researcher is not concerned with how questions are asked, the order they are asked, or anything else to make the interview consistent with the other interviews in a project. The goal is simply to elicit information about a set of topics or issues.

If you were to see a researcher conducting an unstructured interview it would most likely look very much like two people having a conversation, although one person seemed to do most of the talking. The goal for the researcher in an unstructured interview is to get the interviewee to talk about the topic of the research question, and to do so in the way that the interviewee is most comfortable. This means that the interviewee largely explains something to the interviewer, constructing their answer as they go and they wish, emphasizing what they see as important and organizing the story in their own way. The researcher has an interview guide that she uses in this type of interview, but it is very short and basically is a list of topics and issues about the research question that the researcher wants to make sure to cover.

The process of the unstructured interview involves the researcher explaining to the interviewee what they are interested in, and then asking one or two very general questions about the topic, and encouraging the interviewee to talk and explain. The interviewer should say very little in the unstructured interview, with most of their comments or participation being encouragement to the interviewee to continue talking, asking for clarification (probing) and offering supportive comments ("okay," "I see," "yes, I understand now") to demonstrate that they are involved and invested in the conversation.

The overall goal of the unstructured interview is to get the interviewee's subjective experience, in their own words, and to allow them to emphasize what they see as important. The process is a guided conversation, where the interviewer directs the interviewee to general areas of discussion about the topic, and does not restrict the conversation to specific questions or details that they believe are important.

Unstructured Interview Guide

Robbery Victims & Experiences with Prosecutors

When, where and how were you robbed?
How has your case progressed through the criminal justice system? Where is it now?
What types of interactions did you have with the prosecutor in your case?
What did you like and not like about how the prosecutor handled your case?

Elite Interviewing

A fourth, and specialized, form of interviewing is **elite interviewing**. In elite interviewing the investigator allows, if not en-courages, the respondent to teach him or her about the situation, or to seemingly take the lead in structuring the interview. The interview is less standardized, and more exploratory than nonelite interviews. In the elite interview, not all persons are equal. In fact, the information from the respondent in an elite interview is used for reinterpretation, reassessment, and reformulation of research data and information.

The fundamental principle to keep in mind is that the interview should provide a structure in which the respondents can express their own feelings and experiences in their own terms. The method of interviewing must meet the needs of the respondent as well as research needs. If respondents are not given a comfortable framework for response, the information gathered through the interviews will not be of good quality or quantity. Two conventions govern the role of the interviewer in his or her attempt to elicit information from respondents: equality and comparability. The interview situation must be one in which the interviewer and respondent perceive of each as equal in status for the duration of the interview. The structure must also minimize the specific, concrete circumstances of the exchange so that each interview is similar to another. The intrusion of personalities must be minimized.

Lastly, the question of who and how many to interview remains. Obviously, the number of respondents will also be determined by the nature of the information sought. For example, if a researcher is interested in a warden's interpretation of an incident of collective violence in his or her institution, an interview with a warden may be sufficient. However, if the objective is to obtain the reaction of the average inmate in the institution to the riot then interviews with several inmates may be necessary to ensure representativeness and generalizability.

Who to interview will be determined by the type of information sought as well as time, money, and the availability of subjects. Subjects may be interviewed as **informants** or **respondents**. Informants are viewed as surrogate observers, respondents are interviewed when information on the individual subject is of interest. In either case, care must be taken to consider the subject's role in the social setting and how that role will affect their responses.

CONDUCTING INTERVIEWS

While conducting an interview there are many tasks that a researcher is engaged in beyond simply asking questions of the interviewee. While conducting an interview a researcher is engaged in as many as six types of tasks that all must be done simultaneously. First, there is the task of asking questions and responding – participating in the conversation as it occurs.

Second, as the interviewer is listening she needs to be asking herself whether what the interviewee is saying is sufficiently detailed to help her to answer her research questions. If it is, then she need not do anything except continue to listen and participate in the conversation. If what the interviewee is saying is related to the research question being investigated, but not completely clear and thoroughly detailed, the interviewer needs to consider how to ask the interviewee to expand and elaborate on his answers. These follow-up questions are referred to as **probes** by researchers. Probes are the questions that are asked by interviewers to solicit more and more detailed information about topics that are discussed by interviewees.

A third task that all interviewers need to be thinking about is where the conversation is going, and how to direct the conversation in the desired direction. While the interviewer will have an interview guide that may suggest exactly what a next question will be (a structured interview guide), there is a need to think about what the interviewee is saying, and how this information may or may not naturally lead to what the next planned topic/question is.

Fourth, the interviewer needs to be attending to her nonverbal communications that she is giving off as she listens, probes responses and actively thinks about how and where to direct the conversation next. Nonverbal communications are often actions and reactions we do that we do not think about, and often are not aware of. However, so as to ensure that the interview is productive and the interviewee is comfortable, interviewers need to pay attention to their posture, facial expressions, where they look and how they do or do not seem interested and involved in the conversation.

A fifth task, which is parallel to the task of paying attention to one's own nonverbal communication is to pay attention to the nonverbal communication of the interviewee. Basic psychology tells us that when people are uncomfortable or not being fully truthful they typically act differently. This may involve looking away from someone with whom they are talking, fidgeting, licking the lips, pulling at one's hair, ears or clothing, or anything else that is designed to distract either the person who is speaking or the person to whom the less-than-fully-truthful statements are being told. If an interviewer identifies that an intervie-wee is uncomfortable or perhaps not being fully honest, she needs to think about whether it would be best to change the topic of conversation, probe for more information, or simply make a mental note of the reaction and later consider this information when assessing the data from the interview.

Sixth, the interviewer needs to pay attention to the time, other activities in the setting and the tape recorder being used. Regardless of how interesting and engaged someone may be in the process of being interviewed, almost everyone has commitments and responsibilities that take their time, and may mean that will have to leave the interview at a certain time. If an interviewer realizes that the interview is taking longer than anticipated she needs to consider how to either move the conversation more quickly or mentally re-organize her interview guide so as to be sure to get to the most important questions in the interview. Additionally, if the interview is being done in a location where other persons might be able to hear what is being discussed, it is important to control the volume of one's voice and to pace the conversation in such a way as to minimize the opportunities for others to overhear what is being discussed. This is especially important when interviews are conducted at someone's place of work, around family members or anyone else who might have a reason to judge an interviewee based on what they are telling the interviewer. Finally, tape recorders need to be watched so that they do not run out of tape, have batteries run low or otherwise malfunction. If the conversation is not recorded, the interview in all likelihood will provide very, very little useful data.

Interviews with Active Criminals

As an example of the many levels of thinking and working that researchers using interviews have to attend to is the work of Bruce Jacobs who did a major study based on interviews with 54 active, street-level crack dealers.[2] In this study Jacobs made contact with dealers by first simply spending time in an area of the city where many street-level drug dealers operated, and after several months of allowing himself to be seen by dealers, he approached them and told them that he was a researcher and would like to talk to them. At first no one believed that he was not a law enforcement officer, but when he offered to pay each individual for their time, they did consent to interviews. Once he proved to a handful of dealers that he was not a police officer and really was willing to pay for the opportunity to talk to the dealers, they spread the word to others, who then contacted him and agreed to do interviews also.

Interviews with persons actively involved in criminal activity are not a common occurrence in criminal justice research, because it is very difficult to establish credibility with offenders and overcome their fears that the researcher is an undercover law enforcement officer. Jacobs managed to get accepted by street-level crack dealers by investing a lengthy period of time of simply being present in the field and eventually getting lucky and having a handful of dealers agree to be interviewed, if he paid them.

The project proved to be extremely informative. Jacobs explores issues of why dealers work in this high risk and physically dangerous occupation, what dealers associate with law enforcement and how they work to avoid being arrested, and how dealers do and do not cooperate and compete with one another. The social organization of the profession is explored, and provides outsiders (including law enforcement officials) with insights into what is and is not likely to be effective in terms of policing street-level drug dealing. It is only through the subjective experiences of drug dealers that such information could be obtained.

Although it may be difficult to get access to do interviews with active street-level drug dealers (or any types of criminal offenders), this is also the only way to get to this type of information. Picture what would likely have happened if Jacobs had approached dealers on the street with a stack of surveys instead of asking them to talk to him. What about if he had continued simply hanging out in the areas where the dealers worked but had done an observational study and taken notes on what he observed? Or, if Jacobs had decided that instead of learning about how street-level dealers effectively did avoid being arrested, what if he had interviewed drug dealers in jail or prison, who had been arrested? Would his data have been the same? Would it have been as useful as what he was able to get by interviewing "successful" drug dealers?

Transcribing

Once an interview is completed the raw data of the audio recording needs to be transformed into a form that is usable in the analysis stage. In order to transform the interview into a useable form for analysis it is necessary to **transcribe** the audiotape interview so that you can have a printed record of the conversation. The process of transcribing is simply taking an audio recording and typing out the conversation. When transcribing is done by simply listening to the audio recordings of an interview and then typing it out it is important to plan for significant time to get the task done. An experienced and highly skilled transcriptionist can usually transcribe a one hour interview in about two hours. Most researchers find that it takes them anywhere from three to five times longer than the interview to do the transcribing.

There are several ways to do this. A transcribing machine is an audio player that can be controlled with a foot pedal (much like the gas and brake pedals of a car). The transcriptionist turns on the tape, and uses the foot pedals to control the forward playing, stopping and rewinding (so to re-hear portions of the conversation). As the audio plays, the transcriptionist types it out. There are also computer programs that assist in the playing back of the audio so that the speed is controlled automatically and commonly used words are entered into the text. Other technology uses voice recognition to actually type out the transcript as the audio recording plays. While this seems like a much more desirable approach that would save significant amounts of time, most commercially available voice recognition software does not do a very thorough or accurate job of producing a text (and therefore the researcher needs to clean the file and check for errors).

Also, the transcribing process allows the researcher to listen to the entire interview again, focusing on the responses of the interviewee (recall that during the actual interview the interviewer needed to be attending to many levels of awareness). In this way the researcher can begin to listen for patterns and themes in the data, which can inform the actual data analysis stage.

DATA ANALYSIS

The analysis of qualitative interview data is a multi-stage process that works with the transcripts of all of the interviews conducted for a project and works through a data reduction process (as discussed in Chapter Nine). The goal of the data reduction process is to take the many hours of transcripts of conversations and work through a process to identify all of the content related to particular topics (variables) and issues (research questions) and reduce this to a focused record that can be categorized and ordered in ways that will allow the researcher to easily identify and describe the patterns and themes present in the data.

The process of analysis of interview data, the data reduction process, involves seven important stages/tasks beyond the transcribing of the interviews.

1. Developing a coding scheme
2. Initial coding of transcripts
3. Collecting similarly coded passages from transcripts
4. Secondary coding
5. Ordering concepts
6. Outlining concepts
7. Writing the final report

Developing a Coding Scheme

Once all interviews are transcribed the researcher needs to go back to the original research questions that gave rise to the study and identify what specific information (e.g. variables) is needed to get a more complete understanding of the issues in the research question. Once the researcher has identified these issues it is necessary to think about whether each issue can be further broken down (or specified) into more precise, specific concepts, experiences, etc. It is these more precise, specific concepts that the researcher lists along with each research question, and that serve as the guide for what the researcher will look for in the collection of transcribed interviews. These identified concepts are the content that the researcher will use to guide a careful reading of the interviews in step #2.

Initial Coding of Transcripts

After identifying the precise, specific concepts that will inform the researcher about each research question the next task is to take those codes and carefully read each interview transcript looking for instances of interviewees mentioning that concept, event, etc. (that which the code represents).

When doing the coding process it is important to look for no more than three codes at a time. Although it may be tempting for the researcher to look for everything in which he is interested in one reading of the transcripts, this is a very ineffective and inefficient way to work with interview data. When looking for more than three types of specific information at one time it is extremely likely that information will be missed, and the coding will be incomplete. This, in turn, means that the analysis is incomplete, and the final product from the research project will be flawed (invalid and unreliable).

When coding, the researcher carefully reads through all transcripts looking for comments that pertain to the concept for which he is currently coding. When a statement is found in a transcript that addresses the coded for concept it needs to be marked both in the text and a notation made in the margin of the transcript noting what concept the statement addresses. When marking the actual statement in the text it is best to underline the statement (ideally in color) and not highlight. If a statement actually addresses more than one concept for which the researcher is coding and the first time that the statement is identified as pertaining to a code it is highlighted, this means the second time it is found to pertain to a (different) concept, it cannot be marked independently. (Once a sentence is highlighted it cannot be highlighted in a different color. If you use yellow highlighter to note the first concept for which you are coding, and later use blue to highlight for a concept, when you mark blue over yellow you will end up with green. And, green may or may not be the color you are using when coding for a third concept. Regardless, the statement is no longer noted as pertaining to either of the first two concepts/codes.)

The coding process is simply going through the entire collection of transcripts and marking all statements that pertain to a particular concept (which is marked in the transcript with a notation or code).

Collecting Similarly Coded Passages from Transcripts

The third phase of the analytic process is begun once all transcripts are coded for all concepts. In this third stage the data is truly reduced to a smaller collection of statements. The goal in this third phase is to go back through all of the transcripts and collect into a list all of the statements found that pertain to a particular concept/code. Separate lists are made for each concept/code. The movement of the coded statements can be done either by going back into the word processing file of the transcripts and marking and copying the statements into a list in a separate file, or simply retyping the coded statements into a new file. It does not matter how this is actually done, so long as the end product is a listing of all statements from all interviewees that have been coded as related to each important concept.

Secondary Coding

After creating the list of all statements found in the interview transcripts coded for particular concepts the next step is to take those lists and review each statement. When reviewing each statement the researcher is looking to identify what the core idea or focus is of the statement. Whatever is the central meaning of the statement is then marked (in the margins of the list?) for each statement. This step of the process is identifying what the central meaning of the comments are that were offered by interviewees related to the information that informs the research questions.

Ordering the Concepts

After identifying the core meaning of each coded statement the quotations should be reordered, creating subcategories of quotes that have identical or similar meanings. This is the idea of further reducing the data to a collection of concepts and variations on each concept that tell us about how a process works or what the population being studied thinks or perceives about the topic being studied.

Outlining Concepts

After creating the subcategories that group all quotations of similar meaning together the researcher next looks at the "list" of meanings identified and thinks about what would be a logical and meaningful way to discuss these issues. What is the order or flow of these values on the variables (e.g., the concept that was coded for) that make sense and best explain either the process being studied or the dimensions of the subjective way this population experiences whatever it is that is the focus of the study? The subcategories at this point should be moved in the list to reflect this logical order. This re-ordered list of meanings/ideas/concepts/categories then serves as the outline for the order of ideas that will be discussed in the final report when the findings of the study (e.g., the answer to the research question) are presented.

Writing the Final Report

Using the outline of the logical order of meanings/ideas/concepts/categories put together in the previous stage, in the final stage of the process of analysis of interview data the researcher constructs and presents his conclusions about the research question. Remember that the findings of a qualitative research study are essentially an argument that the researcher puts forth in which he claims that based on the data he collected, the answer to the research question is X (whatever his findings are). The outline of the quotations that was developed in phase six is useful for providing the researcher quotes that are available for him to insert into the discussion as illustrations of the concepts he discusses. Remember also that the actual data from a qualitative study (in this case the quotes from the persons who were interviewed) are presented only as support for the argument that the researcher makes. The quotes are used, just as actual observations are used in writing the final report of an observation study, to illustrate or bring to life the ideas that the researcher describes in his own words.

Computerized Interview Coding and Analysis

The data analysis process described above is premised on the idea of doing the analysis by hand and actually working with printed versions of transcripts and the researcher doing multiple readings of each transcript to identify and mark statements pertaining to concepts for which he is coding. An alternative way to do the very time-consuming second and third phases of the process (initial coding of transcripts and collecting similarly coded passages form transcripts) is to use one of the many computer software programs available for qualitative data analysis.

When using these programs it is necessary to keep in mind that they are only doing these two phases of the process. The central idea of all of these software programs is that the researcher can identify a set of key words and/or phrases that the program will find and mark in a computer file of the transcript. Most of the programs will also automatically create the lists of similarly coded passages as well. What all of these computer programs boil down to is a way of more quickly searching transcripts for particular passages containing researcher-identified and programmed key words and phrases.

When using computerized analysis of transcripts the researcher still has to identify what the codes will be, and must still do the thinking work involved in phases four through seven. While the process of searching the transcripts with a software program is obviously must faster than reading through the transcripts multiple times, there is also a potential downside to using these computer programs. The researcher who does the coding by hand reads the transcripts and is focused on what the meanings of interviewees' statements are, not just what the individual words and phrases are that they speak. When using one of the software programs meaning is not necessarily being searched, but only selected key words and phrases that the researcher tells the program to seek out. This means that it is highly likely that some statements spoken by interviewees which in actuality do pertain to a particular concept are not going to be identified and coded, because the interviewee used different words to express an idea, words not thought of by the researcher to include in the search.

Computerized interview analysis is a more efficient way to work with qualitative interview data, but it may not be as accurate and complete as the "old fashioned way." However, especially in projects where a large number of interviews (50 or more) is involved, it may not be feasible to do analysis by hand. In these types of situations investment in one of the many commercially available software packages may be the best move.

FOCUS GROUP INTERVIEWS

A different approach to interviewing, where a researcher interviews a group of people at one time is the **focus group**. This approach, originated and used most frequently by professionals in marketing, is designed to solicit input from multiple persons while also encouraging the individuals participating to listen to and respond to one another. The focus group was developed following World War II as a way for radio programmers to get feedback on programs that they were producing.[3] While the focus group is often thought of as a group interview, when done correctly and well it is actually much more than just an interviewer eliciting responses from multiple interviewees. A well-run focus group will look more like a group conversation, in which all persons involved talk with (not at or to) all of the other group members.

Research endeavors that draw on focus group data may use anywhere from a single focus group to several dozen, depending on the research question being addressed and the population being studied. When focus groups are used as part of an evaluation of a particular program or organization, there are often very few groups conducted, simply because the population being studied is not very large. In other instances there is likely to be many focus groups conducted. The actual number of groups that are conducted will vary, and is a function of sampling and the degree of diversity of the population being studied.

Focus groups are most appropriate for research questions that are primarily about how an organization or program operates, or to identify how a particular population perceives some phenomena. Focus groups are inappropriate for studying individual activities, any type of deviant behavior, any research questions that require any type of personal information or anything that is likely to be controversial. The goals of the focus group interview is to get a group of people both talking and thinking about how they feel about or perceive something, therefore the topic of the discussion needs to be something about which people are comfortable sharing their honest opinions and experiences with others.

Focus groups ideally should have between 7 and 12 people in them.[4] Most researchers who use the focus group methodology believe that it is beneficial to have participants in a focus group not know one another. When a group of people get together who already have a relationship there is likely to be a set of established roles (including leadership) among the individuals, and this will structure the way that the focus group operates. Also, if people in a focus group already have a relationship with one another they are less likely to say things that may contradict or disagree with what others say. This would mean that the data being derived from the focus group may not be valid and reliable.

Two of the authors used focus groups in a study of the perceptions public housing residents held of violence, safety and police in a mid-sized southern city.[5] The larger project looked to identify ways that public housing authorities and local law enforcement officials could enhance the safety of citizens and combat rampant drug trafficking in the public housing complexes of the community. A series of seven focus groups were conducted with residents of public housing communities, in addition to surveys administered door to door to a 10% sample of residents in the communities being studied. While the surveys showed what percent of the residents reported that they had called the police in the last year, how frequently they saw police patrol in their community, how satisfied they were with police services, and whether they had personally participated in any of four crime prevention activities in the community, these data did not provide much information for development of new programs, initiatives or policies.

However, the focus group interviews revealed residents had a "strong sense of fear" and attributed their fears, anxieties and limitations on their out of home activities to a variety of active forms of intimidation practiced by the drug dealers operating in their neighborhoods. Focus groups also elicited a significant amount of data regarding residents' perceptions of and interactions with local law enforcement officials. While the survey data showed that 37% of residents had called the police for assistance in the previous year, the focus group data showed that residents were highly frustrated with the police response, and felt that officers acted aloof, refused to stop when waved down by residents, would not leave their vehicles for conversations, and treated residents with little or no apparent respect. . . . Officers did not take their complaints seriously. As a result, residents did not envision the police as their allies for addressing local safety and crime problems.[6] These detailed views of the police and how residents subjectively experienced their interactions with the police could not have been gained through a survey methodology. In order for a survey to uncover such information the researchers would have had to know to ask whether these were the experiences the residents had. That is unrealistic to expect. However, by engaging the residents of the public housing communities in conversations about their neighborhoods and whether or not the residents felt safe there, these patterns and themes emerged from the discussions. As a result, the researchers, public housing authority officials and local law enforcement officials were provided with a fairly thorough understanding of whether and why residents did or not feel safe. As a result, all three were able to identify and recommend changes for enhancing the safety (and overall quality of life) for these residents.

Conducting a Focus Group Study

The actual process of conducting a focus group study can be thought of as composed of three broad phases, with a number of decisions and tasks that need to be completed during each phase.[7] The three phases of a focus group study are:

1. Conceptualization
2. Interview
3. Analysis and Reporting

Conceptualization Phase

The conceptualization phase is when the goal (or, research question) for the project is identified, as well as determining who can provide the data to address the research question. Identifying the population of interest, and the sample, can be a time consuming task (as discussed in Chapter Six), but is a critical step to ensure that the research question can actually be answered.

The conceptualization phase also includes the actual planning for the focus group. This means identifying who will conduct the group, where it will occur, how long will be planned for it, how individuals will be contacted and invited to participate, what will be the topics and questions posed to the group for discussion, and what type of budget will be needed for the project. Questions of where the focus group will be held are important. As discussed in the chapter on observational research, the physical characteristics of a setting can have important influences on actions and interactions in that setting. Focus groups should be held in settings with minimal distractions, where the group can sit comfortably and all see and hear one another easily. Typically focus groups are done with people either sitting in a circle or around a conference table. This allows all persons to see one another and minimizes the establishment of natural leaders in the conversation. Most focus groups will be planned for no longer than one hour in length. When a group goes longer than one hour people often lose their focus and interest, and the quality of the discussion deteriorates significantly. This means that the planning of topics and questions for discussion need to be done so as to ensure that all of the important issues are addressed in the available time, and that the most important questions/topics are addressed early in the time period.

Interview Phase

The interview phase of a focus group project involves the development of the questions/topics for discussion and the actual conduct of the focus group(s).

When developing the questions/topics it is important for the researcher to think about how questions may be perceived and interpreted by a (likely) diverse group of people, and how what is posed to the group will or will not encourage actual discussion among the group members. As a general rule of thumb, no more than five or six questions should be included in the focus group.

Questions asked in focus groups should be asked in a way that encourages discussion and elaboration, not specific answers. Questions such as "What do you think about the substance abuse program you're enrolled in?" or "What are the things you like about working in this police department?" or "What is it about the program that really makes a difference for the clients?" are questions that will encourage individuals to speak, and very likely promote comments from other group members when individuals offer responses. At the very least, all questions asked in focus groups must be **open-ended questions**. And, questions should always be posed to the group as a whole, not asked directly of individuals (except for any probes that are necessary to clarify a group member's comments).

When actually conducting the focus group it is important to have a team of two researchers working. The team approach has several benefits that help make sure that the focus group runs smoothly and is productive. These benefits include making sure that the researcher actually leading the group discussion can focus on the discussion and not be distracted by having to take notes, watch a tape recorder or manage logistics such as responding to late arriving group members, etc. When the team approach is used the leader of the discussion participates fully in the discussion, and is both engaged in the current conversation and mentally planning how and where to move the discussion as it progresses and how to encourage full participation by all members. The second researcher, sometimes referred to as the back-up role, handles the logistical issues, and is present to assist the lead researcher in whatever ways may be necessary. This may include watching the group members and helping the leader by noting for her if and when particular group members seem to react strongly to an issue and should be encouraged to speak up.

The interviewer in a well run focus group should actually say very little. The interviewer provides the basic structure and topic for the group discussion, and may redirect the conversation if it begins to stray from the original topic and purpose, and the interviewer may need to do some intervention to be sure no individuals either dominate or get closed out of the conversation. At no time, however, should a focus group be conducted in which the interviewer asks questions and simply asks each individual to provide him with an answer. Rather, the interviewer should get the conversation started and encourage individuals to consider and respond to the comments and contributions of other group members.

The leader of the focus group needs to engage in all of the active listening tasks that interviewers in one-on-one interviews do, and they need to react and respond to comments offered by group members in supportive and encouraging ways. One common mistake made by inexperienced focus group leaders is to verbally respond to all comments offered by group members. While on the surface this may appear to be supportive and appropriate what this does is establish a pattern of individual responses, and discourages other group members from speaking in response or support of comments from others. Focus group leaders need to react and respond to comments offered with nonverbal communications, or very short supportive utterances ("I see," or "very good" or "interesting").

The actual process of flow of a focus group needs to be planned as thoroughly as possible, although the researcher needs to be aware that discussions can go in many different directions, and she needs to be ready and able to redirect conversations if they stray from the data needed for addressing her research question. Typically a focus group session will open with a welcome and brief explanation of the purpose of the group, and a brief list of ground rules (being respectful of others, not talking over one another, not dominating the conversation, etc.).

Typically a first question or discussion topic will be used as an icebreaker; this is a topic that is designed to be as non-threatening as possible, but to get people talking. If someone speaks in response to the first question or topic of a focus group discussion they are much more likely to speak again later. Individuals who sit back quietly can be difficult to bring out and get to contribute in meaningful ways, so it is important to get all of the group members in the swing of the discussion early. Icebreaker topics are often something like "How long and where in the institution have you worked here at Friendly Prison?" or "What do you think is the best characteristic of this neighborhood where you live?" While the icebreaker question may produce some interesting general insights, it typically does not yield data directly informing the research question. Responses to it can, however, tell the researcher some background about the group members and how they may react to the real questions of the discussion.

Focus group leaders need to carefully watch the group dynamics, and do their best to manage the group interactions. Encouraging quiet or shy group members to talk, first with nonverbal encouragement and if necessary perhaps asking something similar to, "Mary, what do you think about all of this?" What can be more damaging to a focus group than quiet and reserved participants, however, are group members who dominate conversations, and leave little opportunity for others to participate. Also likely to be damaging for the focus group are group members who present themselves as experts and either speak in such a strongly authoritative way as to discourage others from voicing alternative views or those who actively shut others down. When such individuals are identified in a focus group (and they are present in just about all focus groups) it is the responsibility of the group leader to (nicely and politely) discourage ongoing participation from these individuals and to encourage others to participate. This can be done by avoiding eye contact, not providing supportive utterances to these members comments or when such efforts fail, offering comments such as "Okay, thank you Joe. Now, I really want to hear from some others on this issue." Managing the group dynamics can require a great deal of energy and focus, and it is not always easily accomplished.

Analysis and Reporting

Once all of the focus groups are completed the audio recordings need to be transcribed. Just as with one-on-one interviews, the actual data used for analysis is the set of transcripts of the groups (interviews). Analysis of the transcripts is conducted the same way with focus group data as it is with one-on-one interview transcripts. The researcher needs to engage in the process of data reduction and coding of the data, so as to cull the large amount of statements (e.g. the data about each issue) down to a manageable and organized set of statements addressing each issue of interest for the research question(s) and the various perspectives of the interviewed persons on those issues.

As with all qualitative data analysis, the goal is to identify patterns and themes in the data. The way that research questions are answered and addressed in qualitative research is to identify commonalities in perspective, experience or understanding or explanations of processes experienced by individuals. Finding commonalities means finding recurring instances of a perspective, experience or understanding (a pattern) or general similarities in such issues (a theme) that help consumers of the research to understand either how some process operates or what it is like to be in the shoes of some type of person.

The reporting of the findings from a focus group study is very similar to the reporting of any qualitative research. The report (whether it be a simple summary for an agency or a formal research article) needs to highlight what the research questions were that gave rise to the project, and what the identified patterns and themes are. As is the case with reporting findings from one-on-one interview studies, illustrative quotes should be used to help highlight the patterns and themes. However, also like the case with one-on-one interview findings reporting, the quotes should never be left to stand on their own. It is the responsibility of the researcher to tell the consumer/reader what the patterns and themes are, and to use selected quotes as a way of illustrating or bringing life to the reported patterns and themes.

CONCLUSION

Criminal justice researchers use qualitative interviews when they are interested in identifying and understanding the ways that individuals (whether they are staff, clients or the general public) understand and experience the processes of the criminal justice system. Interviews are unique in that they provide perhaps the greatest depth of understandings of any methodological approach, and the data that are generated by interviews focus on the subjective experiences of persons from whom data is collected.

There are a number of different structures that interviews can take, and the degree of formality that characterizes interviews ranges widely as well. Interviewing is a very time consuming methodology, with both the actual data collection process and the analysis of data processes taking significant amounts of time. It is important to keep in mind that not only are the findings produced by a qualitative interview study focused on the subjective experiences of individuals from whom data is collected, but so too do the processes of collecting and analyzing data in this approach require flexibility and the ability of the researcher to adjust to unanticipated events and information.

Focus groups are one specialized kind of interviewing approach where researchers interested in identifying how some particular process, program or initiative/intervention is perceived by people puts together a group of between 7 and 12 persons to discuss the topic being studied. The focus group interview is really more of a guided group discussion than it is a formal interview. Usually used in evaluation research the focus group interview follows many of the same procedures of a one-on-one interview, but the structure of the event is very different. Analytically, however, focus group data is worked with in essentially the same ways as one-on-one data.

KEY TERMS

Subjective perspective
Structured interview
Rapport
Semi-structured interview
Unstructured interview
Elite interviewing
Informants
Respondents
Probes
Transcribe
Focus group
Open-ended questions

REVIEW QUESTIONS

1. How does qualitative research differ in focus and goals from quantitative research?
2. What are the three different types of interviews and how are they the same and different?

3. What type of qualitative interview is best to use for a study that is a first look at an issue that has not been studied previously?
4. How does a researcher analyze the data from a qualitative interview project?
5. What types of research questions are most appropriate for a focus group methodology?
6. What are the roles of the research team in conducting a focus group?
7. How do the ways that researchers ask questions in a focus group differ from how they ask questions in a one-on-one interview?

REFERENCES

1. Johnson, R. (1998). *Death work: A study of the modern execution process* (2nd ed.). Belmont, CA, Wadsworth.
2. Jacobs, B. A. (1999). *Dealing crack: The social world of streetcorner selling.* Boston, Northeastern University Press.
3. Stewart, D.W., and Shamdasani, P.N. (1990). *Focus groups: Theory and practice.* Applied Social Research Methods Series, Vol. 20. Newbury Park, CA, Sage Publications.
4. Krueger, R.A. (1988). *Focus groups: A practical guide for applied research.* Newbury Park, CA, Sage Publications.
5. Walsh, W.F., Vito, G.F., Tewksbury, R., and Wilson, G.P. (2000). Fighting back in Bright Leaf: Community policing and drug trafficking in public housing. *American Journal of Criminal Justice,* 25(1): 77–92.
6. Ibid.
7. Krueger, R.A. (1988). *Focus groups: A practical guide for applied research.* Newbury Park, CA, Sage Publications.

Chapter Eleven

EVALUATION RESEARCH IN CRIMINAL JUSTICE

CHAPTER OVERVIEW

This chapter introduces the fundamentals of evaluation research, also known as program evaluation. Evaluation research typically involves a wide variety of research techniques. Since evaluation research takes place in the real world, this methodology brings forth a whole set of unique problems and constraints that must be carefully considered. In recent years, evaluation research has assumed a new importance. For example, the Government Performance and Results Act of 1993 requires Federal agencies to determine annual performance targets and to report on results of their efforts to attain them. Total Quality Management approaches require specification of program standards to assess service quality and to identify steps to obtain measurable improvements.[1]

Evaluation research is a systematic way to establish the value and impact of a program or policy. It is designed to inform decision making by determining:

- The cost effectiveness of a program – Should it continue to be funded?
- To continue a program or modify its operation.
- To discontinue a program entirely.

In criminal justice, "evidence based" programs are becoming more common. Typically, they use evaluation research results to determine if programs are efficient, effective and thus should be implemented in other places. This type of research can be used to implement change and improve programs while holding administrators accountable for performance.[2] Evaluation research results can help decision makers when resources are scarce and choices must be made between competing programs and policies. In fact, evaluation research originated as a method for demonstrating to legislatures and other authorities that a program was operating in the prescribed manner – with both effectiveness and efficiency. Therefore, the purpose of evaluation is to inform decisions. It improves our confidence about decisions regarding the future of the program by helping decision makers to determine what works and what does not. It should be tied to project implementation and provide information to guide program operations.

THE PURPOSE OF EVALUATION RESEARCH

Evaluation research is defined as "any scientifically based activity undertaken to assess the operation and impact of public policies and the action of programs introduced to implement these policies."[3] The primary purpose of evaluation research is the determination of the extent to which a program achieves its goals and the assessment of whether that success was a function of program activity. It involves creating an appropriate research design, gathering relevant data, analyzing the data, presenting the research findings while attempting to explain the degrees and reasons behind both program success and program failure.

Evaluation research serves many useful functions. The three most common uses include providing information for: (1) rational decision making, (2) monitoring program performance to provide feedback, and (3) assessment of program impact.

In this complex world, criminal justice administrators must have accurate, concise and timely information to make well informed decisions. For example, it can provide accurate information to address such questions as: Are the services provided producing adequate results? Who is helped by these services? Which program variations are working? Which ones are not? Where are improvements needed?[4] Information from evaluation research can help provide answers to such questions by providing accurate information.

Process Evaluation

A second major function of evaluation research is provide feedback and monitoring information to permit program modification, improvement, or a reduction or reallocation of resources. The purpose of a **process evaluation** is to assess the quality of program delivery. It performs a monitoring function by recording what services are being delivered to whom. It has four major goals:[5]

1. To determine whether the service provided by the program was implemented and delivered to clients in the manner in which it was designed and proposed.
2. To determine whether the program is reaching its intended audience. Who is receiving program services and to what extent?
3. To increase knowledge of what program components are most effective thus enabling managers to design a more effective intervention in the future.
4. To aid understanding of how programs can be successfully implemented.

They should include the perceptions of people close to the program (administrators, staff, and clients) about how things are going:

> A process evaluation requires sensitivity to both qualitative and quantitative changes in programs throughout their development; it means becoming intimately acquainted with the details of the program. Process evaluations not only look at formal activities and anticipated outcomes, but also investigate informal patterns and unanticipated consequences in the full context of program implementation and development.[6]

The key issue here is the determination of whether the program was implemented and its service delivered to the clients for whom it was designed in an effective manner via monitoring – the difference between what was designed and what was desired.[7] As a result, the process evaluation can provide a safety valve for the program by emphasizing problem solving – pointing out malfunctions and recommending adaptations to its design.[8]

For example, a probation department that uses intensive supervision may wish to determine whether or not a high level of contact and services are being provided to clients consistently over time. They may find that certain types of surveillance (curfew checks, job site visits) and treatment modalities (drug counseling) are more effective than others. Providing this type of information on a regular basis allows managers to make changes in service provision and delivery as necessary. In order to make such determinations, researchers typically use a number of methodologies that have been covered in this text with an emphasis upon qualitative techniques (see Chapters Nine and Ten) such as: direct observation of program operations, review of written program records, and interviews with managers, workers and clients of the program.

It gives the researcher a greater appreciation for what the program is about and how operations are conducted. For example, the authors once conducted an evaluation of a drug testing program and conducted visits to the probation officer where the tests were performed. A bulletin board outside the office had a poster that said: "Drug Tests Will Be Conducted on Monday." There is little doubt this method of drug test implementation would have an effect upon the results of the test. The clients now knew when the tests would be conducted. If they were using drugs, they could make plans to attempt to defeat the test. If the evaluators had not visited the program site itself, they would not have known about this flaw in the testing process. Thus, the process evaluation allows the researcher to also serve as an advisor concerning program operations.

Based upon the findings from the process evaluation, the researcher can make recommendations about program operations in the future. These might include expansion, reduction or modification of program operations. In sum, process evaluation informs decisions about programs so their operations can be improved. It helps the program get and stay on track. It helps decision makers anticipate problems due to poor planning and management, unforeseen events and problems in the logic model behind the program. Its monitoring function can detect problems before they become more serious. It is designed to help programs succeed by providing information on program strengths and weaknesses.

Impact Evaluation

The primary purpose of an **impact evaluation** is the determination of the extent to which a program achieves its goals and objectives. It thus involves an assessment of whether this successful attainment had an impact upon crime and/or delinquency.

The first task here is to determine the goals and objectives of the program. Goals are generalized statements of where an organization wants to be at some future time. They tend to be relatively few in number, concise yet not specific, and non-quantitative. The key is to develop objectives that are measurable. For example, law enforcement goals usually include four major desired outcomes:

1. A reduction in the incidence of crime.
2. The repression of criminal activity.
3. The regulation of non-criminal conduct.
4. The provision of services to the public.

The incidence of crime could be measured through the number of crimes reported to the police or through crime statistics generated via a victimization survey (see Chapter 4). The repression of criminal activity could be measured by registering the number of arrests made by officers working under the program. The regulation of non-criminal conduct could also be considered through arrests or less severe sanctions such as warnings to persons engaging in troublesome, but conduct that is not typically criminal, such as trespassing. Finally, the program should document how other services were delivered to the public. For example, a drug prevention program designed to prevent methamphetamine use could engage in public information sessions conducted by officers. The program would then track how many of the sessions were conducted, how many of the sessions were offered, and how many people attended them.

However, designing such measures is not easy to accomplish. One issue is the problem of goal displacement – several levels of program goals often exist. Glaser identifies two levels of goals – manifest and latent. Manifest goals are official statements that are often proclaimed in legislation establishing a program or policy. It is here that universal goal statements like "reducing crime" are typically stated. Latent goals reflect the actual day-to-day procedures and practices of the program.[9] For example, the manifest goal of a halfway house may be to "prevent recidivism" but its programs may be based upon providing treatment to parolees with a drug problem. Preventing drug abuse would be a latent goal of the halfway house program. The official goal cannot be met if the program services are not effectively provided. The prevention of drug abuse must occur in order to meet the goal of preventing recidivism.

Goal displacement can even occur when program objectives are stated in a measurable fashion. For example, the formally stated objectives of a burglary prevention program included:

1. To decrease the number of reported burglaries by 10 percent.
2. To increase by 20 percent the number of arrests for the seven major index offenses over that of the previous year.

Despite the measurable format, questions about these objectives remained. What was the basis for such expectations and were they realistic? How could a multijurisdictional team of seven police officers achieve such goals? Further investigation by the evaluators revealed that program officials had literally copied their objectives from the examples given in the funding agency's request for proposals. The program officials assumed that in order to receive the funds from the grant, they needed to state their objectives in a percentage based format. Of course, this was not the intent of the funding agency. They were simply providing an example of how an objective could be stated. The latent goals of the project would be more directly tied to what the officers were actually doing – proactively targeting suspected burglars, trying to catch them "red-handed," make arrests with strong evidence of guilt and recover stolen property. Thus, the formally stated goals bore no resemblance to what the program was actually doing. If objectives are stated in a quantifiable fashion, but do not reflect program operations, they can serve no purpose with regard to planning and evaluation. If the evaluation is conducted on the basis of such objectives, the result will be a smokescreen or whitewash.[10]

Another problem with goal statements is that they are usually too vague to assess program impact. This may be due to the fact that program administrators do not welcome the evaluation process and the accountability that it promotes. As previously noted, the published program goals may have been overstated to secure funding. Plus, program administrators and staff tend to focus on the process of service delivery. They can control this process but cannot guarantee that the outcomes will indicate success.[11]

Yet, if program measures are vague, then the following problems can result:[12]

1. Success cannot be easily recognized.
2. Makes it difficult to identify and reward key contributors.

3. Failure cannot be detected and corrected in a timely manner.
4. Makes it easy to rationalize inaction.

Goals need to be further defined and quantified into objectives. Objectives set performance targets to be accomplished over a period of time and act as benchmarks that aid decision-making and serve to evaluate progress. They are the specific, measurable targets set for each goal. For example, a delinquency program might want to reduce the number of dropouts from school or the number of runaways or increase the number of youth involved in extracurricular activities. These are all measurable objectives that indicate whether a program has an impact upon the amount of delinquent behavior that occurs. One role of the evaluator is to work with the program administrators and staff to develop objectives that accurately represent what the program is attempting to achieve and whose achievement is a relevant indication of success. Patton suggests that evaluators should ask program administrators and staff the following questions to aid the goal development process: "What are you trying to achieve with your clients? If you are successful, how will your clients be different after the program than they were before? What kinds of changes do you want to see in your clients? When your program works as you want it to, how do clients *behave* differently? What do they say differently? What would I see in them that would tell me they are different?"[13]

Logic Models

The process of establishing goals, objectives and performance indicators can also be facilitated by carefully examining the theory that underlies the basis for the program intervention. In program formation and development, theory performs a number of crucial functions:[14]

1. Drives the selection of treatments.
2. Clarifies the description of the services provided to clients with defined needs.
3. Helps to determine what variables need to be measured.
4. Drives how one interprets a simple comparison of the outcomes of two programs to deeper analyses in terms of research on the topical area in general.

Theory forms the basis for the **logic model** underlying a program – the grouping of variables and the creation of a coherent framework that shows how the program might theoretically produce the desired outcomes and impacts.

The logic behind the program must be described and traced. Typically, program rationales can be divided into four basic components:

1. Inputs: The resources needed by the program to bring about change.
2. Activities: The operations of the project. They demonstrate how the inputs are used.
3. Results: The initial consequences of program operations.
4. Outcomes: Long term program effects upon crime and the criminal justice system.

The Social Development Model

The social development model is a comprehensive developmental approach to preventing youth crime based on an integration of social control and social learning theory in criminology.[15]

> Control theorists argue that most individuals experience strain or frustration of not being able to satisfy their needs and desires and would be tempted to use delinquent means were it not for the restraining influences exerted by their bonds with conventional community institutions such as their family, school, or church. Social learning theorists . . . view the decision to engage in conforming or delinquent behavior as the result of differential social reinforcement, the net effect of all the perceived rewards and punishments associated with a particular pattern of behavior.

Consistent with those theories, the model is based upon the premise that the most important units of socialization (family, schools, peers, and community) influence behavior in a sequential fashion. When youths have the opportunity to engage in conforming behavior within each of these units, positive behavior is the result. To accomplish this, youths must develop necessary skills and be rewarded for positive behavior. These conditions will sponsor the development of the social bonds listed in social control theory (attachment to others, commitment to conforming behavior, and belief in the conventional order).[16] These social bonds inhibit association with delinquent peers and prevent delinquent behavior.[17]

The social development model is supported by research findings from many studies on crime and delinquency. Hawkins and Catalano present data on risk factors associated with a number of problem behaviors, such as violence, drug abuse, teen pregnancy, and school dropout. In the social development model, these **risk factors** are conditions that increase the likelihood that a child will develop one or more behavior problems in adolescence – the greater the exposure to these factors, the greater the likelihood that juveniles will engage in these negative behaviors.[18] Table 11.1 presents an outline of the Social Development Model.

Table 11.1

AN EXAMPLE OF A LOGIC MODEL: THE SOCIAL DEVELOPMENT MODEL

Community Risk Factors and the behaviors they sponsor include:

- **Availability of drugs (substance abuse).**
- **Availability of firearms (delinquency, violence).**
- **Community laws and norms favorable toward drug use, firearms, and crime (substance abuse, delinquency, and violence).**
- **Media portrayals of violence (violence).**
- **Transitions and mobility (substance abuse, delinquency, and dropout).**
- **Extreme economic deprivation (substance abuse, delinquency, violence, teen pregnancy and school dropout).**

Family Risk Factors and the behaviors they sponsor include:

- **A family history of high-risk behavior (substance abuse, delinquency, violence, teen pregnancy and school dropout).**
- **Family management problems (substance abuse, delinquency, violence, teen pregnancy and school dropout).**
- **Family conflict (substance abuse, delinquency, violence, teen pregnancy and school dropout).**
- **Favorable parental attitudes and involvement in the problem behavior (substance abuse, delinquency, and violence).** Children whose parents engage in violent behavior inside or outside the home are at greater risk for exhibiting violent behavior.

School Risk Factors and the behaviors they sponsor include:

- **Early and persistent antisocial behavior (substance abuse, delinquency, violence, teen pregnancy and school dropout).**
- **Academic failure beginning in elementary school (substance abuse, delinquency, violence, teen pregnancy and school dropout).**

Continued on next page

- **Lack of commitment to school (substance abuse, delinquency, violence, teen pregnancy and school dropout).**

Individual/Peer Risk Factors and their indicators consist of:

- **Alienation and rebelliousness (substance abuse, delinquency and school dropout).** It may be a more significant risk for young people of color. Discrimination may cause these youths to reject the dominant culture and rebel against it.
- **Friends who engage in the problem behavior (substance abuse, delinquency, violence, teen pregnancy, and school dropout).** This factor has proven to be a consistent predictor of problem behaviors.
- **Favorable attitudes toward the problem behavior (substance abuse, delinquency, teen pregnancy, and school dropout).** Here, the middle school years are particularly significant. If youths are involved with peers who demonstrate favorable attitudes to these behaviors, they are more likely to engage in them.
- **Early initiation of the problem behavior (substance abuse, delinquency, violence, teen pregnancy and school dropout).** The research review demonstrates that youths who begin to use drugs before age 15 are twice as likely to have drug problems as those who wait until after the age of 19.
- **Constitutional factors (substance abuse, delinquency, and violence).** These factors are biological or psychological in nature. Youths who have problems with sensation-seeking behavior, low harm-avoidance, and lack hf impulse control are more likely to engage in these problem behaviors.

Source: Summarized from Hawkins, J.D. and Catalano, R.F. (1990). *Communities that care.* San Francisco: Jossey-Bass.

Hawkins and Catalano assert that these risks occur in multiple domains. Therefore, the most effective way to combat them is a multifaceted approach across the community. Neighborhood residents and community agencies of all types should join together to deal with these problems. The aim is to provide protection against the sponsorship of risk factors and the spread to problem behaviors that result from them. The goal is to use the public health model to prevent crime. Awareness of these factors is the first step in the development of plans and programs to deal with them in an effective manner. This model has become the framework for a violence prevention strategy mounted by the Office of Juvenile Justice and Delinquency Prevention (OJJDP) – *Comprehensive Strategy for Serious, Violent and Chronic Juvenile Offenders.*[19] By specifying the basis for the program, the logic model can facilitate the development of performance indicators.

Performance Indicators

The crucial task is to develop **performance indicators** that are valid and reliable measures of program effectiveness. They are "benchmark" measures that use available data to quantify the achievement of program progress. They should provide an indication that the program has achieved its desired results and should demonstrate that the program elements are performing well. Such measures should be credible, clear and accurately represent the quality of service provided by the program. In addition, they should reflect what the program is actually attempting to do and have direct linkage to its operations. Here is a review of some familiar criminal justice performance indicators.

Recidivism

Recidivism is a familiar impact measure. It is most often used to evaluate the effectiveness of correctional rehabilitation programs. It is also a measure that people tend to take for granted and whose meaning is accepted by the public without question. Wilkins notes that recidivism "simply means that the offender, once treated/punished, has offended again and that the subsequent offense has been placed on his record." Unfortunately, it is the simplicity of this measure that has lulled decision makers to sleep:[20]

> What has been done to offenders, and particularly to those offenders variously labeled recidivists, has been assumed to be the direct outcome of **their** actions – in a simple cause-effect relationship. This has enabled the false logic to be accepted that the behavior of the recidivist provides sufficient definitions and that it has not been necessary to look any further into the defining process.

Recidivism is typically measured as an offender who has committed a new crime as indicated by a new arrest, conviction or incarceration over a specific time period. In addition, it is possible for an offender to be considered a recidivist without committing a new crime but for failure to maintain the conditions of probation or parole supervision – a "technical violation." However, the choice of one of these indicators of recidivism has a definite impact upon the recidivism rate calculated.

For example, one study followed a 50 percent random sample of federal prisoners (N = 1806) who had served at least one year and a day in prison and recorded their recidivism rate using different indicators. During their first year of release, 29 percent of the prisoners had been rearrested, 15.4 percent had been convicted, 12.6 percent had been sentenced to terms of imprisonment of 60 days or more and 8.7 percent had been sentenced to a new prison term.[21] Thus, depending upon the indicator selected, the range of recidivism rates for this group went from 29 to 8.7 percent.

A related problem with recidivism rates is that their validity is related to the ability of official measures to actually indicate that a new crime has been committed. Not all recidivists are even arrested, let alone reconvicted and incarcerated. To make matters worse, there is a possibility that having a prior record can increase the probability of arrest and further cloud the validity of recidivism measures.

The length of the follow up period is also a crucial influence on the validity of recidivism measures. It has long been held that the longer the offender stays out of trouble with the law, the less likely they are to do it. For example, the President's Task Force on Corrections cited studies on probation and parole outcomes and concluded that they "reveal consistently that most difficulties with offenders occur within the first one or two years under supervision. For those who avoid difficulty through this period, the probability is exceedingly good that they will no longer be involved in criminal activity."[22] However, a six-year follow-up of the same sample of released federal prisoners determined that 60.4 percent of them had been rearrested, 41.7 percent convicted, 34.3 percent had been committed to a sentence of 60 days or more and 27.5 percent resentenced to prison. It was clear that these rates were all significantly higher than those previously reported one year after one year of release.

Thus, we can see that how recidivism is measured clearly has an effect upon its validity as a performance measure. It must be carefully considered in light of the purpose of the program and its ability to avert reoffending. With rehabilitation programs, the causal chain of program operations must also be considered. Returning to our drug treatment program example, the effectiveness of such an effort should be initially considered as freedom from drug abuse – as indicated by drug test results. If a drug abusing offender refrains from drug use, then he/she may not commit a new offense. Such a result could be attributable to the drug treatment program and be considered a performance indicator of success. Recidivism should only be considered if sobriety is established. If the offender returns to drug abuse, there is no need to consider recidivism as an outcome measure. The treatment program would not have met its true purpose and the offender should be considered to be a program failure.[23]

Justice

Justice is a concept that typically defies definition, let alone measurement. Yet, Kobrin has forcefully argued that justice should be considered as an outcome of criminal justice programs and policies.[24]

> Agents of criminal justice assume, perhaps uneasily that improved effectiveness in the control of crime follows improved efficiency in the use of their sanction resources, just as day follows night. In this investigation of this naïve theory, evaluators find themselves obliged to accept program input variables at face value, dutifully assessing their ultimate impact on crime rates.

There is no doubt that due process of law (often defined as "equality of justice") should be considered as a research question for evaluators. As one might expect, justice is difficult to operationally define for measurement purposes. The most common benchmark is that of the Fourteenth Amendment to the U.S. Constitution – promoting equal justice under the law, that all persons should be treated by the law with the same consideration.

For example, Bowers and Pierce analyzed the administration of the death penalty in four states (Florida, Georgia, Texas and Ohio) to determine if the due process procedures established by the *Furman* v. *Georgia* decision were being followed. Their research question focused on due process of law under the capital sentencing system: Had the post-*Furman* statutes eliminated the arbitrary and discriminatory application of the death penalty? They examined the interaction between the race of the offender and the race of the victim in order to determine whether persons sentenced under constitutionally acceptable death penalty statutes were equally likely to be sentenced to death. The results of their analysis in Table 11.2 reveal that there were stark differences in these probabilities in all four states. Black offenders and the killers of white victims were substantially more likely than other racial classifications to receive a death sentence. The authors controlled for the effect of several variables other than race and examined different stages in the criminal process and the general pattern still held. They concluded that "the burden of proof should now be shouldered by those who argue that the death penalty can be imposed without arbitrariness and discrimination."[25]

Table 11.2

PROBABILITY OF RECEIVING THE DEATH PENALTY
IN FLORIDA, GEORGIA, TEXAS, AND OHIO:
BY RACE OF OFFENDER AND VICTIM

Offender/Victim Racial Combinations	Florida	Georgia	Texas	Ohio
Black kills White	.221	.167	.087	.254
White kills White	.046	.042	.015	.046
Black kills Black	.006	.005	.001	.017
White kills Black	.000	.028	.007	.000

Source: Bowers, W.J. and Pierce, G.L. (1980). Arbitrariness and discrimination under post-*Furman* capital statutes, *Crime and Delinquency*, 4, 594.

Crime control methods used by the police are also questioned in terms of justice. Here two related terms, **equity** and **accountability**, are used to assess the due process aspects of police operations. Equity is concerned the distribution of benefits and costs among all citizens in the police service population. Accountability requires that the police act within the constraints set by duly constituted authority – the constraints of laws, rules and regulations, and directives of the governmental bodies with policy making and oversight authority over police.[26] The following indicators have been suggested to measure the extent to which police adhere to the requirements of due process:[27]

1. Officers' Self-Reports: Require reports and randomly audit them with interviews of the citizens who were present.
2. Citizen Reports.
3. Evaluations by Other Professionals.
4. Video Recording of Police/Citizen Encounters.

The nature of citizen contacts should consider such factors as: (1) The number and disposition of citizen complaints against police officers and (2) Whether the reported complaint was sustained or not sustained, (3) If the officer was exonerated, or that (4) The complaint was unfounded. The use of such indicators would permit the evaluator to address the quality of police efforts while delivering the service of a policy or program.

For example, one of the most recent innovations in police operations is **Compstat**. Compstat is a goal-oriented, strategic management process that uses information technology, operational strategy and managerial accountability guide police operations. As designed by the New York City Police Department, this management method asserts that the primary police mission is the reduction of crime and the enhancement of a community's quality of life. The underlying concept of Compstat is that police officers and police agencies can have a substantial positive impact on crime and quality of life problems facing the communities they serve, if they are managed strategically.

Questions about the effectiveness of Compstat have been clouded by what some critics view as its harsh "zero tolerance" crime control methods.[29] However, considering the concepts and indicators discussed previously, researchers have found no support for the conclusion that Compstat enforcement methods have increased community anger and resentment. Researchers at the Vera Institute of Justice demonstrated that police commanders in the South Bronx were able to reduce complaints against their officers below 1993 levels while experiencing the same dramatic decline in crime characteristic of the city as a whole. Both crime and complaints declined in each precinct. They also analyzed statistics supplied NYPD and the Civilian Complaint Review Board, interviewed more than two dozen police officers – from the precinct commanders to the officers on patrol. They concluded that the effective manner used by the precinct commanders to implement crime control policies were the most likely explanation for the decline in civilian complaints against the police.[30] Similarly, Kelling and Souza found that, after an initial increase in complaints filed against NYPD officers from 1994 to 1995, the number of complaints actually declined over the rest of the decade – from 5,618 in 1995 to 4,903 in 1999 – even though the size of the force increased by over 9,000 officers over this period.[31] In this fashion, the question of the quality of police operations regarding due process and justice can be addressed by evaluators.

Measuring Police Performance

Evaluation of police programs have been based upon measures that have become traditional. Typically, these measures attempt to capture the level of security in a community. They include:[32]

1. The vulnerability of its citizens to various crimes of violence.
2. The risk of property loss through theft or vandalism existing in the community.

3. The probability of being a victim from an accident on the highways of the community.
4. The extent of activities defined to be illegal existing in the community.

Thus, research on police effectiveness has always stressed reported crime rates (see Chapter Four) – the "bottom line" is that the police are responsible for crime prevention. Another crime related measure is the number and type of arrests made by an officer. Arrests indicate that something has been done to address and possibly correct a particular problem. In light of our discussion about justice, the quality of the arrest (that it was lawfully done and stood up upon prosecutorial and judicial review) must be considered.

Another crime related police performance measure is the **clearance rate by arrest**. This measure was recommended to police managers by Chief O.W. Wilson – one of the leading authorities on police management. The clearance rate is the percentage of crimes known to the police that they believe has been solved by the arrest of the offender responsible for the crime. The term "cleared" is a police organizational term that bears no direct relation to the administration of criminal law. In short, the clearance rate has nothing to do with the detection of guilt or the attainment of conviction. Also, since it is based upon offenses known to the police, the clearance rate is subject to all of the difficulties surrounding citizen reporting of crimes that were mentioned in our analysis of the Uniform Crime Reports in Chapter Three. It is also important to mention that the arrest of one person can clear several crimes or that several persons may be arrested in the process of clearing one crime.

The social process of clearing crimes also affects the validity of this performance measure. One problem relates to what Pepinsky calls "the policeman's dilemma":[33] "The irony is that although police are supposed to be hired and paid for preventing crime, their importance is likely to be seen as a measure of how many offenses they report or arrests they make."

As with any performance measure, the police may feel pressured to represent themselves in the best possible light and may manipulate rates accordingly. For example, Skolnick lists three incentives that the police can offer in return for the defendant's cooperation in the clearance process: (1) Reduction in the number of charges or counts, (2) concealment of actual criminality, and (3) freedom from further investigation into prior offenses.[34] After all, the defendant who "cops out" also "clears" himself since he is afforded virtual immunity from future arrests on past crimes. Thus, the evaluator who wishes to gauge the efficiency of police performance must be aware of the process surrounding the calculation of clearance rates.

Other measures of police performance are indicators of efficiency. One traditional police performance measure is **response time** on emergency calls. Here, three benchmarks should be considered: (1) when the call is received, (2) when the police unit is dispatched, and (3) when the police unit arrives at the scene. The aim here is to serve citizens as soon as possible to alleviate the extent of the damage caused by the crime or accident and to begin investigation of the crime and hopefully the apprehension of the offender.

Assessing officer workload is another way to determine how the police are using resources. One measure is the number of **calls for service** (from the pubic via the dispatcher) that the officer responds to. Related to this is the amount of self-initiated activity that the officer engages in, including such items as: (1) number of cars stopped, (2) number of traffic tickets issued, (3) number of suspicious subjects checked, (4) number of buildings checked, and (5) field interview reports completed.

The problem with these traditional police performance measures is that they tend to measure what the police do (activities and outputs), rather than their impact upon society. They provide little information about what police action was taken and why. Therefore, new policing methods such as community and problem oriented policing have called for the development of new performance measures that take a closer look at police operations. For example, the Kent Constabulary in the United Kingdom assesses the following measures of police performance:[36]

1. Public satisfaction with police service.
2. Adequacy of police coverage for calls for service
3. Crime victims' satisfaction with police handling
4. Ratios of crimes detected (by the police) to crimes reported (by citizens).
5. Speed in answering telephone calls.
6. Caller satisfaction with the handling of the call.

7. Speed of emergency response.
8. Satisfaction of all people having contact of any sort with police.
9. Public criticism of the police.

These measures are a blend of the old and new and could provide a more complete picture of police operations.

In their assessment of problem-oriented policing in Newport News, VA, Eck and Spellman offered the following indicators for use in the evaluation of this type of effort.[37]

1. Elimination of the problem.
2. Reduction of the number of incidents.
3. Reduction in the seriousness of the incidents or the amount of harm.
4. An improved response to the problem.
5. Shifting responsibility for the problem to a more appropriate agency

Of course, all of these measures shed a different light on the issue of success of a problem oriented policing strategy but all of the possible outcomes should be considered.

Regarding the evaluation of community policing efforts, Skogan advocates special consideration of citizens' attitudes toward the police. Specifically, the evaluator should consider the use of victimization surveys (see Chapter Three) and surveys address the level of the fear of crime in a community. Citizens should also be asked their opinion of the quality and level of satisfaction with the services provided via community policing.[38]

In sum, this review of police performance measures reveals that crime is only one element in the bottom line of policing. Other elements of performance must be recognized and considered in the evaluation of police services.

Utilization-Focused Evaluation

Patton has forcefully argued that program evaluation efforts should not be driven by the determination and measurement of program goals and objectives. Instead, the evaluator should concentrate on the collection of data on a broad array of program effects and the assessment of how these effects met demonstrated needs of clients served by the program – a **goal-free evaluation**. Thus, the main issue not whether program goals are clear, specific and measurable but what information is needed by the primary users of the program.[39]

In a goal-free evaluation, the evaluator pays close attention to the activity and outputs generated by the program without a performance benchmark. Rather than use a goal that is not specific and cannot be stated realistically, this documentation is compiled and then evaluated. For example, a police rape prevention program evaluation that provided a counseling specialist to the department to handle victim counseling and emergency services, assistance to victims who testified in court, prevention programs for the public and training for police officers. The productivity measures for the program are presented in Table 11.3.

Table 11.3

PRODUCTIVITY MEASURES FOR THE RAPE PREVENTION SPECIALIST (SIX-MONTH PERIOD)

Activity	Number
Emergency responses to a crime scene	103
Victim Assistance Provided During Investigation	195
Business Calls Received	1081
Calls Received from Victims	440
Total Contact Hours Spent With Victims	1051

Source: Vito, G.F., Longmire, D.R., and Kenney, J.P. (1983). Preventing rape: An evaluation of a multi-faceted program, *Police Studies*, 6, 34.

The number of business calls received was a measure of the "calls for services" received by the counselor. They included the scheduling of educational presentations and follow-up investigations. They also reflected the actions taken by the counselor to schedule counseling appointments, provide answers to questions and immediate, and emotional support for traumatized victims. The number of contact hours spent with victims includes time spent with the victim during the initial response, assistance during the follow-up investigation, and individual counseling sessions, preparation for court with the district attorney and assistance during court proceedings. Finally, the counselor conducted training sessions with three police departments and 277 public education sessions for a total audience of 10,324 persons. The evaluators concluded that these figures illustrated that the counselor "was extremely active and very productive" and that the "message of prevention was delivered."[40] Documenting activity and then evaluating the outputs is thus a more relevant process than measuring performance against a non-existent or invalid benchmark.

TYPES OF EVALUATION DESIGNS

In order for the evaluator to estimate the effects of a particular program, it is necessary to compare the experiences of recipients of its services with those of some reference or comparison group. In other words, what difference does the intervention make? This effort calls for the development of a research design and the various models that we discussed in Chapter Five. Here, we review research designs with special emphasis upon their use in criminal justice program evaluation.

In general, the research design should make it possible to consider the relationship between the program goals and a variety of independent variables (personal characteristics of the participants, the program components, and the conditions under which the program operates). For example, if you were attempt to determine whether or not drug counseling had an effect on drug users, you would develop a comparison group of drug users who did not receive counseling and then compare them to the participants in terms of such performance indicators as continued drug use, recidivism, or employment. You would also attempt to distinguish whether or not certain characteristics were related to success or failure, such as age, sex, marital status or prior record.

Before and After Program Comparison

This research design compares program results from the same jurisdiction at two points in time – before and after the program was implemented. For example, consider a program designed to reduce jail crowding by releasing first time offenders on home incarceration as a condition of probation. Here, the evaluator could make a simple comparison between the size of the jail population before and after the program was established. Of course, it would be necessary to clearly document the number of prisoners released under the program to attempt to determine whether the change in jail population was due to the program or other factors.

Time Trend Comparison Before and After Program Implementation

In our previous example on jail population reduction, the evaluator could add another comparison by comparing the actual changes to projections on the jail population. The use of population projections would make it possible to consider the differences between the pre and post program conditions and the projection estimate – an indication of where the jail population would stand if conditions remained the same over time.[41]

The Classical Experiment

The domestic violence experiments discussed in Chapter Five were excellent examples of using an experimental design to evaluate a policy. The aim was to determine whether arresting individuals for misdemeanor assault as opposed to simply restoring order and leaving the premises would make a difference. Of course, the comparison of recidivism rates between the groups who were and were not arrested initially revealed that arrest was an effective deterrent to future domestic violence. Upon replication, this conclusion did not hold true. Yet, the benefit of the experimental design help to make these conclusions more relevant because it insured that the two groups, assigned at random in the field experiments, were directly comparable.

Quasi-Experimental Designs

In addition, the researcher can propose the use of a quasi-experimental design (see Chapter Five). Here the researcher evaluates the program through the use of information generated by a comparison of the performance of the experimental and comparison groups. The cases are not randomly assigned so this method gives the researcher an option to pursue when random assignment is either impermissible or impossible. An example of this type of design was utilized by Vito in his study of a drug and alcohol program called "Project Papillon." The comparison group was constructed through a procedure in which inmates that were eligible for but not admitted to the program due to "non-prejudicial reasons" (such as men who were paroled early, or who had entered alternative programs). The assumption was that this "self drop" group was comparable to the experimental group. The recidivism rates of the two groups were not substantially different – indicating that the treatment was not significantly effective.[42]

There may also be natural experiments where quasi-experimental designs are useful because they can be developed quickly to respond to recent events. For example, the *Furman* decision resulted in the reversal of all death sentences in 1972 to life imprisonment. Years later, a number of these inmates were eligible for release on parole. In Kentucky, Vito and Wilson tracked the parole progress of these former death row inmates and found that their recidivism rate was not dramatically high and that none of them committed another homicide.[43] Thus, their release did not represent a severe threat to public safety.

What Works in Crime Prevention

In a government report, researchers from the University of Maryland conducted an evaluation research synthesis of crime prevention programs in criminal justice. They developed the "Maryland Scale of Scientific Methods" to assess the quality of the research design and methodology used by the studies. Research that was judged to be valid under this scale was then analyzed to make the determination of what works and what does not work in crime prevention.[44] The results of their review are presented in Table 11.4.

In this manner, evaluation research studies can be compiled to give criminal justice administrators an idea of what types of programs can be used to address particular types of crime problems.

Table 11.4

WHAT WORKS IN CRIME PREVENTION

- **For infants**: Frequent home visits by nurses and other professionals.
- **For preschoolers**: Classes with weekly home visits by preschool teachers.
- **For delinquent and at-risk preadolescents**: Family therapy and parent training.
- **For schools**:
  –Organizational development for innovation.
  –Communication and reinforcement of clear, consistent norms.

Continued on next page

Table 11.4 – *Continued*

–Teaching of social competency skills.

–Coaching of high-risk youth in "thinking skills."

• **For older male ex-offenders**: Vocational training.

• **For rental housing with drug dealing**: Nuisance abatement action on land-lords.

• **For high-crime hot spots**: Extra police patrols.

• **For high-risk repeat offenders**:

–Monitoring by specialized police units.

–Incarceration.

• **For domestic abusers who are employed**: On-scene arrests.

• **For convicted offenders**: Rehabilitation programs with risk-focused treatments.

• **For drug-using offenders in prison**: Therapeutic community treatment programs.

WHAT DOES NOT WORK IN CRIME PREVENTION

• Gun "buyback" programs.

• Community mobilization against crime in high-crime poverty areas.

• Police counseling visits to homes of couple's days after domestic violence incidents.

• Counseling and peer counseling of students in schools.

• Drug Abuse Resistance Education (D.A.R.E.).

• Drug prevention classes focused on fear and other emotional appeals, including self-esteem.

• School-based leisure-time enrichment programs.

• Summer jobs or subsidized work programs for at-risk youth.

• Short-term, nonresidential training programs for at-risk youth.

• Diversion from court to job training as a condition of case dismissal.

• Neighborhood watch programs organized with police.

• Arrests of juveniles for minor offenses.

• Arrests of unemployed suspects for domestic assault.

• Increased arrests or raids on drug market locations.

• Storefront police offices.

• Police newsletters with local crime information.

• Correctional boot camps using traditional military basic training.

• "Scared Straight" programs whereby minor juvenile offenders visit adult prisons.

• Shock probation, shock parole, and split sentences adding jail time to probation or parole.

• Home detention with electronic monitoring.

• Intensive supervision on parole or probation (ISP).

• Rehabilitation programs using vague, unstructured counseling.

• Residential programs for juvenile offenders using challenging experiences in rural settings.

Source: Sherman, L.W., Gottfredson, D.C., MacKenzie, D.L., Eck, J., Reuter, P., and Bushway, S.D (1998), *Preventing crime: What works, what doesn't, what's promising*, Washington, D.C., National Institute of Justice, 1 and 7.

PROBLEMS AND ISSUES IN EVALUATION RESEARCH

There are additional problems that typically plague the criminal justice evaluator. One is the political nature of social programs. Many programs are political creatures that have emerged from political bargaining. The performance of programs are linked to the reputation of sponsors, the careers of administrators and politicians, the jobs of staff members as well as the expectations of clientele. The continued existence and funding of programs are often tied to the results of the evaluation.[45] New and innovative programs in criminal justice are particularly fraught with such political considerations. The ensuing pressures for a positive evaluation can place the researcher in a precarious position. Early involvement of the administrator and program in the evaluation effort cannot only reduce friction but also facilitate the development of performance measures and establishing the expectations of all parties. Without the support and cooperation of the program administrators and staff, a successful evaluation is nearly impossible.

Another potential problem is the relationship between the program administrator and the evaluator. For these participants, the rewards provided by the research study are markedly different and related to their status. Typically, researchers are members of a profession in which status and advancement depend upon productivity in ways that have more to do with their ability to develop information about the quality of the research than with the success or failure of a program. A researcher may be willing and often eager to criticize program assumptions, but reluctant to question the research techniques that were implemented. On the other hand, the career of the administrator could be tied to the performance of the program.[46] One suggested solution to this problem calls for the administrator to adopt an "experimental" stance toward evaluation and be more pragmatic and forward looking – interested in finding solutions to a problem rather than trying to justify one that was selected in advance.[47] It is clear that some negotiation between the evaluator and the administrator is in order with the interests of each party clear defined and represented. The researcher must demonstrate the value of the project in terms of its ability to develop solutions to social and agency problems.

It is also important to note that often a slow but definite process of cooptation occurs in evaluation in which the researcher associates closely with the program and all of its participants. This process may be the result of financial need, friendship or the desire for future research opportunities. It is important that the researcher maintain an objective and unbiased view and avoid "going native" (as was discussed in Chapter Nine). One suggestion is to have colleagues review the research and offer criticisms. Evaluation results are generally considered as "all or nothing" propositions, magnifying the pressures and constraints in the effort. Of course, there may be situations where the evaluation results dictate that the program should be abandoned, but only after considerable consideration and thought about the impact of the program. If the evaluation is properly conducted, it should provide information for monitoring, adjusting and improving a program. Only after these considerations have been rejected should a program be considered for termination.

Ethical issues also surround evaluation research. One of the foremost concerns is the use of random assignment of subjects to construct a classical experimental design. As discussed in Chapter Five, random assignment is used to assign clients to an experimental (receives the treatment) or control group (does not receive the treatment). The objection is that it is improper to deny or withhold a presumably beneficial treatment from eligible subjects in order to conduct research.[48] However, this objection fails to consider the benefits of random assignment in such instances.

First of all, random assignment is a much more democratic method of determining program entry than is typically used. Literally, all of the subjects who are eligible for the program have an equal chance of being selected. Once eligibility is determined, no other form of screening other than random assignment can be considered. Often, eligible clients are denied access to treatment due to the unavailability of treatment slots in the program. Under such conditions, random assignment is a benefit to subjects. Experiments also eliminate "creaming" – the selection superior applicants by program officials to make the program look good.[49] Second, denial of treatment under random assignment may only be temporary. Members of the control group could enter treatment after the evaluation is completed. Finally, waiting until the evaluation is conducted could also be a benefit. If the research results are positive, then the previously rejected client will either gain entry to a program of proven quality or not enter a program judged to be ineffective.[50]

The final major obstacle facing the researcher in the evaluation of criminal justice programs is the "data net problem" or the condition of the program's information system. This problem is due in large part to legal constraints and bureaucratic inertia that hinders the gathering of data that is vital to the evaluation effort. Program records and agency files are sources of evaluation data. Programs usually collect a fairly large amount of information about what they do and the subjects that they deal with. Unfortunately, experience has suggested that organizational records are not as useful as they could be. Records may be missing, inaccurate, unverified, out of date, and incomplete. The evaluator must meet with program administrators and staff to insure that data that are vital to the performance measures and outcomes for the program are collected and safely maintained. Unless careful attention is given to the program's information system, vital data may not be requested at the proper time or be maintained in an improper format that defies analysis and interpretation. For example, a program designed to provide volunteer assistance to parolees was based upon the match between the volunteer's special interests, skills, and personality in relation to the client's needs, preferences, and limitations. Unfortunately, data on the matching process was never collected and the program evaluation was unable to address the effectiveness of the heart of the program as a result.[51] Unless program administrators recognize what data elements must be collected and maintained, the evaluation will be unable to examine program effectiveness in the truest sense. Such problems will be eliminated if the evaluation research begins *with* the program, not as a late developing afterthought. Research results are more dependable when the information system is built into the program from the start.

Obtaining outcome information from official data to measure program output is a related data difficulty. For example, to obtain accurate data on recidivism results (arrest, conviction, incarceration), it may be necessary to contact several different agencies in the criminal justice system. Receiving permission to gain access to such records is often difficult at best. One method to track the official criminal record of individuals is through a "rap sheet" – data maintained by the Federal Bureau of Investigation. Understandably, the FBI does not provide such personal information for research purposes. As a result, recidivism information can be fragmented and incomplete and evaluators are often forced to make the best of their limited outcome measure.

Overall, the quality of evaluation research in criminal justice must be viewed with these constraints in mind. An awareness of such problems, coupled with thorough planning can help minimize these obstacles to evaluation.

CONCLUSION

This chapter reviewed the basic steps and issues surrounding evaluation research in criminal justice. Evaluation research is designed to provide information concerning the operations, effectiveness, and impact of a program or policy. It should provide criminal justice administrators with reliable information to make decisions on program operations. As with all research processes, it is fraught with pitfalls and problems, most of which can be overcome through careful planning and awareness of the environment.

KEY TERMS

Process Evaluation
Impact Evaluation
Logic Model
Performance Indicators
Equity
Accountability
Compstat
Clearance Rate by Arrest
Response Time
Calls for Service
Goal-free Evaluation

REVIEW QUESTIONS

1. What are the primary purposes of evaluation research?
2. How can evaluations aid decision makers in criminal justice?
3. What constraints are commonly imposed upon evaluators?
4. What are the differences between a process and an impact evaluation?

5. Discuss the strengths and weaknesses of each of the performance indicators listed in the chapter.
6. What is a goal-free evaluation and is it feasible?

REFERENCES

1. Newcomer, K.E., Hatry, H.P., and Wholey, J.S. (1994). Meeting the need for practical evaluation approaches: An introduction, in Wholey, J.S., Hatry, H.P., and Newcomer, K.E., eds., *Handbook of practical program evaluation*, San Francisco, Jossey-Bass Publishers, 3–5.
2. Latessa, E.J. (2004). The challenge of change: Correctional programs and evidence-based practices. *Criminology and Public Policy* 3: 554–558.
3. Rossi, P.H., and Wright, S.R. (1977). Evaluation research: An assessment of theory, practice, and politics, *Evaluation Quarterly*, 1, 5–52.
4. Newcomer, Hatry, and Wholey, Meeting the need, 1.
5. Scheirer, M.A. (1994). Designing and using process evaluation, in Wholey, J.S., Hatry, H.P., and Newcomer, K.E. eds., *Handbook of practical program evaluation*, San Francisco, Jossey-Bass Publishers, 42.
6. Patton, M.Q. (1997). *Utilization-focused evaluation: The new century text*, Thousand Oaks, CA, Sage Publications, 206.
7. Senese, J.D. (1998). *Applied research methods in criminal justice*, Chicago, Nelson-Hall, 72.
8. Sylvia, R.D., and Sylvia, K.M. (2004). *Program planning and evaluation for the public manager*, Long Grove, IL, Waveland Press, 107.
9. Glaser, D. (1973). *Routinizing evaluation: Getting feedback on the effectiveness of crime and delinquency programs*, Rockville, MD, National Institute of Mental Health, 22; Kobrin, S. (1980). Outcome variables in program evaluation: Crime control, social control, and justice, in Klein, M.W., and Teilman, K.S., eds., *Handbook of cri-minal justice evaluation*, Beverly Hills, CA, Sage Publications, 447–448.
10. Vito, G.F., Longmire, D.R., and Kenney, J.P. (1983). Cracking down on crime: Issues in the evaluation of crime suppression programs, *Journal of Police Science and Administration*, 11, 38–41.
11. Patton, *Utilization-focused evaluation*, 157.
12. Nutt, P.C. and Backoff, R.W. (1992). *Strategic management of public and third sector organizations: A handbook for leaders*, San Francisco: Jossey-Bass Publishers, 47.
13. Patton, *Utilization-focused evaluation*, 154.
14. Baruch, R.F. (1998). Randomized controlled experiments for evaluation and planning, in Bickman, L., and Rog, D.J., eds., *Handbook of applied social research methods*, Newbury Park, CA, Sage Publications, 172.
15. Greenwood, P.W. (1995). Juvenile crime and juvenile justice, in Wilson, J.Q., and Petersilia, J., eds. *Crime*, San Francisco, CA: Institute for Contemporary Studies, 91–120.
16. See Hirschi, T. (1969). *The causes of delinquency*. Berkeley: University of California

Press; Reckless, W.C. (1973). *The crime problem.* New York: Appleton, Century, Crofts.

17. Hawkins, J.D., and Weis, J.G. (1985). The social development model: An integrated approach to delinquency prevention, *Journal of Primary Prevention,* 6, 7397.

18. Hawkins, J.D., and Catalano, R.F. (1990). *Communities that care.* San Francisco: Jossey-Bass.

19. Wilson, J.J., and Howell, J.C. (1995). Comprehensive strategy for serious, violent, and chronic juvenile offenders, in Howell, J.C., Krisberg, B., Hawkins, J.D., and Wilson, J.J., eds., *A sourcebook: Serious, violent, and chronic juvenile offenders,* 36–46, Thousand Oaks, CA, Sage Publications.

20. Wilkins, L.T. (1969). *The evaluation of penal measures,* New York, Random House, 43–44.

21. Hoffman, P.B., and Stone-Meierhoffer, B. (1980). Reporting recidivism rates: The criterion and follow-up issues, *Journal of Criminal Justice,* 8, 53–60.

22. The President's Commission on Law Enforcement and the Administration of Justice (1970). *Task force report: Corrections,* Washington, D.C., U.S. Government Printing Office, 320.

23. Vito, G.F. (1999). What works in drug testing and monitoring, in Latessa, E.J., ed. *Strategic solutions: The International Community Corrections Association examines substance abuse,* Lanham, MD: American Correctional Association, 137–160.

24. Kobrin, Outcome variables in evaluation.

25. Bowers, W.J., and Pierce, G.L. (1980). Arbitrariness and discrimination under post-*Furman* capital statutes, *Crime and Delinquency,* 4, 563–635.

26. Mastrofski, S.D., and Wadman, R.C. (1991). Personnel and agency performance measurement, in Geller, W.A., ed. *Local government police management,* Washington, D.C., International City Management Association, 380.

27. Mastrofski, S.D. (1996). Measuring police performance in public encounters, in Hoover, L.T., ed., *Quantifying quality in policing,* Washington, D.C., Police Executive Research Forum, 223–224.

28. Walsh, W.F., and Vito, G.F. (2004). The meaning of Compstat: Analysis and response. *Journal of Contemporary Criminal Justice,* 20, 51–69.

29. Eck, J.E., and Maguire, E.R. (2000). Have changes in policing reduced violent crime? An assessment of the evidence," in Blumstein, A. and Wallman, J., eds. *The crime drop in America,* Cambridge, UK, Cambridge University Press, 251.

30. Davis, R.C., and Mateu-Gelabert, P. (1999). *Respectful and effective policing: Two examples from the South Bronx,* New York, NY, The Vera Institute of Justice.

31. Kelling, G.L., and Sousa, W.H. (2001). *Do police matter? An analysis of the impact of New York City's police reforms,* New York, Center for Civic Innovation at the Manhattan Institute.

32. Ostrom, E. (1973). On the measurement and meaning of output and efficiency in the provision of urban police services, *Journal of Criminal Justice,* 1, 98.

33. Pepinsky, H.E. (1980). *Crime control strategies: An introduction to the study of crime,* New York, Oxford Press, 104, 247.

34. Skolnick, J. (1975). *Justice without trial: Law enforcement in democratic society,* New York, John Wiley & Sons, 164–175.

35. Stephens, D.W. (1996). Community problem-oriented policing: Measuring impacts, in Hoover, L.T., ed. *Quantifying quality in policing*, Washington, D.C., Police Executive Research Forum, 103–108.
36. Bayley, D.H. (1996). Measuring overall effectiveness or, Police-force show and tell, in Hoover, L.T., ed., *Quantifying quality in policing*, Washington, D.C., Police Executive Research Forum, 46.
37. Eck, J.E., and Spelman, W.S. (1987). Who you gonna call? The police as problem busters, *Crime and Delinquency*, 33, 31–52.
38. Skogan, W.G. (1999). Measuring what matters: Crime, disorder, and fear, in Langworthy, R.H., ed., *Measuring what matters: Proceedings from the policing research institute meetings*, Washington, D.C., National Institute of Justice and the Office of Community Oriented Policing Services, 47, 51.
39. Patton, *Utilization-focused evaluation*, 181–184.
40. Vito, G.F., Longmire, D.R., and Kenney, J.P. (1983). Preventing rape: An evaluation of a multi-faceted program, *Police Studies*, 6, 30–36.
41. Hatry, H.P., Winnie, R.E., and Fisk, D.M. (1973). *Practical program evaluation for state and local government officials*, Washington, D.C., The Urban Institute, 45.
42. Vito, G.F. (1983). Does it work? Problems in the evaluation of a correctional treatment program, *Journal of Offender Counseling, Services and Rehabilitation*, 7, 5–21.
43. Vito, G.F., and Wilson, D.G. (1991). Back from the dead: Tracking the progress of Kentucky's Furman-commuted death row population, *Justice Quarterly*, 5, 101–112.
44. Sherman, L.W., Gottfredson, D.C., MacKenzie, D.L., Eck, J., Reuter, P., and Bushway, S.D. (1998). *Preventing crime: What works, what doesn't, what's promising*, Washington, D.C., National Institute of Justice.
45. Weiss, C. (1975). Evaluation research in the political context, in Struening, E. and Guttentag, M., eds., *Handbook of evaluation research*, Beverly Hills, Sage, 13–26.
46. Twain, D. (1975). Developing and implementing a research strategy, in Struening, E., and Guttentag, M., eds., *Handbook of evaluation research*, Beverly Hills, Sage, 27–52.
47. Campbell, D. (1973). Reforms as experiments, in Caporaso, J.A. and Roses, L.L., eds., *Quasi-experimental approaches*, Evanston, IL, Northwestern University, 224.
48. Adams, S. (1975). *Evaluation research in corrections*, Washington, D.C., U.S. Department of Justice, 66–73.
49. Baruch, Randomized controlled experiments, 166.
50. Petersilia, J. (1989). Implementing randomized experiments: Lessons from BJA's intensive supervision project, *Evaluation Review*, 13, 435–458.
51. Carlson, E.W., Vito, G.F., and Parks, E.C. (1980). Effectiveness of volunteer assistance to parolees: Race as a factor, *Evaluation Review*, 4, 323–338.

INDEX

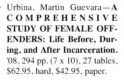
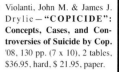